光輝歷程
香港聖樂團65載
The Hong Kong Oratorio Society - 65 Glorious Years

1956-2021

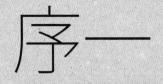

序一

楊健明教授 | 香港聖樂團會長

香港聖樂團成立於 1956 年，至今已有 67 年的發展歷史，舉辦超過三百多場音樂會，成為香港歷史最悠久和最活躍的合唱團，為數以萬計的古典音樂愛好者提供優質精神食糧與文化生活。

2006 年，香港聖樂團慶祝成立 50 周年金禧紀念時，已經開始有籌備出版樂團歷史的意向，但因種種原因，未能如願。現在看到樂團完整 65 年（1956-2021）歷史的出版，令我感到無限欣慰！

香港聖樂團成立至今，目標和使命都十分清晰，就是要演繹和推廣西方大型合唱作品，特別是「神曲」（oratorio），供市民欣賞。 這些樂曲一般都有優美的旋律，無論是聽眾或歌者，往往都能感受到音樂的震撼，心靈得到觸動和鼓舞。

我自從 1970 年加入香港聖樂團後，樂團活動已成為我生活的一部份。正如很多團員說，每星期二晚的排練已經成為他們的習慣，團員們都熱愛聲樂合唱，除了音樂上的互相切磋，生活上亦彼此關懷與照顧，很多成為終身好友！

我很榮幸有機會能夠為香港聖樂團服務，擔任主席長達 18 年之久。在過往五十多年，我親身見證樂團茁壯成長，曲目範疇不斷擴大，演出水準不斷提升。香港聖樂團長久以來，在演唱西方神劇及大型合唱作品方面， 擔任了重要的角色，不但讓愛好聲樂的團員在過程中成長， 還為香港聽眾帶來優美的聖樂欣賞機會， 對香港的聲樂文化可謂貢獻良多。另外，香港聖樂團 65 年來在海外 8 個國家、地區的 25 個城市，一共演出 53 場音樂會，對香港及海外的音樂交流，可稱得上居功至偉。同時這些愉快的海外音樂之旅也提升了樂團的凝聚力。

香港聖樂團今天取得的成就是得到社會各界人士的積極支持和參與的結果， 包括：贊助人、無私奉獻的委員、熱愛歌唱的團員、擔任獨唱的聲樂家、伴奏、樂團的樂手、指揮及音樂總監等等，還有很多忠實的聽眾。容我在這裏，向他們表示衷心的感謝和崇高的敬意。我深信香港聖樂團將繼續努力為社會大眾提供更多優美的合唱音樂，為香港的音樂舞台作出貢獻。

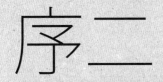

序二

陳永華教授｜香港聖樂團音樂總監

我是 1995 年獲時任香港聖樂團主席余漢翁先生邀請出任聖樂團音樂總監的。其後我與聖樂團共同見證了好幾個歷史場面，包括九七回歸及邁進二十一世紀，其中與團員在非典肺炎及新冠疫情期間，堅持排練和演出，用音樂與市民共渡時艱，記憶猶新。

出任了接近三十年的聖樂團音樂總監，我重演大家喜愛唱、聽的經典名曲之餘，也嘗試一些在香港很少演出以至沒有演過的古典音樂，同時也委約香港作曲家譜寫新曲。

聖樂團的伴奏樂隊由我還沒加入時的香港管弦樂團，到余漢翁先生後來創立的香港小交響樂團，到近二十年合作無間的香港弦樂團，都是聖樂團的最佳夥伴。而聖樂團出席最多及水準最高超的鋼琴伴奏一定是黃健瑜老師，黃老師幾乎每週都抽空出席，更是聖樂團的專用管風琴師。

聖樂團不間斷在本地及海外演出，過程中建立了不少珍貴友誼。合唱團方面包括明儀合唱團，以及澳門、溫哥華、卡加里、三藩市等地合唱團，及內地的專業合唱團，本地的大、中、小學及幼稚園合唱團等。特別一提的是曾合作十七年的香港日本人俱樂部合唱團每年一次的慈善音樂會，以及曾合作十年的聖公會林護紀念中學合唱團。樂隊方面除上述樂團，以及香港中樂團外，還有澳門、深圳、北京、上海、三藩市、多倫多等當地樂團。客席指揮、聲樂家及作曲家當然也不少。通過逾六十年的聲樂音符，香港聖樂團的友誼遍佈海內外。

合唱能凝聚不同年齡及背景的人，通過和諧的聲音及情懷，跟隨指揮的帶引下唱出統一的音色，音量強弱及心神一致的樂音，其間還要經過嚴格的訓練，才到台上演出，整個過程是人類合作的高峰。社會多些合唱活動對個人可以抒懷減壓，提供藝術活動，創造就業，帶出社會和諧。

人類有史以來就唱歌，希望歌聲能繼續消解矛盾，帶來和平喜樂，就像貝多芬《歡樂頌》的主旨一樣！能夠擔任香港聖樂團音樂總監近三十年是我的榮幸！

序三

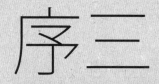

歐陽志剛執事 | 香港聖樂團執行委員會主席

1956 年，一群熱愛合唱、對生活充滿激情的人士在緣份中相聚，攜手成立非牟利的香港聖樂團（聖樂團）。無關利益、無關得失，他們始終堅信，總有一句歌詞、一段旋律，能滋養人們的心靈，帶領人們走過精神世界的荒蕪，豐富香港的文化生活。

時光荏苒，聖樂團發展至今已有 67 年歷史，一直以來同舟共濟，初心不改，致力推動合唱團的發展與壯大。歷經幾代大師的音樂指導，由最初的幾名音樂愛好者壯大到現今擁有百多名團員，由本地到世界各地舉行音樂會，成為香港歷史最悠久及最活躍的合唱團。團員來自五湖四海，但音樂無國界，他們用最真摯的歌聲與旋律跨越文化和語言障礙，將彼此緊密地聯繫在一起，再將這份赤誠的情感傳遞出去，讓世界各地的人們觀賞和細味，也展現出香港的音樂文化魅力。

身為聖樂團的團長，我很榮幸並驕傲能參與到合唱團的發展，見證合唱團的不斷成長與成功。聖樂團的輝煌成果離不開創辦人黃明東先生、黃飛然老師、黃永熙博士、現在我們的音樂總監陳永華教授等指揮及歷屆執行委員會成員，以及各位充滿創造力的歷代團員們的努力。通過他們不辭勞苦的付出和貢獻，聖樂團才能從不見經傳的小合唱團，發展成為能獨挑大樑，將經典合唱藝術帶給不同人士，也和不同地區音樂家合作，交流音樂。六十多年的歌聲成為香港音樂文化不可或缺的一部份。

香港聖樂團致力推廣優美聖樂和培育年輕有才華的合唱者，我誠摯希望有更多年輕人加入其中，為合唱團注入新血脈，用音樂的力量將人們凝聚一起。這是傳統與創新的結合，繼承與傳承的相融。

由於聖樂團有着這源遠流長的歷史，我們這一代就責無旁貸地要將過去好好記錄下來。我們能將這豐厚的歷史素材結集成書，實得蒙周光蓁博士及其團隊為聖樂團收集整理資料、重新數碼化珍貴的圖像及編訂內容；又得到周大福慈善基金慷慨捐助，作為獲得香港藝術發展局配對資助計劃的起動款項；另有個別資深團員無私提供史料和口述材料；他們都是為我們落實這個計劃的好朋友和夥伴，永誌難忘。

序四

陳達文博士 | 香港聖樂團名譽顧問

我很榮幸能為香港聖樂團成立 65 周年紀念書撰寫序言。自 1962 年香港大會堂開幕以來，我一直擔任香港政府的文化藝術發展工作。在 60、70 和 80 年代，香港聖樂團幾乎所有的公開演出都在大會堂舉行，而我在這二十多年裏都在那裏工作。因此，我有幸能夠參加並欣賞香港聖樂團這些音樂會，並與許多表演藝術家交談。

香港聖樂團的演唱，主要是神劇音樂。這聲樂形式，起源於 16 世紀，並在 17 和 18 世紀達到了高峰。通常以基督教的頌拜為基礎，由獨唱家、合唱團和管弦樂隊演出，不需要舞台、服裝或佈景。這種形式使得神劇音樂可以在教堂或音樂廳等不同的場合演出，並吸引了不同的觀眾群體。神劇音樂展現了人類聲音的表達力和戲劇性的可能性，並致力傳達宗教的意義和盼望。神劇音樂也培養了合唱團成員和觀眾之間的社區和靈性感，因為他們分享了一種超越時間和空間的共同音樂體驗。

香港聖樂團通過其眾多音樂會，充份發揮神劇音樂的特點，促進合唱音樂的欣賞。它不僅在教徒之外建立了觀眾群，而且對培養合唱歌手、獨唱家和伴奏家作出了貢獻，並為合唱指揮提供機會，為廣大音樂愛好者演繹所有主要聖樂作品。

香港聖樂團的表演藝術家們都是非常優秀的音樂推廣者，在過去六十多年裏，他們對音樂的熱愛和個人的才華，為香港的藝術發展立下了汗馬功勞，發揮了重大作用。

此外，我們還要向香港聖樂團在促進香港與各地區之間的國際文化交流方面所做的開創性努力表示敬意。

我們也要向多年來香港聖樂團的領導致敬，特別是其主席和執行委員會成員。他們都是志願者，負責籌辦眾多音樂會，給香港市民欣賞，並親自參加所有排練和演出，真的做到身體力行、以身作則。希望他們加倍奮勉，進一步推動音樂的欣賞和參與。

我們還要感謝本書的主編周光蓁博士，通過他的辛勤研究，產生了這本涵蓋 65 年的香港音樂史。本書提供 1956 年至 2021 年香港聖樂團音樂會的完整列表，並採用注釋和分析音樂節目的大數據，來呈現一個重要的音樂團體的歷史。

最後，我們要肯定保存音樂團體歷史的重要性和意義，並讚揚香港藝術發展局通過其口述歷史項目和書籍出版贊助，為記錄香港藝術歷史所作出的巨大努力。

香港是一個多元文化的城市，香港聖樂團 65 年來的成就，是一個好例子。而本書記錄的資料，不單傳承了前人的理念，還會啟發讀者了解：美麗的香港，不單是世界金融中心，還是一個文化交流的中樞！

目錄

附錄

凡例

s：女高音 soprano

a：女中音 alto

m：女次中音 mezzo soprano

t：男高音 tenor

ct：假聲男高音 countertenor

b：男中音 baritone

bb：男低音 / 男中低音 bass/bass-baritone

*：參看附錄成員名單 Additional details in Appendix I

**：參看附錄文字選編 Additional details in Appendix II

序曲

「上星期五晚上，一群熱愛音樂者聚集在大埔道142號，成立香港聖樂團，通過提倡和組辦合唱團『演唱、演繹和演出神劇』。該合唱團組成後將由黃明東擔任指揮。」以上是 1956 年 1 月 22 日星期日《南華早報》以標題〈香港聖樂團成立〉的報道。

報道亦提到樂團 1956 年 1 月 20 日成立時，選出方榮康為樂團主席，Miss M.M. Wong 及程周景真（Louise Ching）分別為秘書、司庫。另外亦選出一個五人委員會，成員是 Harold Metcalf、卓明達、鄺象祖、Ernst Meier、李淑嫻，其中鄺夫人李淑嫻擔任樂團鋼琴伴奏。樂團亦邀請當時擔任教育督學的 Donald Fraser 和 John Bechtel 牧師為贊助人。

報道介紹黃明東畢業於福州協和大學後，到美國普林斯頓西敏合唱學院深造，考獲音樂學士、碩士。黃明東亦經常演出鋼琴獨奏，也伴奏獨唱演出。

報道亦宣佈：「香港聖樂團首次排練將於 1 月 27 日晚上 8：30 在九龍塘窩打老道真光書院進行，有興趣人士歡迎參加成為會員。」一星期後，《南華早報》再次報道，香港聖樂團首次排練的合唱成員為四十五人，選唱兩段《彌賽亞》合唱曲：*Surely He Hath Borne Our Griefs*、*Lift Up Your Heads, O Ye Gates*。 🕮

Formation of H.K. Oratorio Society

On Friday evening, at 142 Taipo Road, a group of people interested in music gathered to form the Hongkong Oratorio Society to promote and organise a Choir "for the singing, rendition and performance of oratorios." The Choir, when organised, will be directed by Mr Theodore Huang.

Officers of the Society elected on Friday were: Mr W. H. Fong, Chairman; Miss M. M. Wong, Hon. Secretary, and Mrs R. Ching, Hon. Treasurer. Five Committee members chosen were: Mr Harold Metcalf, Mr Cheuk Ming-tai, Mr J. C. Kwong, Mr Ernst Meier, and Mrs J. C. Kwong.

Mr Theodore Huang received his BA from Fukien Christian University. After further training in the United States, he received his BM and M. Mus. from the Westminster Choir College, Princeton, New Jersey. As part of his practical training, Mr Huang served as Minister of Music at the Methodist Church of East Stroudsburg, Penna., and the First Presbyterian Church of Vineland, New Jersey.

On December 22 last year, Mr Huang conducted a 70-voice choir at the Kowloon Tong Church of the Chinese Christian and Missionary Alliance.

Mrs Kwong has been selected to be the pianist for the Hongkong Oratorio Society Choir.

Mr D. J. Fraser and the Rev. John Bechtel, were invited to become patrons of the newly formed Society.

Those interested in becoming members of the Hongkong Oratorio Society are requested to contact the Hon. Secretary of the Society, Miss M. M. Wong, 71 Granville Road, Kowloon, for further particulars concerning membership.

The first rehearsal of the Hongkong Oratorio Society Choir will be held on Friday, January 27, at the True Light Middle School, 115 Waterloo Road, Kowloon Tong, at 8.30 p.m.

National day talk

In commemoration of Indian National Day, January 26, the Secretary of the Indian Chamber of Commerce, Mr A. E. Thomas will give a talk entitled, "India After Republic," at the Y's Men's Club luncheon on that date.

工商晚報, 1956-01-22

香港聖樂會 音樂界組織

【本報專訊】 此間熱

心音樂之人士，最近組織一香港聖樂會，以促進及組織聖樂歌唱班，現理莎與約翰伯同牧師，已被邀為贊助人。

凡有意參加該會者，可向荔連威老道七十號黃小姐接洽。

該合唱團之第一次預演，將於廿七日晚八時，假九龍眞光學校舉行。（日）

五，三公斤收七角十五公分，二公斤收一元，餘則亦類推。一。斤收由本港元寄澳則同。一，樣收個位。

1956-1959 年

導讀：

1956 年成立的香港聖樂團，繼當時三大合唱團（香港歌詠團、香港歌劇會、香港樂進團），成為最新的民辦合唱團。創辦人兼指揮是從美國留學回港的黃明東，與一眾熱愛合唱藝術人士攜手成團，其中包括不少教會及教育界專才。

在沒有大會堂的日子，樂團早年排練及演出主要在教會及學校進行，包括創團演出及之前的一場慈善籌款音樂會。後者擔任女高音獨唱是當時準備留學法國的費明儀，她的丈夫許樂群是黃明東在福州協和大學的同學，費明儀也是香港聖樂團第一位成員。她因準備出國而辭演創團演出，由張有興夫人周保靈代替，她亦由此成為樂團早期合作的獨唱家之一。

本章敍述的四年，樂團一共演出十三場音樂會，曲目固然大部份是聖樂，但也有個別非神曲作品，包

括貝多芬、海頓、布拉姆斯的聲樂作品，以及歌劇
《三王夜訪》的香港首演。這段時期最重要演出是
1956 年底與三大合唱團合演莫扎特《安魂曲》，
以紀念作曲家誕辰二百周年。該演出一星期後，美
國西敏合唱團到訪，在璇宮戲院演出。演出後，通
過校友黃明東，兩團在尖沙咀樂宮樓一起聯歡，由
西敏創辦人威廉臣指揮兩個樂團大合唱。

另一場重要演出是 1957 年藝術節閉幕音樂會，由
剛剛從中英樂團改名為香港管弦樂團合演海頓《四
季頌》的春、夏，指揮是從上海移居香港的富亞。

黃明東 1958 年初返美，由 Dennis Parker 接任，
同年聖誕期間演出《彌賽亞》全曲。1959 年初，
麥堅尼（L. G. McKinney）牧師出任樂團第三任指
揮，以演出海頓《四季頌》全曲告別五十年代。🌸

黃明東

為興建教會、
學校籌款音樂會

韓德爾《彌賽亞》選段

指揮：
黃明東

獨唱：
費明儀 [s]、Maureen Clark [a]、
Harold Metcalf [t]、陳定國 [bb]

伴奏：
鄺李淑嫻

地點：
九龍塘基督教中華宣道會

1956 年 10 月 26 日

創團音樂會

布拉姆斯《安魂曲》選段、
韓德爾《彌賽亞》
第二部份、
貝多芬《合唱幻想曲》

指揮：
黃明東

獨唱：
周保靈 [s]（布拉姆斯）、
黃祉賢 [s]（韓德爾）、
Maureen Clark [a]、
Robert Witcher [t]、
郭慶昌 [bb]

伴奏：
鄺李淑嫻、李柏芳、
麥雲卿（貝多芬）

地點：
九龍伊利沙伯中學

費明儀與黃明東

Mrs. Pauline Cheong-Leen, soprano, leading a choir at the Choral Concert given by the Oratorio Society at Queen Elizabeth School, Kowloon, on Oct. 26.—B. C. Hsiung

周保靈創團音樂會演出

《華僑日報》

CHORAL CONCERT

Oratorio Society's Programme At Queen Elizabeth School

CREDITABLE PERFORMANCE

(BY ERNEST GOTTSCHALK)

The Hongkong Oratorio Society presented itself for the first time with a promising choral concert on Friday night in the hall of the Queen Elizabeth School before a full house. Its conductor, Mr Theodore Huang, appeared to be efficient and spirited leader who had succeeded in a relatively short time to create out of the fifty-five singers a responsive chorus already able to render creditable performances of oratorios and works of similar character.

The programme distinguished itself by a well-considered diversity offering selections of choruses and arias from the second part from Handel's "Messiah," four choruses from the "German Requiem" by Brahms and concluded with the "Choral Fantasia" by Beethoven.

Evelyn Kwong played the organ and orchestra parts of the works, on a Hammond organ needing quite a while before she got the right feeling for her instrument; with the effect that the performed at the beginning rather timidly thus not

wean, lacks musical maturity and expressions to be entrusted with such an important undertaking.

The necessity to substitute organ or piano for an orchestra must be always a handicap. While it was less felt at the selections from the "Messiah" and even at the choruses from the "German Requiem", it was to be deplored during the performance of the "Choral Fantasia." Here the transcriptions for the Hammond organ became

《南華早報》

**香港音樂協會主辦
四大合唱聯合演出**

**莫扎特《安魂曲》
（香港歌詠團、香港歌劇會、
香港樂進團）**

指揮：Hector McCurrach

獨唱：
周保靈 s、
Maureen Clark[a]、
John Sung[t]、鄒慧新 [bb]

伴奏：
鄺李淑嫻、李柏芳、
麥雲卿 （貝多芬）

地點：
九龍伊利沙伯中學

1956 年 12 月 9 日
與訪港西敏合唱團聯歡

1956 年 12 年 14 日
重複創團音樂會節目

地點：
尖沙咀香港基督教青年會

「香港聖樂團，假樂宮樓歡迎美國西敏合唱團菰港聯歡大會。在歡迎會上，西敏合唱團[威廉臣]指揮兩個樂團全體團員大合唱。」《工商日報》

1957 年 7 月 12 日
海頓《四季》－春、
布拉姆斯《命運之歌》、
舒伯特《米利暗之歌》、
Randall Thompson *The*
Peaceable Kingdom
（無伴奏四部合唱）

指揮：
黃明東

獨唱：
周保靈[s]、黃祉賢[s]、
Maureen Clark[a]、
Robert Witcher[t]、
Harold Metcalf[b]

伴奏：
鄺李淑嫻、李柏芳

地點：
九龍華仁書院

《華僑日報》

"The soprano, as frequently happens, was even fuller and stronger in the chorus parts than in the solos...The chorus worked up to a splendid crescendo in 'God of Light', and all concerned produced good all-round volume in 'Hark the Deep Tremendous Voice'."

《南華早報》

Hong Kong Philharmonic Orchestra

and

HONG KONG ORATORIO SOCIETY

FESTIVAL OF ARTS CONCERT

Conductor — **Arrigo Foa**
Leader — **S. M. Bard**
Choir Master — **Theodore Huang**

with **GEOFFREY TANKARD**, pianoforte

Programme

Cimarosa — Overture "The Secret Marriage"
Beethoven — Piano Concerto No. 3 in C Minor
Haydn — "The Seasons" (Spring and Summer)
Edna Chen, soprano
Robert Witcher, tenor
Chan Ting Kwok, bass

LOKE YEW HALL
University of Hong Kong

Thursday, 31st October, 1957 at 8.30 p.m.

Tickets now on sale at
Moutries, Chater Road, Hong Kong.

$5, $3 and $2.

女中音陳之霞："[In] the early days of HKOS, quite a number of Mr. Theodore Huang's pupils, including myself...had been singing together once a week West Lounge of the YMCA. Those were the evenings we always looked forward to attending. The chairman's opening prayers always made the members sing joyfully and thoughtfully. The tea breaks also helped to draw the members closer together."

（三十五周年紀念場刊）

1957 年 10 月 31 日

1957 年香港藝術節
閉幕演出

海頓《四季頌》春及夏

指揮：
富亞

獨唱：
Edna Chen[s]、
Robert Witcher[t]、陳定國[bb]

伴奏：
香港管弦樂團

地點：
香港大學陸佑堂

聖誕音樂會

曼諾第歌劇《三王夜訪》及聖誕曲頌唱

指揮：
黃明東

獨唱：
Robin Grist[t]、周保靈[s]、
Robert Witcher[t]、黃德懷[bb]、
陳定國[bb] 等

地點：
九龍覺士道童軍禮堂

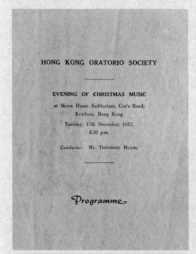
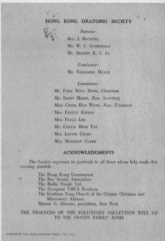

AMAHL AND THE NIGHT VISITORS *
by GIAN CARLO MENOTTI

Amahl	ROBIN GRIST
His Mother	PAULINE CHEONG-LEEN
King Kaspar	ROBERT WITCHER
King Melchior	TACTWAY WONG
King Belthazar	CHAN TING KWOK
The Page	CHAN SHUI PAK
Shepherds	JOSEPH WONG, PAUL CHANG, JOHN BECHTEL, GLENN KRANZOW, WILLAM CHEUK
Shepherdesses	LA MAE MARK, ESTHER CHEN, CAROL HSU, BARBARA CHAN, CECILIA CHAN, AMY WU

"This amusing Christmas musical play, with its touch of sadness interspersed, featured Robin Grist as Amahl, and Pauline Cheong-Leen as his mother. Musical direction was by the Society's founder and stalwart, Theodore Huang. It was a bitter-sweet occasion, for it marked the Society's last performance under the leadership and encouragement of Mr. Huang, who...will leave soon for the United States to take up an important musical post."

(by K.C.H from a news clipping)

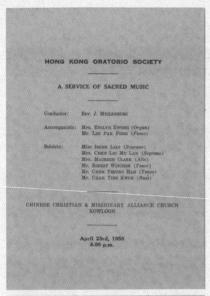

HONG KONG ORATORIO SOCIETY

A SERVICE OF SACRED MUSIC

Conductor: Rev. J. Muilenburg

Accompanists: Mrs. Evelyn Kwong (Organ)
Mr. Lee Pak Fong (Piano)

Soloists: Miss Irene Liao (Soprano)
Mrs. Chen Liu Mu Lan (Soprano)
Mrs. Maureen Clark (Alto)
Mr. Robert Witcher (Tenor)
Mr. Chen Tseung Han (Tenor)
Mr. Chan Ting Kwok (Bass)

CHINESE CHRISTIAN & MISSIONARY ALLIANCE CHURCH
KOWLOON

April 23rd, 1958
8.00 p.m.

MEMBERS OF THE CHORUS

Soprano

Chen Liu Mu Lan, Pola Lee, La Mae Mark, Vivian Woo, Esther Chen, Virginia Lee, Lillian Mark, Florence Der, Irene Liao, Virginia Muilenburg, Rebecca Kan, Elaine Mark, Ching-Han Wong

Alto

Barbara Chen, Lee Law Tak, Amy Wu, Cecilia Chan, Marina Lee, Rose Cheng, Jessi Tsai, Maureen Clark, Ming Ming Wong

Tenor

Paul Chang, Fong Wing Hong, Paul Chau, Lee Chau Yuan, Chen Tseung Han, Robert Witcher, Peter Hu

Bass

John Bechtel, Chu Man Wai, Lee Pak Fong, Tsetway Wong, Chan Kwok Chiu, John Ducker, George Lau, Chan Ting Kwok, Ho Wing Chee, Loren E. Noren, William Cheuk, Glenn Kranowe, S. C. Wong

ACKNOWLEDGMENTS

The Hong Kong Oratorio Society expresses its gratitude to the Chinese Christian & Missionary Alliance Church for permission to use the church hall.

布拉姆斯《安魂曲》選段、
Heinrich Schütz
*The Seven Words of Christ
on the Cross*

指揮：
J. Muilenburg 牧師

獨唱：
廖新靄[s]、陳劉沐蘭[s]、
Maureen Clark[a]、Robert
Witcher[t]、陳宗翰[t]、陳定國[bb]

伴奏：
鄺李淑嫻、李柏芳

地點：
九龍塘基督教中華宣道會

"The Oratorio Society's chorus rose above all interference and produced some very creditable tone, and responsive and expressive interpretations...I would say that this body of singers has definitely improved in every way since I last heard them, and it is certain that with patience and encouragement, the improvement will continue."

《南華早報》

韓德爾 Acis and Galatea

指揮：
富亞

獨唱：
Patti Duncan[s]、
Robert Witcher[t]、
Alexander Wong[t]、
Alan Sainsbury[bb]

聯合演出：
香港歌詠團

伴奏：
香港管弦樂團

地點：
香港大學陸佑堂、
九龍伊利沙伯中學

2 CONCERTS

presented by

HONGKONG PHILHARMONIC ORCHESTRA
THE HONGKONG SINGERS
HONG KONG ORATORIO SOCIETY

(Symphony Orchestra & 100 Voices)

Thursday, 27th November at 8.30 p.m.
LOKE YEW HALL, H.K. UNIVERSITY

Thursday, 4th December at 8.30 p.m.
QUEEN ELIZABETH SCHOOL, Kowloon

Conductor: Arrigo Foa   Chorusmasters: Donald Fraser
Leader: S. M. Bard   Dennis Parker

PROGRAMME

1. Overture: II Seraglio .... *Mozart*
2. Suite of Russian Songs .... *arr. Liadov*
3. Suite of English Folk Songs .. *Vaughan Williams*
4. Acis & Galatea .... *Handel*

SOLOISTS:—Patti Duncan (Galatea) . *Soprano*
Robert Witcher (Acis) ... *Tenor*
Alexander Wong (Damon) . *Tenor*
Alan Sainsbury (Polypheme) *Bass*

Booking: MOUTRIES Tickets: $7, $5 & $3

"The concert on Thursday night by the Hongkong Singers, the Oratorio Society and the Philharmonic Orchestra represents the biggest effort by local musicians in Hongkong for a long time...The Hongkong Oratorio Society, before the regretted departure of Theodore Huang, gave promise of becoming a fine spirited choir of youthful voices...it naturally suffered after the departure of the force behind it, but it has not lost its original intention, and a good deal of hope is still centred upon it."

《南華早報》

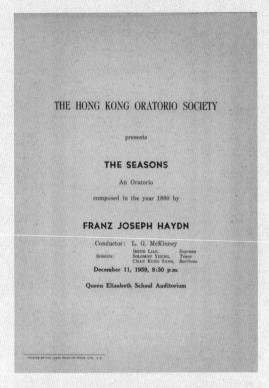

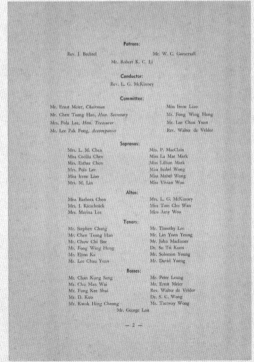

韓德爾《彌賽亞》

指揮：
Dennis Parker

獨唱：
Edna Chen[s]、
Maureen Clark[a]、
Robert Witcher[t]、鄒慧新[bb]

伴奏：
鄺李淑嫻

地點：
九龍伊利沙伯中學

海頓《四季頌》

指揮：
L. G. McKinney 牧師

獨唱：
廖新靄[s]、楊毓智[t]、陳供生[b]

伴奏：
李柏芳

地點：
九龍伊利沙伯中學

1960-1969 年

導讀：

進入 1960 年代的香港聖樂團，十年間一共演出二十二場音樂會。早年由麥堅尼（L. G. McKinney）牧師指揮，繼續演出以聖樂為主的作品，包括巴赫、海頓等清唱劇。此外 George Wilson 博士亦客席指揮莫扎特、孟德爾遜大型聲樂作品，頗獲好評。多才多藝的黃飛然，在這期間經常指揮。除了指揮樂團首次演出孟德爾遜《以利亞》等大型聲樂作品，也擔任男高音獨唱，以及領奏樂隊大提琴聲部等。

1962 年大會堂開幕後，樂團開始更多與樂隊合作演出，包括由林聲翕創辦的華南管弦樂團，以及由香港管弦樂團小提琴家鄭植沛領奏的普歌管弦樂團（Poco Musica Society）。1966 年黃飛然指揮業餘時期的香港管弦樂團，演出布拉姆斯《安魂曲》，

受到英文樂評的負面批評，時任樂團主席朱文偉去信反駁，為樂團名聲辯護，字字珠璣。翌年樂團獲邀參與慶祝大會堂成立五周年的「香港音樂美術節」。在這期間，樂團在復活節、聖誕等日子在電視台播放演出，亦先後在大會堂主辦周文珊、袁恩光獨唱音樂會。

1967 年 12 月，從美國回港的黃永熙博士首次指揮樂團，演出《彌賽亞》。自此開始長達三十五年的樂緣。在他的領導下，樂團合唱成員倍增，首次演出威爾第《安魂曲》，指揮香港管弦樂團的同時，請來江樺、李冰擔任獨唱，開始了兩位聲樂家與聖樂團近半世紀的合作關係。在此之前，樂團先後與著名獨唱家費明儀、徐美芬、周宏俊、譚天眷、田鳴恩、林祥園等合作演出，甚獲好評。🎼

1960 年 4 月 13 日

巴赫《聖約翰受難曲》

指揮：
L. G. McKinney 牧師

獨唱：
陳劉沐蘭 [s]、何肇珍 [s]、
鄭樂時 [a]、楊毓智 [t]、
陳宗翰 [t]、陳供生 [bb]、
黃德懷 [bb]、Ernst Meier[bb]

伴奏：
鄺李淑嫻、李柏芳

地點：
九龍塘基督教中華宣道會

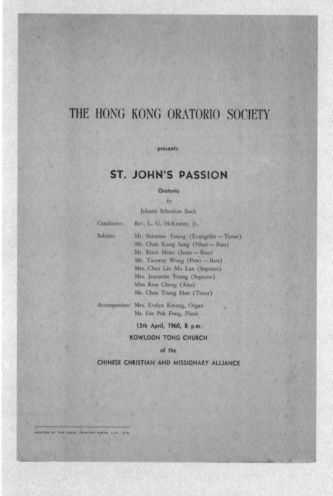

THE HONG KONG ORATORIO SOCIETY

presents

ST. JOHN'S PASSION

Oratorio
by
Johann Sebastian Bach

Conductor: Rev. L. G. McKinney, Jr.

Soloists: Mr. Solomon Young (Evangelist — Tenor)
          Mr. Chan Kung Sang (Pilate — Bass)
          Mr. Ernst Meier (Jesus — Bass)
          Mr. Tactway Wong (Peter — Bass)
          Mrs. Chen Liu Mu Lan (Soprano)
          Mrs. Jeannette Yeung (Soprano)
          Miss Rose Cheng (Alto)
          Mr. Chen Tsung Han (Tenor)

Accompanists: Mrs. Evelyn Kwong, Organ
              Mr. Lee Pak Fong, Piano

13th April, 1960, 8 p.m.
KOWLOON TONG CHURCH
of the
CHINESE CHRISTIAN AND MISSIONARY ALLIANCE

PRINTED BY THE LOCAL PRINTING PRESS, LTD., H.K

HONG KONG ORATORIO SOCIETY

presenting

REQUIEM

by

WOLFGANG AMADEUS MOZART

Conductor: Dr. GEORGE WILSON

Soloists:
Mrs. CHEN LIU MU LAN .... **Soprano**
Miss ROSE CHENG .... **Alto**
Mr. SOLOMON YOUNG ...... **Tenor**
Mr. CHAN KUNG SANG ..... **Bass**

Accompanist: Miss LA MAE MARK .... **Piano**

Friday, 25th November, 1960
at 8.30 p.m.

QUEEN ELIZABETH SCHOOL,
Kowloon

TICKETS AT $5.00, $3.00 and $2.00

Obtainable at:
MOUTRIES CO.) HONG KONG and
TOM LEE PIANO CO.) KOWLOON

Words And Music

ORATORIO SOCIETY'S
"REQUIEM" PLEASES
(BY "EEYORE")

The Hongkong Oratorio Society gave a most satisfactory performance of Mozart's "Requiem" under their conductor, Dr George Wilson, at the Queen Elizabeth School auditorium on Friday evening, before a large audience.

《南華早報》

1960 年 11 月 25 日

莫扎特《安魂曲》

指揮：
George Wilson

獨唱：
陳劉沐蘭 [s]、鄭樂時 [a]、
楊毓智 [t]、陳供生 [bb]

伴奏：
麥雲卿

地點：
九龍伊利沙伯中學

1960 年 12 月 11 日

韓德爾《彌賽亞》、
莫扎特《安魂曲》、
貝多芬《哈利路亞》選曲

地點：
九龍閩南中華基督教會

1961 年 5 月 23 日

孟德爾遜《聖保羅》

指揮：
George Wilson

獨唱：
費明儀 [s]、Edna Chen[s]、
Lillian Zau[a]、Thomas
Cheng[t]、黃飛然 [t]、
黃德懷 [bb]、Ernst Meier[bb]

伴奏：
鄺李淑嫻、麥雲卿

地點：
九龍塘基督教中華宣道會

HK ORATORIO SOCIETY PRESENTS "ST PAUL"

Work With Message Of Contemplative Worship

The Hongkong Oratorio Society last night presented the oratorio, "Saint Paul" by Felix Mendelssohn-Bartholdy, to a large congregation at the Kowloon Tong Church of Chinese Christian and Missionary Alliance.

《南華早報》

THE HONG KONG ORATORIO SOCIETY

presents

Elijah

An Oratorio

Composed by

F. MENDELSSOHN - BARTHOLDY

Friday, 11th May, 1962, 8.30 p.m.
City Hall, Concert Auditorium
Hong Kong.

The Hongkong Oratorio Society on stage at the City Hall last night for their presentation of Mendelssohn's "Elijah."—(Staff Photographer).

《南華早報》

孟德爾遜《以利亞》

指揮：
黃飛然

獨唱：
李同嚴[s]、Maureen Clark[a]、Peter Beale[t]、Thomas Cheng[t]、McKinney[bb]

伴奏：
鄺李淑嫻、Ruth Galster

地點：
香港大會堂（演奏廳）

海頓《創世記》

指揮：
L.G. McKinney 牧師

獨唱：
徐美芬[s]、Peter Beale[t]、
Gordon Lockhart[b]、
尹慶樑[b]

伴奏：
華南管弦樂團、Ruth Galster

地點：
香港大會堂音樂廳 / 循道會

高盧《聖城》

指揮：
黃飛然

獨唱：
徐美芬[s]、周宏俊[a]、
田鳴恩[t]、陳供生[bb]

伴奏：
華南管弦樂團、鄺李淑嫻、
屠月仙

地點：
香港大會堂音樂廳

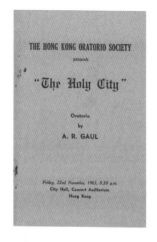

THE HONG KONG ORATORIO SOCIETY
presents

"The Holy City"

Oratorio
by
A. R. GAUL

Friday, 22nd November, 1963, 8.30 p.m.
City Hall, Concert Auditorium
Hong Kong

「四部聲強弱適中，混唱時極之和諧，聲質之清晰，幾與職業合唱團不分伯仲。此非排練不為功，亦足證麥堅理牧師之指揮得當及努力。」

《華僑日報》

「……《聖城》之音樂會，可說是集本港著名之音樂家於一堂。合唱團擁有團員六十人，皆為對聲樂訓練有素之士……至於擔任伴奏之華南管弦樂隊，經常由林聲翕教授指揮，為本港最有成績之樂隊，首席小提琴由青年交響樂團指揮文理小姐擔任，此外為范孟桓先生之中提琴、黃呈權醫生之長笛、阮三根先生之定音鼓、李淑嫻女士之電風琴，及屠月仙之鋼琴，皆屬一時之選。」

《華僑日報》

ORATORIO CONCERT AT CITY HALL

The South China Sinfonietta and singing cast as seen at last night's City Hall oratorio concert of Mendelssohn's "St Paul" given by the Hongkong Oratorio Society. The solo part were sung by Nancy Zi (soprano), Miss Ruth Chow (contralto), Mr Ho Kwan-ching (tenor) and Mr Chan Kung-sang (baritone).

《南華早報》

HONG KONG ORATORIO SOCIETY
presents
"SAMSON"
Oratorio by
G. F. HANDEL

Conductor: Frank Huang

Soloists: Nancy Zi — Soprano
Ruth Chow — Alto
Ho Kwan Ching — Tenor
Chan Kung Sang — Baritone
Wilson Hsueh — Baritone

Pianist: Irene Lo

Orchestra: POCO Orchestra

at City Hall Concert Auditorium
on Friday, 11th December, 1964, 8.30 p.m.
Tickets at HK$10, $5 and $3
on sale at
Hong Kong: Tsang Fook Piano Co., Marina House, Queen's Rd. C.
Kowloon: Tom Lee Piano Co., Carnarvon Road, Tsimshatsui.

1964 年 5 月 30 日 **

孟德爾遜《聖保羅》

指揮：
黃飛然

獨唱：
徐美芬 [s]、周宏俊 [a]、
何君靜 [t]、陳供生 [b]

伴奏：
華南管弦樂團、鄺李淑嫻

地點：
香港大會堂音樂廳

1964 年 12 月 11 日

韓德爾《參孫》

指揮：
黃飛然

獨唱：
徐美芬 [s]、周宏俊 [a]、
何君靜 [t]、陳供生 [b]、薛偉祥 [b]

伴奏：
普歌管弦樂團、羅玉琪

地點：
香港大會堂音樂廳

香港華人基督教聯會
金禧音樂會

韓德爾《猶大 • 瑪喀比》

指揮：
黃飛然

獨唱：
程雅南[s]、周宏俊[a]、
田鳴恩[t]、陳供生[bb]

伴奏：
普歌管弦樂團、羅玉琪

地點：
香港大會堂音樂廳

"The Oratorio Society is to be congratulated on its sincere efforts throughout the year, to keep alive the tradition of Oratorio presentations. It has now established the custom of giving one or more concerts each year and its choice of works has always been ambitious."

《南華早報》

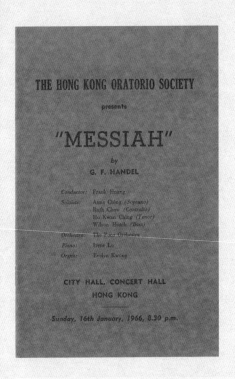

韓德爾《彌賽亞》

指揮：
黃飛然

獨唱：
程雅南[s]、周宏俊[a]、田鳴恩[t]、
薛偉祥[bb]

伴奏：
普歌管弦樂團、鄺李淑嫻、
羅玉琪

地點：
香港大會堂音樂廳

Members of Hong Kong Oratorio Society and
Poco Orchestra at "Messiah"—Rehearsal

1966 年 9 月 23 日

布拉姆斯《安魂曲》

指揮：
黃飛然

獨唱：
徐美芬 [s]、陳供生 [b]

伴奏：
香港管弦樂團、羅玉琪

地點：
香港大會堂音樂廳

1966 年 12 月 30 日

主辦周文珊師生聯合音樂會

鋼琴伴奏：
葛邦懿、胡德倩、洪溫

地點：
香港大會堂音樂廳

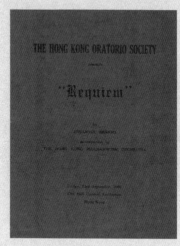

「十年的『神曲』演唱已令許多團員獲得豐富的經驗⋯⋯在技巧方面，我們不能自躋於職業歌唱家之林。我們只是愛好歌唱，並盼本團與樂隊今晚演出這首宏偉莊嚴、照耀古今的作品時，能予閣下深刻印象，從而樂於欣賞我們下次的音樂會。」

（場刊）

"To prepare for the gigantic 'Requiem', our members did spend an enormous measure of time an strength over a period of six months. During the final month, HK Philharmonic Orchestra joined in for combined rehearsals...In denying the efforts of these two well established organisations, your critic has knowingly or unknowingly done a disservice to the culture of Hong Kong."

《南華早報》 *Letter to editor* by Chu Man Wai, HK Oratorio Society chairman

1967 年 3 月 24 日

巴赫《聖約翰受難曲》
電視演出

1967 年 5 月 19 日

主辦袁恩光獨唱音樂會
地點：
香港大會堂音樂廳

大會堂落成五周年：
香港音樂美術節

莫扎特第十二彌撒曲、
孟德爾遜《讚美之歌》

指揮：
黃飛然

獨唱：
程雅南[s]、Teresa Wong[a]、
何君靜[t]、陳供生[bb]

伴奏：
鄺李淑嫻、蔣璧煇

地點：
香港大會堂音樂廳

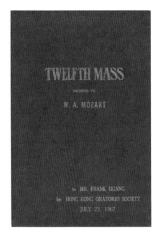

市政局為慶祝大會堂落成五週年舉辦

一九六七年香港音樂美術節

音樂會入場券：二元及一元，每日十時至六時及每次音樂會前在大會票房出售。
電話：229928，229511

日期	節目	日期	節目
七月十三日 星期四 八時 音樂廳	香港管絃樂團 指揮：富亞	七月二十二日 星期六八時半 劇院	鋼琴二重奏 林小湛，吳綺玲
七月十四日 星期五 八時 音樂廳	聲樂演唱 王若詩(女高音) 袁恩光(男中音) 伍淑英(鋼琴) 香港音樂協會主辦	七月二十三日 星期日 三時 音樂廳	青年小提琴演奏會 汪西三主持
七月十五日 星期六 八時 音樂廳	室樂會 徐美芬(女高音) 高士文(橫笛) 梅雅麗(鋼琴)	七月二十三日 星期日 八時 音樂廳	聖樂演唱 香港聖樂團
七月十五日 星期六 八時半 劇院	聲樂及鋼琴 愛樂合唱團	七月二十四日 星期一 八時 音樂廳	聲樂及器樂 男青年會黃大仙中心主持
七月十六日 星期日 三時 音樂廳	中國名歌演唱會 角聲合唱團	七月二十五日 星期二 八時 音樂廳	鋼琴演奏會 許曹露潤女士主持
七月十六日 星期日 八時 音樂廳	歐西民歌演唱會	七月二十六日 星期三 八時 音樂廳	女皇軍團第二營軍樂團
七月十七日 星期一 八時 音樂廳	輕歌劇「快樂的英格蘭」 香港歌詠團	七月二十七日 星期四 八時 音樂廳	聲樂演唱 藝風合唱團
七月二十日 星期四 八時 音樂廳	聲樂演唱 費明儀(女高音) 明儀合唱團	七月二十八日 星期五 八時 音樂廳	鋼琴與小提琴演奏 趙不爐(小提琴) 林鴻熹(鋼琴) 香港音樂協會主持
七月二十一日 星期五八時十五分 音樂廳	現代中國作曲家作品演奏會 麗的呼聲主持	七月二十九日 星期六 八時 音樂廳	國樂與西樂 香港商業電台主持
七月二十一日 星期五 八時半 劇院	聲樂演唱 容可爲(男高音) 洪溫(女高音)	七月二十九日 星期六八時半 劇院	聲樂演唱 香港仔工業學院舊生會
七月二十二日 星期六 八時半 音樂廳	聲樂演唱 羅賓賓兒合唱團	七月三十日 星期日 八時 音樂廳	歌劇選演 江樺(女高音) 林祥園(男高音) 蘇孝良(鋼琴) 盧景文導演

《音樂生活》

HONG KONG ORATORIO SOCIETY

presents

"MESSIAH"

Oratorio by

G. F. HANDEL

Conductor:	Wong Wing-hee
Soloists:	Anna Cheng (Soprano)
	Ruth Chow (Contralto)
	Frank Huang (Tenor)
	Chan Kung Sang (Bass)
Organ:	Evelyn Kwong
Accompanied by	Ad hoc-Orchestra

CITY HALL (Concert Hall)

on TUESDAY, 5th DECEMBER, 1967, 8.00 p.m.

Tickets at $5.00 and $3.00

BOOK NOW at HARRY ODELL PRODUCTIONS LTD.
Room 414, 9, Ice House Street, Telephone: 231488

"SHOWBOX" BOOKING OFFICE,
(Shop No. 2, Alexandra House, West Arcade)

UNION HOUSE ARCADE THEATRE TICKET SERVICE
PRINCE'S BUILDING ARCADE THEATRE TICKET SERVICE

Shanghai Commercial Bank Ltd.,
666, Nathan Road.

Tickets on Sale Daily at the City Hall from 6.00—9.00 p.m.

陳浩才：「[演出] 為五月以來最熱鬧的一場音樂會，打破了多月來樂壇的沉悶局面，當晚在黃永熙指揮下，不只成為該聖樂團成立以來最動人的一次演出，在本地合唱音樂會中像如此成功的亦屬罕見。」

《星島晚報》

1967 年 12 月 5 日 */

韓德爾《彌賽亞》

指揮：
黃永熙

獨唱：
程雅南 [s]、周宏俊 [a]、
黃飛然 [t]、陳供生 [bb]

伴奏：
樂隊（領奏：白德醫生）、
鄺李淑嫻、蔣璧煇

地點：
香港大會堂音樂廳

Members of The Hong Kong Oratorio Society at their Rehearsal

香港學校音樂協會主辦
聖誕音樂會

韓德爾《彌賽亞》（選段）

指揮：
黃永熙

伴奏：
英華男校、拔萃女書院、
伊利沙伯中學等聯合樂隊
（**指揮：**文理）

Good Friday
麗的電視播放

Stainer:《十架受難曲》

指揮：
黃永熙

獨唱：
黃飛然 [t]、陳供生 [bb]

伴奏：
鄺李淑嫻

錄音地點：
北角循道衛理堂

The Hong Kong Oratorio Society
present
A Concert of Good Friday Music

On Good Friday at 6:30 p.m. the Hong Kong Oratorio Society will once again appear on RTV singing Crucifixion by J. STAINER. Like Handel's Messiah, this piece of music is certainly one of the best known and most often sung pieces by the local churches.

The very prominent Dr. Wong Wing-hee will again conduct the chorus. Dr. Wong Studied conducting with late Pierre Monteux and received his doctorate from Columbia University in music and music education. Ever since he conducted the Messiah Concert by Hong Kong Oratorio Society last year, Dr. Wong has gained a very definite place in the heart of many of local music lover.

The Soloists for the evening will be Mr. Frank Huang,

tenor and Mr. Chan Kung Sang, bass. At the organ is none other than Mrs. Evelyn Kwong. At present HKOS has over 100 singing voices.

The programme is detailed as follows:—

1. And they came to a place named Gethsemane.
2. The Agony.
3. Processional to Calvary.
4. The Majesty of the devine Humiliation.
5. God so loved the world.
6. Jesus said, "Father, forgive Them"
7. So Liftest Thy Devine Petition.
8. And one of the Malefactors.
9. When Jesus therefore saw his mother.
10. The Appeal of the Crucified.
11. After this, Jesus knowing that all things were now accomplished.
12. For the Love of Jesus.

The programme is produced by David Doe and recorded at the North Point Methodist Church.

CLOSE-UP

TV Times

PIANIST: EVELYN LEE

「在全場滿座的熱烈氣氛中,演出極為成功。這次音樂會薈萃了全港的精英,其規模的盛大,籌備的周密,演出的感人,實書本港樂壇寫下又一光輝之頁。」

《工商晚報》

1968 年 4 月 15 日

香港華人基督教聯會 主辦復活節聖樂音樂會

指揮:
黃永熙

獨唱:
程雅南 [s]

伴奏:
鄺李淑嫻

地點:
香港大會堂音樂廳

1968 年 5 月 19 日／6 月 2 日

威爾第《安魂曲》

指揮:
黃永熙

獨唱:
江樺 [s]、譚天眷 [m]、何君靜 [t]、陳供生 [bb]

伴奏:
香港管弦樂團

地點:
香港大會堂音樂廳

CITY HALL
POPULAR
CONCERT
presented by
the Urban Council

VERDI'S
REQUIEM

H.K. Oratorio Society
H.K. Philharmonic Orchestra
Conductor: Dr. Wong Wing-Hee

Ella Kiang, soprano
Giulietta Tann, mezzo-soprano
Ho Kwan Ching, tenor
Chan Kung Sang, bass

Sunday, 2nd June
at 3 p.m.
Tickets ($1) at City Hall

1968 年 12 月 1 日 **

海頓《創世記》

指揮：
黃永熙

獨唱：
徐美芬 [s]、許元貞 [m]、
黃飛然 [t]、袁恩光 [b]

伴奏：
管弦樂隊、鄺李淑嫻、
羅玉琪

地點：
香港大會堂音樂廳

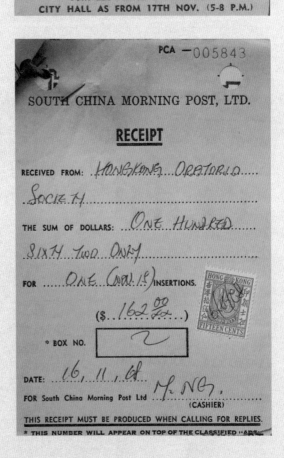

COMMERCIAL RADIO

8.02 p.m.

HAYDN'S CREATION AS
PERFORMED BY THE
HONG KONG ORATORIO SOCIETY
— LIVE FROM THE CITY HALL
CONCERT HALL.

HONG KONG ORATORIO SOCIETY

PRESENTS

CREATION

BY J. HAYDN

CONDUCTOR: DR. WONG WING HEE

SOLOISTS : NANCY ZI as GABRIEL
FRANK HUANG as URIEL
CHAN KUNG SANG as RAPHAEL
GUAN CHENG WONG as EVE
YUEN YAN KWONG as ADAM

ORCHESTRAL ACCOMPANIMENT
with EVELYN KWONG (organ)
and IRENE LO (piano)

SUNDAY, 1ST DECEMBER, 1968, 8:00 P.M.
CITY HALL, CONCERT HALL.

TICKETS ON SALE NOW AT

MOUTRIE & CO. (H.K.) LTD.,
TOM LEE PIANO CO. KOWLOON.
CITY HALL AS FROM 17TH NOV. (5-8 P.M.)

PCA — 005843

SOUTH CHINA MORNING POST, LTD.

RECEIPT

RECEIVED FROM: HONGKONG ORATORIO
SOCIETY
THE SUM OF DOLLARS: ONE HUNDRED
SIXTY TWO ONLY
FOR ONE (NOV. 18) INSERTIONS.
($ 162 00)
* BOX NO. 2
DATE: 16. 11. 68
FOR South China Morning Post Ltd M. NG.
(CASHIER)

THIS RECEIPT MUST BE PRODUCED WHEN CALLING FOR REPLIES.
* THIS NUMBER WILL APPEAR ON TOP OF THE CLASSIFIED "ADS"

FESTIVAL OF CHRISTMAS MUSIC

Hong Kong Oratorio Society
Friday 20 December at 7.30 p.m.

Melba Choir
Sunday 22 December at 2.30 p.m.

Victoria Chamber Symphony
Sunday 22 December at 5 p.m.

**Robin Boyle Singers
& Deena Webster**
Monday 23 December at 7.30 p.m.

聖誕音樂會

獨唱：
陳劉沐蘭 [s]、歐陽慕貞 [a]、
Donald McComb [t]、陳供生 [bb]

伴奏：
鄺李淑嫻

地點：
香港大會堂音樂廳

凱魯畢妮《C 小調安魂曲》、羅西尼《聖母悼歌》

指揮：
黃永熙

獨唱：
江樺[s]、李冰[m]、林祥園[t]、
Malcolm Barnett[bb]

伴奏：
管弦樂隊、鄺李淑嫻

地點：
香港大會堂音樂廳

THE HONG KONG ORATORIO SOCIETY
AFTER A PERFORMANCE OF CHERUBINI'S "REQUIEM" & ROSSINI'S "STABAT MATER"
AT THE CITY HALL CONCERT HALL ON 10 MAY 1969

THE HONG KONG ORATORIO
SOCIETY
presents

REQUIEM
by Cherubini
and
STABAT MATER
by Rossini

Conductor: **Dr. Wong Wing Hee**
Soloists: **Ella Kiang, Soprano**
   Lee Bing, Mezzo-Soprano
   Lin Siang Yuen, Tenor
   Malcolm Barnett, Bass

Orchestral accompaniment with
Evelyn Kwong (organ)

CITY HALL, CONCERT HALL
Saturday, 10th May, 1969, 8.00 p.m.

Tickets: $10, $6, $3, available at:

Moutries' (Alexandra House)
Tom Lee Piano Co. (Carnarvon Road, Kowloon)
City Hall (from 27th April)

THE HONG KONG ORATORIO SOCIETY

presents

BEETHOVEN's

MASS IN C OP. 86   THE MOUNT OF OLIVES OP. 85

Soloists: Soloists:
Iris To, Soprano   Tuan Pei Lan, Soprano
Barbara Chen, Contralto Ho Kwan Ching, Tenor
L. G. McKinney, Tenor   Chan Kung Sang, Bass
Chan Kung Sang, Bass

Conducted by Dr. Wong Wing Hee
with orchestral accompaniment

City Hall, Concert Hall
Friday, November 7th, 1969, 8 p.m.

Tickets: $10, $6, $3 available at

Moutrie & Co. (Alexandra House, H.K.)
Tom Lee Piano Co. (Cameron Rd., Kowloon)
Tsang Fook Piano Co. (Marina House, H.K.)
City Hall Ticket Office (from Oct. 25)

"Dr Wong has welded the members into an excellent co-ordinated group of well-balanced voices, and the chorus sections were the best part of the performances of the two choral masterpieces."

《南華早報》

貝多芬《C 大調彌撒曲》[1]、
《橄欖山》

指揮：
黃永熙

獨唱：
杜少端 [1s]、陳之霞 [1a]、
McKinney [1t]、段白蘭 [s]、
何君靜 [t]、陳供生 [bb]

伴奏：
管弦樂隊

地點：
香港大會堂音樂廳

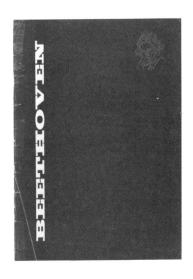

H.K. ORATORIO SOCIETY PERFORMANCE AT H.K. TVB

1969 年 12 月 2 日

**聖誕 carols
on TVB 4-6 pm**

THE HONG KONG ORATORIO SOCIETY
CHRISTMAS CONCERT
21 DECEMBER 1969, CITY HALL CONCERT HALL

1969 年 12 月 21 日

聖誕音樂會

指揮：
黃飛然

獨唱：
陳劉沐蘭[s]、陳之霞[a]、
何君靜[t]、Loren Noren[b]、
孫永輝[bb]

地點：
香港大會堂音樂廳

1970-1979 年

導讀：

1970 年代是香港音樂，以至整個表演藝術界的歷史轉折時期。其間政府調整資助策略，由市政局主導藝術發展，職業藝團相繼成立。香港聖樂團雖然不在此列，但仍受益於政策的改變所帶來更多演出的機會，包括首次與本地及著名海外樂團的合作演出，以及每套節目由一場增加到兩場演出。

在這十年間，有記錄音樂會一共有三十八次，其中不少極具歷史意義，包括首次外訪到菲律賓、台灣和澳門演出。樂團自黃永熙博士領導後，水平有一定提升。1970 年代初開始樂團音樂會更多與市政局聯合主辦，報章廣告更刊登了「售罄」。此外各電視台以至商業電台也播放樂團演出，足證樂團在社會的認受性逐漸提升。

樂團在這個時期開始使用團徽，場刊製作也明顯更精美，節目預告亦恆常化。合唱隊伍亦銳意擴大成

員人數，例如兩個女聲部由 1972 年的 48 人增至 1978 年的 64 人。後者名單中包括阮妙芬、譚允芝、盧業瑂等本地新生代成員。

客席獨唱家方面，這十年期間先後有費明儀、江樺、楊羅娜三大女高音參與演出，成為歷史佳話。隨着樂團首訪菲律賓演出後，菲國獨唱家也來港參與演出。至於客席指揮最重要的演出，是 1972 年紐約聖樂團 Charles Lee 博士來港親自指揮自己的合唱作品。

至於與樂隊演出，1974 年職業化前後的香港管弦樂團均與聖樂團演出。較為重要的是 1971 年由林克昌指揮的貝多芬第九交響曲，那可能是首次由香港本地樂隊與合唱團演出全曲。港樂和聖樂團在 1979 年兩度演出《貝九》，分別由陳亮聲、董麟指揮。此外，聖樂團 1978 年與成立不久的泛亞交響樂團聯袂演出。

更為重要的，是聖樂團兩度與外國樂團在香港藝術節聯合演出，1977 年、1978 年分別與 BBC 蘇格蘭樂團和伯恩茅斯交響樂團合演。另外，樂團在 1976 年第一屆亞洲藝術節首演黃自《長恨歌》，載入史冊。🎵

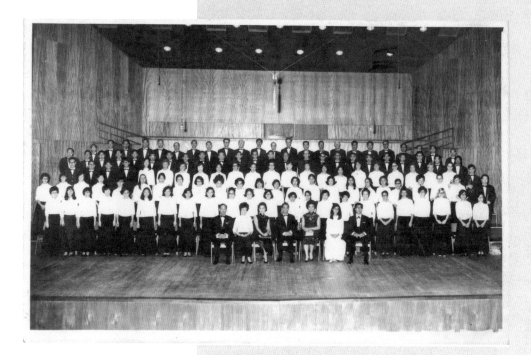

1970 年 4 月 19 日 *

韓德爾《彌賽亞》

指揮：
黃永熙

獨唱：
陳劉沐蘭 [s]、周宏俊 [a]、
黃飛然 [t]、李少偉 [bb]

伴奏：
鄺李淑嫻、蔣璧輝

地點：
香港大會堂音樂廳

"All in all the performance was very enjoyable, and one in which Mr Wong and the Oratorio Society can take pride."

《南華早報》

SOLOISTS
獨　唱

Ella Kiang
Soprano
江　樺
女高音

Lee Bing
Mezzo Soprano
李　冰
女中音

Ho Kwan Ching
Tenor
何君靜
男高音

Chan Kung Sang
Bass
陳供生
男低音

「比較高格而有意義之演唱大會……演出的
合唱部份，由香港聖樂團的逾百名團員擔
任……伴奏方面，有該團自組龐大的管弦樂
隊擔任，全曲由黃永熙博士指揮。」

《華僑日報》

貝多芬誕辰二百周年

貝多芬
《莊嚴彌撒曲 D 大調 》

指揮：
黃永熙

獨唱：
江樺 [s]、李冰 [m]、何君靜 [t]、
陳供生 [bb]

伴奏：
42 人管弦樂隊、鄺李淑嫻

地點：
香港大會堂音樂廳

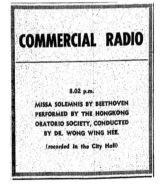

1970 年 12 月 19 日

聖誕音樂節

地點：
香港大會堂音樂廳

1970 年 12 月 24-25 日

麗的電視播放聖誕歌詠

指揮：
黃永熙

《工商晚報》

The Urban Council & the Hong Kong Philharmonic Society

jointly present

BEETHOVEN'S SYMPHONY NO. 9

貝 多 芬 第 九 交 響 曲

市 政 局 與 香 港 管 弦 協 會 聯 合 主 辦

CITY HALL CONCERT HALL 大 會 堂 音 樂 廳
MAY 15 & 16, 1971 一 九 七 一 年 五 月 十 五 及 十 六 日

THE HONG KONG PHILHARMONIC ORCHESTRA
AND THE HONG KONG ORATORIO SOCIETY
AFTER A PERFORMANCE OF
BEETHOVEN'S NINTH SYMPHONY (CHORAL)
15 MAY 1971, CITY HALL CONCERT HALL, HONG KONG

"...Ode to Joy sung well by a choir of local residents is a gratifying demonstration of the development of standards of performance by the musicians of our community...The Oratorio Society provided an excellent Chorus for the Finale, and the singers showed the result of careful rehearsals with Chorus Master Dr. Wong Wing-hee."

《南華早報》

1971 年 5 月 15-16 日

市政局與香港管弦協會聯合主辦

貝多芬《第九交響曲》

指揮：
林克昌

獨唱：
江樺[s]、周宏俊[m]、張寶華[t]、
McKinney[bb]

伴奏：
香港管弦樂團

地點：
香港大會堂音樂廳

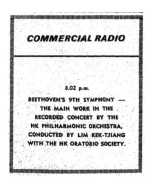

COMMERCIAL RADIO

8.02 p.m.

BEETHOVEN'S 9TH SYMPHONY —
THE MAIN WORK IN THE
RECORDED CONCERT BY THE
HK PHILHARMONIC ORCHESTRA,
CONDUCTED BY LIM KEK-TJIANG
WITH THE HK ORATORIO SOCIETY.

1971 年 7 月 17 日 /18 日

威爾第《讚美貞女瑪利亞》、《聖母讚歌》、莫扎特《安魂曲》

指揮：
黃永熙

獨唱：
徐增綏 [s]、歐陽慕貞 [a]、David Lee[t]、楊允田 [bb]

伴奏：
43 人管弦樂隊（領奏：Lous Garcia）、鄺李淑嫻

地點：
香港大會堂音樂廳

The Urban Council & The Hong Kong Oratorio Society jointly present

TE DEUM *by Verdi*
REQUIEM *by Mozart*

Conductor: Wong Wing Hee

Soloists:
Alice Wong, soprano
Barbara Chen, contralto
David Lee, tenor
Yeung Wan Tin, bass

(with orchestral accompaniment)

CITY HALL CONCERT HALL

Saturday, 17 July & Sunday, 18 July 1971 at 8 p.m.
Tickets: $1 (students), $3, $5
at the City Hall Box Office

THE HONG KONG ORATORIO SOCIETY
AFTER A PERFORMANCE
OF VERDI'S "TE DEUM" & "MOZART'S" "REQUIEM"
AT THE CITY HALL CONCERT HALL ON 17th & 18th JULY 1971

"For those of us who have been attending concerts by the Society since the early days of its activities, there is much satisfaction in noting the large membership and the steady progress in the performance of increasingly demanding works."

《南華早報》

THE HONG KONG ORATORIO SOCIETY AND THE CHUNG CHI COLLEGE CHOIR
AFTER A PERFORMANCE OF HANDEL'S "ISRAEL IN EGYPT"
6th NOVEMBER 1971, CITY HALL CONCERT HALL

THE URBAN COUNCIL AND THE HONG KONG ORATORIO SOCIETY
JOINTLY PRESENT

MASS IN G by F. SCHUBERT

AND TWO WORKS BY CONTEMPORARY COMPOSERS:

TRANSFIGURATION by HOVHANESS

FAREWELL, VOYAGER by T. CHARLES LEE

SOLOISTS:	BARBARA FEI	(Soprano)
	DAVID LEE	(Tenor)
	JAMES McKINNEY	(Bass)
CONDUCTOR:	T. CHARLES LEE	
CHOIR DIRECTOR:	WONG WING HEE	
ACCOMPANISTS:	EVELYN LEE	
	WONG KIN YU	

SATURDAY, 27 MAY 1972 AT 8.00 P.M.
CITY HALL CONCERT HALL
ADMISSION TICKETS: $5 $3 $1 (STUDENT)
AVAILABLE AT CITY HALL TICKET OFFICE

THE HONG KONG ORATORIO SOCIETY AFTER THE PERFORMANCE OF "FAREWELL VOYAGER"
CONDUCTED BY DR. CHARLES T. LEE OF ORATORIO SOCIETY OF NEW YORK
CITY HALL CONCERT HALL, MAY 27, 1972.

劉森:「聲部之比例十分平均,於混聲演唱時,其聲音極其和諧與渾然成一體,成為一種沛然莫禦之音色,即使未聽其歌詞之演唱,亦已顯得先聲奪人了。」

(剪報)

慶祝崇基學院成立 20 周年暨香港聖樂團成立 15 周年聯合演出

韓德爾《出埃及記》

指揮:
黃永熙

獨唱:
潘志清[s]、Poppy Crosby[s]、周宏俊[a]、黃飛然[t]、McKinney[bb]、陳供生[bb]

伴奏:
管弦樂隊、黃健瑜

地點:
香港大會堂音樂廳

舒伯特《G 大調彌撒曲》、哈夫納《基督易容曲》、查思理《航行者,前途無量》

指揮:
T. Charles Lee

獨唱:
費明儀[s]、David Lee[t]、McKinney[bb]

伴奏:
黃健瑜、李淑嫻

地點:
香港大會堂音樂廳

[馬尼拉] 威爾第《安魂曲》

指揮：
David Yap（1125）、
黃永熙

獨唱：
Conching Rosal[s]、Kathy Sternberg[m]、Francisco Aseniero[t]、Noel Velasco[bb]

聯合演出：
菲律賓合唱團

伴奏：
馬尼拉交響樂團

地點：
馬尼拉菲律賓文化中心

SPECIAL ANNOUNCEMENT

SECOND GALA: Sunday, November 26, 1972
6:20 in the evening

Guest Conductor: DR. W. HEYWARD WONG

HONG KONG ORATORIO SOCIETY

Tickets are available at:

1. CCP Lobby (During Intermission tonight)

2. MRS. LILY A. BACHO (Knox Church)
   Telephone No. 76-84-37

3. ST. JOHN'S METHODIST CHURCH
   Mrs. Sonia Velasco (Tel. 99-57-16)

4. UNION CHURCH OF MANILA
   Mr. Vittorio Clavette or Miss Clemente
   Tel. 88-99-81

5. ELLINWOOD (Malate) CHURCH
   Mr. Gregorio Alarcon (A.M. only)
   Tel. 59-36-37

6. CCP Box Office or Lobby (Before Curtain)
   For reservations, please call: Tel. 500691

Limited Tickets Available:

Sponsor Seats	P 25.00
Orch. Center Front	20.00
Orch. Sides	10.00
Balcony I	5.00
Balcony II	(Sold Out)

"Doubtless, Requiem has been a singularly-outstanding presentation for the year 1972, a stupendous opus superbly rendered."

（菲律賓 *Bulletin Today*）

THE HOLY CARPENTER CHURCH

presents

VERDI'S REQUIEM

to be performed by

THE HONG KONG ORATORIO SOCIETY

ELLA KIANG Soprano
RUTH CHOW Mezzo-Soprano
HO KWAN CHING Tenor
CHAN KUNG SANG Bass
EVELYN LEE Organist
DIANA TSEUNG Pianist
DR. WONG WING-HEE Conductor

17 January, 1973 Wednesday 8 p.m.

City Hall Concert-Hall,

Tickets at $6. $3. From City Hall

1-8 p.m. Saturdays, Sundays &

Public Holidays

12.30-1.30 p.m.; 5-8 p.m. Weekdays.

1972 年 12 月 20-23 日

聖誕音樂會

韓德爾《彌賽亞》選段

地點：
香港大會堂音樂廳

1973 年 1 月 17 日

聖匠堂主辦

威爾第《安魂曲》

指揮：
黃永熙

獨唱：
江樺[s]、周宏俊[a]、何君靜[t]、
陳供生[bb]

伴奏：
李淑嫻、蔣璧輝

地點：
香港大會堂音樂廳

1973 年 6 月 1-2 日

孟德爾遜《以利亞》

指揮：
黃永熙

獨唱：
Victoria Kincaid[s]、
周宏俊[a]、
Francisco Aseniero[t]、
Constantino Bernardez[b]

伴奏：
李淑嫻、管弦樂團（領奏：
Victor Chamberlain）

地點：
香港大會堂音樂廳

MENDELSSOHN'S
ELIJAH

"...the standard of singing was very high, probably at its very best of the many oratorios performed in recent years. "

《南華早報》

THE URBAN COUNCIL
and
THE HONG KONG ORATORIO SOCIETY
jointly present

MENDELSSOHN'S
ELIJAH
with
Orchestral Accompaniment

Victoria Kinkaid   (soprano)
Ruth Chow   (mezzo-soprano)
Francisco Aseniero   (tenor)
Constantino Bernardez (baritone)

(Messrs. Aseniero and Bernardez, famous vocalists from Manila, Philippines, are coming to Hong Kong specially for the performances)

Conductor: Dr Wong Wing-hee

1st (Friday)   June, 1973, 8 p.m. – City Hall
2nd (Saturday)   Concert Hall

Tickets at $5, $3, $1 (for students only) available at City Hall Box Office

1974 年 4 月 18-19 日

韓德爾《參孫》

指揮：
黃永熙

獨唱：
Joyce Bell[s]、周宏俊[a]、
Francisco Aseniero[t]、
Constantino Bernardez[b]

伴奏：
樂隊（領奏：Victor
Chamberlain）、李淑嫻、
劉善言

地點：
香港大會堂音樂廳

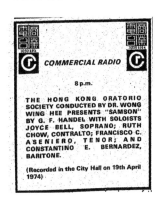

"Dr Wong's excellent training of the Choir and his firm control of dynamics resulted in a very good standard of performance throughout the evening...The Oratorio Society gives pleasure to many by their concert and television performances, and much pleasure to their members who enjoy the rehearsals every week."

《南華早報》

1974 年 9 月 28 日、11 月 12 日**

海頓《四季頌》

指揮：
黃永熙

獨唱：
楊羅娜[s]、Michael Ryan[t]、
榮德淵[b]

伴奏：
黃健瑜、李淑嫻，加圓號、
小號、定音鼓

地點：
香港大會堂音樂廳

「此次演唱會規模之盛大，及陣容之強壯，係前所未見。」

《福音週報》

1974 年 12 月 20 日

聖誕音樂會

A Day for Dance
by Lloyd Pfautsch

指揮：
黃永熙

伴奏：
管弦樂隊

地點：
香港大會堂音樂廳

1975 年 3 月 30-31 日 **

[馬尼拉] 孟德爾遜《以利亞》

指揮：
黃永熙

獨唱：
Irma Enrile[s]、
Erlinda Ascuna[a]、
Francisco Aseniero[t]、
Constantino Bernardez[b]

伴奏：
菲律賓愛樂樂團

地點：
馬尼拉菲律賓文化中心

1975 年 7 月 5 日

海頓《創世記》

指揮：
黃飛然

獨唱：
徐美芬 [s]、David Lee [t]、
榮德淵 [b]、李少偉 [bb]

伴奏：
黃健瑜、李淑嫻

地點：
香港大會堂音樂廳

《華僑日報》

"The chorus was in very good voice, managing one especially fine pianissimo, and some controlled but most forceful loud passages."

《南華早報》

 8 p.m.
THE HONG KONG ORATORIO SOCIETY DIRECTED BY DR.
WONG WING HEE.
B Minor Mass by Bach

Listen to the new
personal sound of 1050 Radio

THE URBAN COUNCIL AND THE HONG KONG ORATORIO SOCIETY

JOINTLY PRESENT

市政局及香港聖樂團聯合主辦

BACH'S B minor mass
巴赫：B 短調彌撒曲

Soloists
獨唱

Lola Young, Soprano	女高音：	楊羅娜
Ruth Chow, Mezzo Soprano	女次高音：	周宏俊
Barbara Chen, Alto	女低音：	陳之霞
David Lee, Tenor	男高音：	李大衛
L.G. McKinney, Baritone	男中音：	秦堅理
Evelyn Lee, Organist	風琴：	李淑嫻

And Orchestral Accompaniment
管絃樂獨伴奏

Victor Shum, Leader
首 席：岑國緯

Conducted by Wong Wing Hee
指 揮：黃永熙

City Hall Concert Hall
Saturday, 22, Nov. 1975, 8:00 p.m.
Sunday, 23, Nov. 1975, 8:00 p.m.

大會堂音樂廳
一九七五年十一月廿二日下午八時
一九七五年十一月廿三日下午八時

— 3 —

1975 年 11 月 22-23 日

巴赫 B 小調彌撒曲

指揮：
黃永熙

獨唱：
楊羅娜[s]、周宏俊[m]、
陳之霞[a]、David Lee[t]、
McKinney[b]

伴奏：
管弦樂隊（首席：岑國緯）、
李淑嫻

地點：
香港大會堂音樂廳

《華僑日報》

1976 年 4 月 9-11 日

韓德爾《彌賽亞》

指揮：
蒙瑪

獨唱：
江樺[s]、周宏俊[a]、
Francisco Aseniero[t]、
Aurelio Estanislao[b]

伴奏：
香港管弦樂團

地點：
香港大會堂音樂廳

THE HONG KONG ORATORIO SOCIETY AND THE HONG KONG PHILHARMONIC ORCHESTRA
AFTER A PERFORMANCE OF HANDEL'S "MESSIAH"
ON 10 APRIL 1976 AT THE CITY HALL, CONCERT HALL, HONG KONG

SOB O PATROCÍNIO DA DIOCESE DE MACAU
澳門天主教會聖樂藝進

HONGKONG ORATÓRIO SOCIETY
香港聖樂團

Apresenta
演出

MISSA IN C MINOR
de
WOLFGANG AMADEUS MOZART
莫扎特作品C短調彌撒曲

Conduzida por
Dr. Wong Wing Hee
黃永熙博士指揮

Data: dia 1 de Agosto de 1976 - às 20.00 horas
日期：一九七六年八月一日晚上八時正
Local: Auditório Diocesano
地點：聖羅撒教區音樂廳

The Hong Kong Oratorio Society after a performance in the Asian Arts Festival on 11th November 1976 at the City Hall Concert Hall, Hong Kong.

AN URBAN COUNCIL PRESENTATION
市政局主辦

HONG KONG 香港聖樂團
ORATORIO 中國藝術歌曲
SOCIETY 及民歌演唱會

CONCERT HALL 香港大會堂音樂廳

亞洲藝術節
THE FESTIVAL OF
ASIAN ARTS
10-24 NOVEMBER 1976 HONG KONG CITY HALL
一九七六年十一月十日至廿四日香港大會堂

1976 年 8 月 1 日

[澳門] 莫扎特
《C 小調彌撒曲》

指揮：
黃永熙

地點：
聖羅撒教區音樂廳

1976 年 11 月 11 日 **

第一屆亞洲藝術節

黃自《長恨歌》及
中國民歌選唱

指揮：
黃永熙

獨唱：
胡佳 [s]、李冰 [m]、何君靜 [t]、
程路禹 [b]

伴奏：
李淑嫻、賈那素、黎如冰
（中國民歌）

地點：
香港大會堂音樂廳

莫扎特《C 小調彌撒曲》

指揮：
黃永熙

獨唱：
江樺 [s]、譚天眷 [m]、王帆 [t]、
楊允田 [b]

伴奏：
管弦樂隊

地點：
香港大會堂音樂廳

HONG KONG ORATORIO SOCIETY AND URBAN
COUNCIL JOINTLY PRESENT

MOZART'S GRAND MASS IN C MINOR

ON SUNDAY, DECEMBER 5TH, 8 P.M.,
AT THE CITY HALL CONCERT HALL

CONDUCTOR: WONG WING HEE
SOLOISTS: ELLA KIANG, SOPRANO
          GIULIETTA TAM, MEZZO SOPRANO
          WONG FANG, TENOR
          YEUNG WAN TIN, BASS
       WITH ORCHESTRAL ACCOMPANIMENT.

TICKETS OBTAINABLE AT CITY HALL BOX OFFICE

The Society is recruiting more members. If you are an experienced choralist, you are invited to call at the West Lounge, Y.M.C.A., Salisbury Road, Kowloon, on any Tuesday evening at 8 p.m. before December 29th, 1976, for an audition.

The Society's projects for 1977 include:—

The Dream of Gerontius   Elgar
   (With BBC Scottish Symphony Orchestra—
   February 28th and March 1st)

Te Deum   Bruchner

Ninth Symphony   Beethoven
   (With H.K. Philharmonic—Soloists from
   Germany—September 22nd, 23rd and 24th)

A Choral Work with the Hong Kong Philharmonic
   (December 16th and 17th)

Old members of the Society are urged to re-join its regular rehearsals on Tuesdays, 8 p.m., at the Y.M.C.A., Salisbury Road, Kowloon.

《華僑日報》

Monday	BBC Scottish Symphony Orchestra with Hong Kong Oratorio Society
28	Conductor: Christopher Seaman Soloists: Bernadette Greevy, Contralto, John Mitchinson, Tenor Delme Bryn-Jones, Baritone
	Elgar: Dream of Gerontius, op.38
Tuesday	BBC Scottish Symphony Orchestra with The Hong Kong Oratorio Society
1	Conductor: Christopher Seaman Soloists: Bernadette Greevy, Contralto, John Mitchinson, Tenor Delme Bryn-Jones, Baritone
March	Elgar: Dream of Gerontius, op.38

黃永熙："It was not only the dream of Gerontius, but mine too. Since I joined the society we have performed many major works never sung in Hong Kong before and we had waited a long time to do the [Dream of Gerontius by Elgar]"

《南華早報》

1976 年 12 月 16 日

聖誕音樂會

指揮：
黃永熙

地點：
香港大會堂音樂廳

1977 年 2 月 28 日 -3 月 1 日 ★★

第五屆香港藝術節
埃爾加《格隆提爾斯之夢》

指揮：
Christopher Seaman

伴奏：
BBC 蘇格蘭交響樂團

1977 年 5 月 21 日

貝多芬《C 大調彌撒曲》、
《平靜的海洋》

地點：
九龍城浸信會

《華僑日報》

1977 年 9 月 23-25 日

紀念貝多芬逝世
150 周年

布魯克納《讚美頌》、
貝多芬《第九交響曲》

指揮：
蒙瑪

伴奏：
香港管弦樂團

地點：
香港大會堂音樂廳

THE HONG KONG ORATORIO SOCIETY AND THE HONG KONG PHILHARMONIC ORCHESTRA
AFTER A PERFORMANCE OF BRUCKNER'S "TE DEUM" & BEETHOVEN'S "SYMPHONY No. 9"
ON 26 SEPTEMBER 1977 AT THE CITY HALL, CONCERT HALL, HONG KONG

貝多芬《第九交響曲》

香港聖樂團主席鄭崇羔：「今晚的音樂會，旨在讓公眾人士欣賞個別團友獨唱。全場收入，用以貼助來春[到台北]旅行演唱費用。」

（場刊）

韓德爾《彌賽亞》

指揮：
黃永熙

獨唱：
江樺[s]、周宏俊[a]、
Noel Velasco[t]、
McKinney[bb]

伴奏：
香港管弦樂團

地點：
香港大會堂音樂廳

THE HONG KONG ORATORIO SOCIETY AND THE HONG KONG PHILHARMONIC ORCHESTRA
AFTER A PERFORMANCE OF HANDEL'S "MESSIAH"
ON 16 DECEMBER 1977 AT THE CITY HALL, CONCERT HALL, HONG KONG

"The chorus forms the strongest single element of Dr Wong's
interpretation of the Messiah. He uses 160 or so voices like an
instrument, bringing out light and shade, pathos and ecstasy
by turn...For colour and conviction it would be hard to improve
or to equal this year's Messiah."

《南華早報》

日 期	大會堂音樂廳	時 間
30 星期一	伯恩茅斯交响樂團,香港聖樂團 指揮:巴夫奧 · 貝格倫 獨唱:費莉絲蒂 · 龐瑪(女高音) 羅拔 · 戴維斯(男中音) 狄伯特:雙弦樂團協奏曲 舒伯特:C小調第四交响曲(「悲劇的」,D.417) 佛瑞:安魂曲(作品48)	晚上八時
31 星期二	伯恩茅斯交响樂團,香港聖樂團 指揮:巴夫奧 · 貝格倫 獨唱:費莉絲蒂 · 龐瑪(女高音) 羅拔 · 戴維斯(男中音) 凱魯畢尼:「安納克瓦」序曲 西貝流士:C大調第三交响曲(作品52) 佛瑞:安魂曲(作品48)	晚上八時

1978 年 1 月 30-31 日

第六屆香港藝術節

佛瑞《安魂曲》

指揮:
Paavo Berglund

伴奏:
伯恩茅斯交響樂團

地點:
香港大會堂音樂廳

海頓《四季頌》

指揮：
黃永熙

獨唱：
楊羅娜 s、陳榮光 t、榮德淵 b

伴奏：
台北市立交響樂團

地點：
台北孫中山紀念堂

（中華民國第一屆聖樂展連鎖活動之一）
**香港聖樂團
慈善演唱會**
「HONG KONG ORATORIO SOCIETY」CHARITY CONCERT
（全部收入轉捐台灣麻瘋救濟協會為麻瘋病胞醫治工作之用）

演唱歌曲：海頓「四季頌」　　獨唱：女高音／楊羅娜
指　揮：黃永熙博士　　　　　　　　男高音／陳榮光
鋼　琴：李淑嫻　　　　　　　　　　男中音／榮德淵
電子琴：Huge MACDONALD
法國號：丁長勤・葉可欣
定音鼓：朱宗慶
時間：民國67年3月26日(星期日)下午八時
地點：國父紀念館
主辦：中華民國音樂學會　協辦：台灣麻瘋救濟協會等十單位
策劃：「香港聖樂團」慈善公演籌備委員會

「合唱的優點很多，由於香港學習外文的環境較好，所以
演唱時的發音相當流暢⋯⋯香港聖樂團的另一個優點是音
量夠大、也夠均衡，團員中，男女人數的比例雖然是二比
三，可是男女聲部的音量相當平衡⋯⋯聽來渾然一體，可
見一個訓練有素的合唱團。」

《中央日報》

THE HONG KONG ORATORIO SOCIETY WITH THE PAN ASIA SYMPHONY
ORCHESTRA AFTER A PERFORMANCE OF HAYDN'S SEASONS ON
2 MAY 1978 AT THE CITY HALL CONCERT HALL, HONG KONG

1978 年 5 月 2 日

海頓《四季頌》

指揮：
黃永熙

獨唱：
楊羅娜 [s]、陳榮光 [t]、榮德淵 [b]

伴奏：
泛亞管弦樂團

地點：
香港大會堂音樂廳

1978 年 5 月 20 日

元朗區文藝協進會主辦

海頓《四季頌》

指揮：
黃永熙

獨唱：
楊羅娜 [s]、張汶 [t]、楊允田 [b]

伴奏：
李淑嫻、戚明儀

地點：
元朗安寧路信義會生命堂

香港聖樂團
下週二演出
泛亞管弦樂隊伴奏
素來以演唱巨型聲

的訓練及發展，將會更
能迎合社會的需要，是次酒會的舉辦目
的，除旨在給予學生作實際經驗上的體察外，
並希望外界人士對兩校在旅遊業及酒店業上人
才的訓練方面有所認識

樂作品馳名之香港聖樂
團定於五月二日星期二
在大會堂音樂廳與市政
局合辦規模龐大之音樂
會演唱海頓之活潑輕鬆
「四季曲」將陽春烟景
多日心緒，炎夏風光，秋天興緻
刻劃人微

其中農夫，農女及農女
之情人分別由享譽至高
之聲樂家楊羅娜，名男
中音榮德淵及留學維也
納音專之抒情男高音陳
榮光擔任獨唱，除了聖
伴奏。

樂團之一百五十位合唱
團員並有泛亞管弦樂隊
五十多人伴奏，由黃永
熙博士指揮，朗誦部份
由英籍麥唐納先生電琴

規模龐大籌備認真
，定有美滿成績，票價
三種在大會堂票房發售
，演出只一場。楊羅娜
小姐，欲聘從

分五元，十元，十五元
速。

1978 年 10 月 1 日 *

韓德爾《出埃及記》

指揮：
黃永熙

獨唱：
潘志清 [s] 、陳愛堅 [s] 、
陳之霞 [a] 、張汶 [t]

伴奏：
黃健瑜、戚明儀

地點：
香港大會堂音樂廳

The Hong Kong Oratorio Society, The Wong Tai Sin Children's Choir and The Hong Kong Philharmonic Orchestra after a performance of Carl Orff's "Carmina Burana" on 19.1.1979 at the City Hall Concert Hall.

1979 年 1 月 19-20 日

奧爾夫《布蘭詩歌》

指揮：
蒙瑪

聯合演出：
黃大仙兒童合唱團
（指揮：楊羅娜）

伴奏：
香港管弦樂團

地點：
香港大會堂音樂廳

January 19 & 20 (Friday & Saturday) 1979, at 8 p.m.
City Hall Concert Hall

Conductor: Hans Günter Mommer
Soloists: Anne Pashley, soprano
Ronald Murdock, tenor
Robert Carpenter-Turner, baritone

Choir: Hong Kong Oratorio Society
Choirmaster: Wong Wing Hee
Choir: Wong Tai Sin Children's Choir
Choirmistress: Lola Young

Mozart   Il Seraglio Overture
Britten   Les Illuminations for Solo Voice & Orchestra, Op. 18
Orff   Carmina Burana

Tickets at $20, 15, 10 & 3 (for students) from the City Hall Box Office

an Urban Council presentation
in association with The Hong Kong Philharmonic Society Limited

FORTHCOMING
JANUARY CONCERTS

THE HONG KONG ORATORIO SOCIETY AND THE HONG KONG PHILHARMONIC ORCHESTRA PRESENTING BEETHOVEN'S "9th SYMPHONY" AT THE QUEEN'S BIRTHDAY CONCERT ON 21st & 22nd ~~MAY~~, 1979 AT THE CITY HALL CONCERT HALL, H.K.
APRIL

1979 年 4 月 21-22 日

女皇壽辰音樂會

貝多芬《第九交響曲》

指揮：
陳亮聲

獨唱：
江樺[s]、陳之霞[a]、翁克強[t]、
程路禹[bb]

伴奏：
香港管弦樂團

地點：
香港大會堂音樂廳

羅西尼《莊嚴彌撒曲》

指揮：
黃永熙

獨唱：
李冰 [m]、陳之霞 [a]、
鄭棣聲 [t]、陳供生 [bb]

伴奏：
黃健瑜、戚明儀、翁偉儀

地點：
香港大會堂音樂廳

貝多芬《合唱幻想曲》

指揮：
George Hurst

伴奏：
香港管弦樂團

市政局主辦

聖誕音樂會系列 '79

指揮：
黃永熙

伴奏：
戚明儀

地點：
香港大會堂劇院

THE HONG KONG ORATORIO SOCIETY PRESENTING ROSINI'S "MESSE SOLENNELLE"
ON 29TH SEPTEMBER, 1979 AT THE CITY HALL CONCERT HALL

> **HONG KONG ORATORIO SOCIETY**
> **Performance of**
> **ROSSINI'S MESSE SOLENNELLE**
> **City Hall Concert Hall**
> **29 September 1979 (Saturday), 8 p.m.**
> **Tickets: $5, $10, $15**
> **From City Hall Box Office**
>
> *****************
>
> The Society will perform Beethoven's Choral Fantasia in November and Ninth Symphony in December with the Hong Kong Philharmonic Orchestra. Experienced choralists who are interested in these works and oratorio music are invited to call at the West Lounge, YMCA, Salisbury Rd., Tsimshatsui, Kowloon, on Tuesday, 2 October 1979, or any Tuesday, at 8 p.m. for an audition.

貝多芬《第九交響曲》

指揮：
董麟

獨唱：
駱秀端[s]、陳之霞[a]、王帆[t]、
程路禹[b]

伴奏：
香港管弦樂團

地點：
香港大會堂音樂廳

《工商日報》

1980-1989 年

導讀：

1980 年代承接 1970 年代職業藝團相繼成立，發展一系列的演出場地：由 1980 年的荃灣大會堂開始，沙田、屯門等，到 1989 年的香港文化中心。另外伊利沙伯、紅磡等大型體育館亦相繼落成。香港聖樂團在大部份新建音樂廳都留下音符。

在這十年間演出增至五十二次有記錄的音樂會，其中八次是在境外演出，包括首次出訪新加坡、北京、上海和漢城（即今天首爾），歷史意義重大，也為聖樂團各成員之間增加凝聚力。此外亦與到訪外國樂團合演，包括倫敦巴赫合唱團、阿姆斯特丹管弦樂團，以及 1989 年為文化中心揭幕的波士頓交響樂團。

這段時期本團最重要的事情，莫過於首席指揮黃永熙博士 1983 年新加坡演出回港後宣佈退休。之後幾年往返美國與香港，繼續帶領聖樂團外訪演出，

到 1988 年正式定居美國。這段期間主要由張毓君擔任指揮，陳晃相、曾葉發等也以客席指揮身份領導演出，也包括從北京來港指揮首演兒子黃安倫新作品的黃飛立教授。

聖樂團 1986 年全年，進行了成立三十周年紀念演出。也在這一年，團徽的設計作出微調，將圍繞十字架的五位小天使／聖樂者從上方移到下方，較貼切反映演出受眾的位置。新的設計一直沿用至今。

至於聯合演出，除了上述與倫敦、波士頓藝術團體演出外，還有兩次重要的合演。首先是 1985 年在紅磡體育館參加「黃河音樂節」，與本地近三十個合唱團體，在中央樂團團長嚴良堃指揮下，與中央樂團合唱團一起演出千人《黃河大合唱》。另一個重要演出是 1988 年與香港日本人俱樂部合唱團合演貝多芬第九交響曲。這項慈善音樂會之後連續舉行十七年，成為一項記錄。另一個新記錄是 1983 年開始每年均有外訪演出，其中 1986-1989 連續四年前往澳門，與新成立的澳門室樂團演出。🔰

1980 年 6 月 13-14 日

威爾第《安魂曲》

指揮：
黃永熙

獨唱：
海外客席獨唱家

伴奏：
香港管弦樂團

地點：
香港浸會學院（今大學）
大專會堂

《工商日報》

聖樂團與管絃樂團
聯合舉行音樂會

香港聖樂團與香港管弦樂團，將於本月十三、十四日，星期五、六，晚上八時在大專會堂，舉行盛大音樂會，演唱弗爾第第四作品「安魂頌」。音樂會由黃永熙博士指揮，合唱部份由一百二十人組成之香港團擔任，獨唱部份則由四位海外名歌唱家專程來港擔任演出。是次音樂會門票分卅元，廿元，十五元，十元及三元「學生票」，現已在大會堂票房發售。

THE URBAN COUNCIL AND THE HONG KONG ORATORIO SOCIETY JOINTLY PRESENTING A CHORAL CONCERT ON "ALLELUJA" by J.S. Bach, G.F. Handel, R. Thompson, "MASS IN G MINOR" by R.V. Williams, AND "DIXIT DOMINUS" by G.F. Handel ON 26th NOVEMBER, 1980 AT THE CITY HALL, CONCERT HALL, HONG KONG.

1980 年 11 月 26 日

巴赫 / 韓德爾 / 湯普森
《阿利路亞》、
佛漢 • 威廉斯
《G 調彌撒曲》、
韓德爾《上主的話》

指揮：
黃永熙

獨唱：
潘志清[s]、陳嘉璐[m]、王帆[t]、
楊允田[b]

伴奏：
黃健瑜、戚明儀

地點：
香港大會堂音樂廳

1981 年 2 月 14 日

民歌及藝術歌曲

地點：
元朗趙聿修紀念中學

1981 年 4 月 24 日

為香港佑寧堂支持精神
患者籌款演出

巴赫 / 韓德爾 / 湯普森
《阿利路亞》、
孟德爾遜《以利亞》
合唱部份

1981 年 6 月 13-14 日

二十五周年紀念音樂會

孟德爾遜《以利亞》

指揮：
黃永熙

獨唱：
任蓉[s]、陳之霞[a]、
岡本僑生[t]、麥志成[b]

伴奏：
香港管弦樂團

地點：
荃灣、香港大會堂音樂廳

HONG KONG PHILHARMONIC ORCHESTRA
Music Director: Ling Tung   General Manager: John Duffus

CONCERTS IN JUNE 1981

CITY HALL CONCERT HALL

Fri 5th Sat 6th 8pm	Milhaud Ravel Berlioz	La Creation du Monde Piano Concerto in G major Symphony Fantastique	
	Conductor: Soloist:	Maurice Peress Monique Duphil	

TSUEN WAN TOWN HALL/CITY HALL CONCERT HALL

Sat 13th Tsuen Wan 7:30pm Sun 14th City Hall 8pm	Mendelssohn Conductor: Soloists: Choir:	Elijah Wong Wing Hee Jenny Ren Barbara Chen Mak Chi Shing Takao Okamura Hong Kong Oratorio Society

THE HONG KONG ORATORIO SOCIETY JUBILEE CONCERT
PRESENTING MENDELSSON'S ELIJAH
SUNDAY, 14th JUNE 1981, CITY HALL CONCERT HALL, HONG KONG

港聖樂團慶祝銀禧
與港管弦樂團聯演
十三十四晚分在荃灣本港舉行

為慶祝香港聖樂團銀禧紀念，香港管弦樂團，本月十三晚七時半假益荃灣大會堂，及十四晚（星期日）八時，假大會堂音樂廳，與香港聖樂團聯台舉行兩晚香港聖樂團銀禧紀念音樂會。屆時，將由聖樂團指揮黃永熙博士執棒，演出孟德爾遜盛名的神曲「以利亞」。四位著名聲樂家，被請參加演出，他們包括專程由德國返回港的女高音任蓉之外，男高音岡本僑生，及曾贏獲法國杜魯斯國際大賽首獎的日本男低音岡村喬生等。大會堂的門票現已售罄，荃灣音樂會，只餘下少量門票，於荃灣商生書局發售。

《華僑日報》

THE HONG KONG ORATORIO SOCIETY PRESENTS MASS IN B FLAT (THERESA)
BY F.J. HAYDN AND CHORAL AND OTHER WORKS BY OTHER COMPOSERS.

4th OCTOBER, 1981   CITY HALL CONCERT HALL, H.K.

李秀蓮（女高音）

畢業於九龍拔萃女書院，現攻讀於香港大學法律學院，對聲樂具濃厚興趣。

一九七九年，李秀蓮首次參加香港校際音樂節獨唱項目得冠軍，應嘉修士獎學金，進修聲樂，自此師事名女高音歌唱家江樺。一九八一年度香港大學學生節歌唱比賽，李秀蓮更盡取錦標，成爲港大學生節佳話。

雖然李秀蓮所受的聲樂訓練，只有兩年，成績已可觀。她的修養與抱負在年輕的一代中，頗堪注意。　　➡

譚允芝

譚允芝現年二十歲，爲港大法律學院二年級學生，自幼習琴，肄業於聖保羅男女中學時，爲該校合唱團之中堅分子，多次在歌劇製作中担任重要角色，一九七七年於校內贏獲伍伯就教授紀念獎學金，遠開始追隨鄭漢成先生研習聲樂，同年七月偕同銀禧樂團遠赴英倫巡迴演唱，深獲好評。曾在歷屆校際音樂節個人及號組項目中奪得多項榮譽，今屆在公開組個人項目中更囊括藝術歌曲獨唱及聖樂獨唱兩項冠軍，評判讚譽其「技巧控制純熟、吐字清淅、表達細膩」。譚允芝現任港大法律學院合唱團及港大學生會合唱團之指揮，並曾與李秀蓮合作爲香港電台灌錄藝術歌曲重唱及獨唱節目。

1981 年 10 月 4 日

海頓《降 B 大調彌撒曲》

指揮：
Leonard Pegg

獨唱：
李秀蓮[s]、譚允芝[a]、王帆[t]、楊允田[bb]

伴奏：
香港室樂團

地點：
香港大會堂音樂廳

1981 年 12 月 22 日

聖桑《聖誕神曲》、
聖誕歌曲

指揮：
黃永熙

獨唱：
馮志麗[s]、陳嘉璐[m]、
嚴仙霞[a]、王帆[t]、楊允田[bb]

伴奏：
嚴賀潔、戚明儀

地點：
香港大會堂劇院

THE HONG KONG ORATORIO SOCIETY PRESENTING A CHRISTMAS CONCERT ON 22.12.81
AT THE CITY HALL THEATRE, HONG KONG.

《華僑日報》

「白遼士所寫的安魂曲註明要用幾百人的合唱團，樂隊要用上十六個定音鼓，另外有四個銅樂隊分佈在會場的四個角落。香港演唱這曲時是在體育館裏舉行的，因為連音樂廳也不能容納這樣多的人。」

（黃永熙「指揮的話」，一九八四年北京場刊）

與倫敦巴赫合唱團合演
慶祝大會堂成立二十周年

白遼士《安魂曲》

指揮：
Sir David Willcocks

聯合演出：
明儀合唱團、香港巴赫合唱團、
香港兒童合唱團、香港雅樂社等

伴奏：
香港管弦樂團、
香港青年管樂團、皇家香港團隊
（義勇軍）軍樂團等

地點：
香港伊利沙伯體育館

VIVALDI: GLORIA　　GIACOMO PUCCINI: MESSA DI GLORIA
Presented by Hong Kong Oratorio Society with Pan Asia Symphony Orchestra
June 13, 1982　　City Hall Concert Hall, Hong Kong
Dr. W.H. Wong　conductor

1982 年 6 月 13 日

大會堂二十周年音樂會

韋華第《榮耀頌》、
浦契尼《榮耀彌撒曲》

指揮：
黃永熙

獨唱：
潘若芙[s]、馮志麗[s]、
陳愛堅[s]、嚴仙霞[a]、王帆[t]、
阮品強[b]

伴奏：
泛亞交響樂團、嚴賀潔

地點：
香港大會堂音樂廳

"Choral singing was excellent in textures varying between boldly declaimed homophonic and sharply focused polyphony. Phrasing was often beautifully moulded and dynamics well-controlled."

《南華早報》

廿載繽紛大會堂　市局文娛遍香江

Choral Concert
by the
**Hong Kong
Oratorio
Society**
香港聖樂團
演唱會

City Hall — Where the arts have flowered for 20 years

THE SEASONS by HAYDN
Performed by the HONG KONG ORATORIO SOCIETY at the TSUEN WAN TOWN HALL on October 30, 1982
Conductor, Dr. WONG WING HEI

1982 年 10 月 30 日

紀念海頓誕辰 250 周年

海頓《四季頌》

指揮：
黃永熙

獨唱：
黃少萍 [s]、劉森坪 [t]、楊健明 [b]

伴奏：
嚴賀潔、戚明儀

地點：
荃灣大會堂演奏廳

The Hong Kong Oratorio Society
in
"The Seasons"
(To Commemorate the 250th Anniversary of
the Birth of Joseph Haydn)

October 30, 1982 (Saturday)
8.00 p.m.
Auditorium, Tsuen Wan Town Hall

Conductor: Dr. Wong Wing-hee   Soprano: Justina Wong
Tenor: Sam Lau   Baritone: Enoch Young
Pianist: Cindy Chik   Organist: Kitty Yim

Tickets at $5, $10, $15
Tickets are now available at the
Tsuen Wan Town Hall Box Office and

Presented by the Cultural Services Department (N.T.)

團員音樂會（為 1983 年新加坡之旅籌款）

地點：
香港大會堂劇院

聖誕音樂會

指揮：
黃永熙

獨唱：
嚴仙霞[a]、王帆[t]、阮品強[b]

伴奏：
嚴賀潔、戚明儀

地點：
香港大會堂音樂廳

香港聖樂團團員演唱會
（籌募海外演唱會）
Vocal Recital by members of the
H. K. Oratorio Society
(In aid of Overseas Concert Tour)

Monday, 8th November, 1982. 一九八二年十一月八（星期一）
City Hall Theatre 大會堂劇院
8 p.m. 下午八時

「[王帆說:]我們一路出機艙,橫着眼前的是『歡迎香港聖樂團』的橫額,跟着就獻上花束。這個花園城市的氣溫雖然很高,但我們的情緒更高。」

《晶報》

「在[新加坡]國家劇場演唱返港後,該團首席指揮黃永熙博士正式表示行將告別樂團⋯⋯『我在聖樂團得到無限歡欣,而且時間長達十六年之久⋯⋯現在聖樂團已成為東南亞最有聲望的合唱團⋯⋯我不敢說我一定會來。不過,如有機會我必定再來探望各位。』」

《華僑日報》

1983 年 2 月 17 日 **

[新加坡] 國家劇場俱樂部成立十五周年

海頓《四季頌》

指揮:
黃永熙

獨唱:
馮志麗 s、王帆 t、陳晃相 b

伴奏:
嚴賀潔、嚴仙霞

地點:
國家劇場

工作委员会
Organising Committee

名誉顾问	：杨健明博士
	梁耀杨博士
	黄永熙博士
	陆伟煜
演出顾问	：陈团生，王帆
顾问	：刘旭文
主席	：李岳祥
副主席	：梁德儒
	叶保应
秘书	：司徒乐庆
	黄萍
财政	：司徒乐庆
	吴立江
查账	：施光祖
	峇士卡
舞台监督	：叶保应
	李嘉仪
宣传与特刊	：李嘉仪
	黄萍
票务	：刘珍丝
	美娜，峇士卡
招待组	：吴永享，刘静霞
	王玢，郭景如，郑心益
	张春香，刘珍丝
后台小组	：陈序理，陈振成
	苏雅勉，林振嘉
	美娜，峇士卡

Honarary Advisers	: Dr. Enoch Young
	Dr. Peter Liang
	Dr. Wong Wing Hee
	Michael Loke
Concert Advisers	: Tan Tuan Seng
	Wong Fang
Adviser	: Low Hiok Boon
Chairman	: Lee Ngak Siang
Vice-Chairmans	: Liang Teck Yee
	Yap Pau Eng
Secretaries	: Seetoh Lock Heng
	Ng Peng
Treasurers	: Seetoh Lock Heng
	Goh Lik Kung
Auditors	: See Kwang Chow
	K.P. Bhaskar
Stage Managers	: Yap Pau Eng
	Lee Kiah Ngee
Publicity & Programme	: Lee Kiah Ngee
	Ng Peng
Ticketing	: Liew Tien See
	Meenachye Bhaskar
Reception	: Goh Yong Hiang
	Lau Chay Hia
	Ong Foon
	Quek Keng Joo
	Cheng Sum Aik
	Cheong Choon Hiong
	Liew Tien See
Stage Management	: Tan Sze Lee
	Tan Cheng Seng
	Soh Ah Bian
	Lim Chin Kah
	Meenachye Bhaskar

国家剧场俱乐部庆祝成立十五周年特邀香港圣乐团呈献
A Presentation by National Theatre Club to Commemorate its 15th Anniversary

海顿四季颂演唱会
HAYDN'S IMMORTAL ORATORIO
"The Seasons"
By Hong Kong Oratorio Society

National Theatre · 17-2-1983 · 7.30pm · Singapore

Jointly presented by the Urban Council &
the Hong Kong Oratorio Society
市政局及香港聖樂團合辦

HONG KONG ORATORIO SOCIETY

香港聖樂團

Conductor: Dr. Wong Wing Hee
指揮：黃永熙博士

Friday, 29 April 1983 at 8pm   City Hall Concert Hall
一九八三年四月廿九日（星期五）晚上八時
香港大會堂音樂廳

**凱魯畢尼《C 大調彌撒曲》、
韓德爾《同心頌主》**

指揮：
黃永熙

獨唱：
陳愛堅 [s]、嚴仙霞 [a]、劉森坪 [t]、
阮品強 [b]

伴奏：
嚴賀潔、戚明儀

地點：
香港大會堂音樂廳

**韓德爾《 C 大調彌撒曲》
（with Jubilee Singers）**

地點：
香港大會堂音樂廳

MESSIAH by G. F. HANDEL
Conducted by Dr. Wong Wing Hee　October 2, 1983　City Hall Concert Hall
Organised by The Hong Kong Oratorio Society as a tribute to Dr. Wong Wing Hee

1983 年 10 月 2 日 / 4 日

韓德爾《彌賽亞》

指揮：
黃永熙

獨唱：
江樺[s]、鄭慧芊[m]、王帆[t]、
Emanuel Gregorio[b]

伴奏：
香港室樂團、嚴賀潔

地點：
香港大會堂音樂廳、荃灣
大會堂演奏廳

《華僑日報》

1983 年 12 月 21 日

聖誕音樂會

指揮：
張毓君

地點：
香港大會堂音樂廳

1984 年 4 月 14 日

海頓《四季頌》
（北京巡演預演）

指揮：
黃永熙

獨唱：
馮志麗 [s]、王帆 [t]、楊健明 [b]

伴奏：
嚴賀潔、戚明儀

地點：
循道衛理教會九龍堂

「為了檢閱一下，香港 [聖樂團] 在行前特別半公開地
來了一次彩排……聞風而至者也有幾百人，佔了基督教
循道會教堂的大部份。事實上排練也很認真，除了中間
停頓了片刻由黃博士和伴奏者略談兩句之外，整晚由頭
至尾就像一場完整的音樂會。」

《華僑日報》

黃飛立（左）與楊健明（右）

1984 年 4 月 21-22 日 */**

[北京] 海頓《四季頌》

指揮：
黃永熙

獨唱：
馮志麗 [s]、王帆 [t]、楊洪基 [b]

伴奏：
嚴賀潔 [o]、戚明儀 [p]

地點：
北京民族文化宮禮堂

「[聖樂團北京演唱會籌委會主席梁耀揚]：這次到北京的演出，是最雄壯的嘗試，因為這是第一個應邀訪京的大音樂團體，對香港和北京的文化交流，足以作很有價值的貢獻。」

《大公報》

"From all accounts, our musician ambassadors were received with great enthusiasm by the audience of more than 2000 and made something of a cultural coup in proving the ability of an amateur choral group"

《南華早報》

"Its tour to Peking was the most ambitious to date and was particularly important in terms of musical representation and in forging cultural links between Hong Kong and China"

《南華早報》

《工商日報》

Choral Concert by the Hong Kong Oratorio Society

1984 年 6 月 4 日

**韓德爾《加冕頌歌》、
巴赫《耶穌，我喜悦》、
海頓《納爾遜彌撒曲》**

指揮：
黃永熙、張毓君

獨唱：
黃少萍 [s]、嚴仙霞 [a]、
劉森坪 [t]、阮品強 [b]

伴奏：
嚴賀潔、戚明儀

地點：
香港大會堂音樂廳

**阿姆斯特丹管弦樂團和
香港合唱團合演**

貝多芬《第九交響曲》

指揮：
Paavo Berglund

獨唱：
馮志麗 [s]、Katherine Lewis[a]、
王帆 [t]、Norman Anderson[bb]

地點：
香港大會堂音樂廳

**普及合唱選曲：
聖桑《詩篇 150》、
海頓《主是偉大的》、
孟德爾遜《聽我禱告》、
伯恩斯坦《夢斷城西》選曲**

地點：
元朗聿修堂 / 陸佑堂 /
九龍城浸信會

左起：王帆、Berglund、馮志麗、客席樂師、黃永熙。

**Josef Rheinberger
《伯利恆之星》及聖誕曲**

指揮：
黃永熙、張毓君

地點：
荃灣大會堂演奏廳

「黃永熙……雖然曾一度放下工作回美享受天倫樂，但由
於抵不住團員與觀眾的熱誠，過去也合作愉快而又獲得很
大滿足，因此還是回港，重新擔任聖樂團指揮工作。」

《華僑日報》

《華僑日報》

"We have come to depend upon the [HK] Oratorio Society for large scale choral works of quality and enthusiasm."

《南華早報》

巴赫《復活節神曲》、韓德爾《上主的宣告》

指揮：
黃永熙

獨唱：
（巴赫）趙麗儀[s]、
趙曼姿[a]、曾永耀[t]、
Norman Howarth[bb]、
（韓德爾）Nancy Goff[s]、
陳愛堅[s]、嚴仙霞[a]、
曾永耀[t]、楊允田[bb]

伴奏：
余必達、嚴賀潔及獨奏家

地點：
香港大會堂音樂廳

普及聖樂晚會

指揮：
黃永熙、張毓君

伴奏：
嚴賀潔

地點：
循道衛理教會九龍堂

黃河音樂節

千人《黃河大合唱》
（二十九個本地合唱團與
中央樂團合唱團聯合演出）

指揮：
嚴良堃

伴奏：
香港交響樂團

地點：
香港（紅磡）體育館

演出貝多芬、孟德爾遜、
柯普蘭、黃自、林聲翕等
作品

指揮：
黃永熙、張毓君

伴奏：
嚴賀潔

地點：
元朗聿修堂

韓德爾《彌賽亞》

指揮：
黃永熙

獨唱：
江樺 [s]、嚴仙霞 [a]、王帆 [t]、
陳維昕 [b]

地點：
荃灣大會堂演奏廳

楊健明與江樺

黃永熙博士：「一九三五年夏，上海的聖樂團首創音樂文化交流的先河，組團訪問了香港、廣州、佛山……現在經過了五十年，香港的聖樂團才來到上海回訪，不能不說是一個最緩慢的『交流』。」

（場刊）

樂團主席 Joan Jasper："The choir were moved to tears such was the great enthusiasm generated by the Chinese. After the performance, people came to backstage proclaiming it was the best Christmas present they'd ever had."

《南華早報》

1985 年 12 月 30-31 日 */**

上海文化局邀請演出

貝多芬《C 大調彌撒》[1]、
韓德爾《彌賽亞》 第一部份 [2]

指揮：
黃永熙

獨唱：
馮志麗 [1s]、江樺 [2s]、
嚴仙霞 [a]、呂國璋 [t]、
楊允田 [1b]、溫可錚 [2bb]

伴奏：
上海樂團管弦樂隊

地點：
上海音樂廳

三十周年紀念音樂會

韓德爾 《出埃及記》

指揮：
張毓君

獨唱：
Nancy Goff[s]、趙麗坤[m]、
黃超梅[m]、譚允芝[a]、
呂國璋[t]、朱承恩[b]、
郭顯揚[b]、蘇惠生[b]、
楊健明[b]

伴奏：
戚明儀、鄔賈那素、
John Wilson

地點：
香港大會堂音樂廳

HONG KONG ORATORIO SOCIETY
30th ANNIVERSARY CONCERT
presents Handel's "Israel in Egypt"

Conductor: Andrew Cheung 張毓君指揮

香港聖樂團卅週年紀念音樂會

演唱韓德爾作曲之「出埃及記」

SPONSORED BY URBAN COUNCIL
市政局贊助

張毓君：「我們在卅周年紀念音樂會上再一次選唱此曲，有一個特別的理由：因為這是一首真正專門為給合唱團演唱的神曲……需要良好的合唱技巧和辛勤的練習。香港聖樂團團員們的專注和努力使本人深受感動。他們在練習中竭力以赴。深信觀眾們從今天晚上的演出中可分享他們的快慰和滿足。」

（場刊「指揮的話」）

" GREAT ORATORIO FAVOURITIES "
Presented by the HONG KONG ORATORIO SOCIETY
August 24, 1986 Tsuen Wan Town Hall
Conductor: Dr. WONG Wing Hei

1986 年 8 月 24 日 /31 日

三十周年紀念音樂會

**聖樂精選（《以利亞》、
《創世記》、《參孫》、
《彌賽亞》選段）**

指揮：
黃永熙

獨唱：
江樺 [s]、馮志麗 [s]、李冰 [m]、
王帆 [t]、呂國璋 [t]、陳晃相 [b]、
楊健明 [b]

地點：
荃灣大會堂、元朗聿修堂

1986 年 11 月 12 日 / 16 日

三十周年紀念音樂會

孟德爾遜《以利亞》

指揮：
黃永熙

獨唱：
馮志麗 s、嚴仙霞 a、王帆 t、
陳榮貴 b

伴奏：
港樂成員管弦樂隊

地點：
香港大會堂音樂廳

1986 年 12 月 22 日

三十周年紀念音樂會

**巴赫《有嬰孩為我而生》
及聖誕曲**

指揮：
黃永熙

獨唱：
潘若芙 s、陳之霞 a、
Michael Ryan t、李建真 b

伴奏：
戚明儀、徐增毓、
John Wilson

地點：
香港大會堂音樂廳

"If the glory of Felix Mendelssohn's Elijah has faded somewhat in the West, the original splendour still lives on in Hong Kong, thanks to the Hong Kong Oratorio Society."

《南華早報》

HONG KONG ORATORIO SOCIETY
30th ANNIVERSARY CONCERT
presents "Christmas Concert, 1986."
Conductor: Wong Wing Hee 黃永熙指揮

香港聖樂團卅週年紀念音樂會
演唱（聖誕音樂會）

22nd December, 1986.　City Hall Concert Hall
一九八六年十二月廿二日　　大會堂音樂廳
SPONSORED BY URBAN COUNCIL
市政局贊助

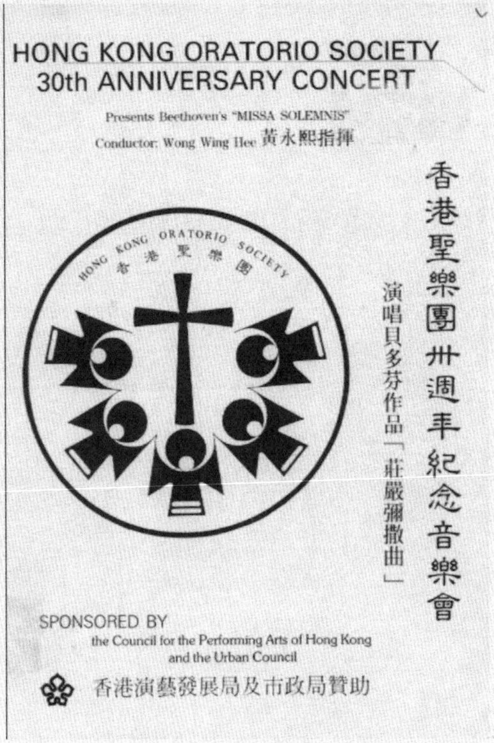
HONG KONG ORATORIO SOCIETY
30th ANNIVERSARY CONCERT
Presents Beethoven's "MISSA SOLEMNIS"
Conductor: Wong Wing Hee 黃永熙指揮
香港聖樂團卅週年紀念音樂會
演唱貝多芬作品「莊嚴彌撒曲」
HONG KONG ORATORIO SOCIETY
香港聖樂團
SPONSORED BY
the Council for the Performing Arts of Hong Kong
and the Urban Council
香港演藝發展局及市政局贊助

1987年3月21日

三十周年紀念音樂會

韓德爾《彌賽亞》

指揮：
張毓君

獨唱：
江樺[s]、梁麗麗[m]、
Arlis Hiebert[t]、
Hugh Phillipson[bb]

伴奏：
港樂成員管弦樂隊

地點：
沙田大會堂演奏廳

三十周年紀念音樂會

貝多芬《莊嚴彌撒曲》

指揮：
黃永熙

獨唱：
任蓉 [s]、陳嘉璐 [a]、呂國璋 [t]、
陳晃相 [bb]

伴奏：
港樂成員管弦樂隊、唐燕玉

地點：
香港大會堂音樂廳

「今年是『師傅』與聖樂團合作的二十周年紀念（『師傅』是
香港聖樂團的團員和本港一些音樂家們對黃博士較親切的稱
呼）……黃博士態度隨和，與他作為一位指揮家的身份好不相稱。
但當他踏上指揮台上，人們對他的形象完全改觀。被他指揮過的
人都會同意，他的確是一位名副其實的『師傅』。」

（場刊）

THE KINGDOM by Elgar
Performed by The Hong Kong Oratorio Society
11th October, 1987.

"As for the Oratorio Society itself, they had the right glowing
sounds for this very glowing, very exciting manifestation of
the English oratorio at its best."

《南華早報》

埃爾加 《神的國度》

指揮：
黃永熙

獨唱：
黃少萍[s]、嚴仙霞[a]、王帆[t]、
Brian Rayner Cook[b]

伴奏：
港樂成員管弦樂隊、
余必達

地點：
香港大會堂音樂廳

聖誕音樂會（香港兒童合唱團男童合唱組）

指揮：
曾葉發

獨唱：
潘志清[s]、丘玉鳳[s]、
朱慧堅[a]、曾永耀[t]、
郭顯揚[bb]

伴奏：
弦樂組（領奏：黃衛明）、
戚明儀、John Wilson

地點：
沙田大會堂演奏廳

1987年12月27日

［澳門］

**韓德爾《彌賽亞》[1]、
海頓《創世記》選曲**

指揮：
黃永熙

獨唱：
江樺 [1s]、呂國璋 [1t]、
馮志麗 [s]、王帆 [t]、
楊允田 [bb]

伴奏：
澳門室樂團

1988年3月20日

赴韓國預演

**布魯克納《經文歌》、
浦契尼《榮歸主頌》、
韓德爾《彌賽亞》
（第二、三部份）**

指揮：
黃永熙

獨唱：
江樺 [s]、陳嘉璐 [a]、呂國璋 [t]、
陳偉超 [b]

伴奏：
弦樂組、戚明儀、
John Wilson

地點：
香港大會堂音樂廳

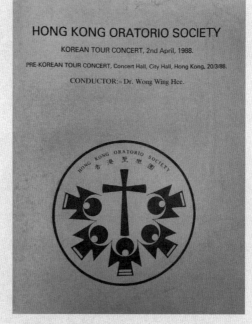

'88 부활절 기념 음악회

홍콩 오라토리오 합창단 내한공연
HONG KONG ORATORIO SOCIETY SEOUL CONCERT

ART KOREA MANAGEMENT

1988 年 4 月 2 日

[漢城（今首爾）]

布魯克納《經文歌》、浦契尼《榮歸主頌》及靈歌三首

指揮：
黃永熙

地點：
世宗文化回館

Conductor makes his final bow

[F]IFTY years ago a young conductor from Shanghai came to Hongkong for the first time to conduct a concert in what was then the only suitable venue — Hongkong University's Lok Yu Hall.

On Sunday, at the City Hall Concert Hall at 8 pm that still "young" conductor, Dr Wong Wing-hee, will conduct his final concert in Hongkong with the Oratorio Society before leaving for the United States.

It was 20 years ago that Dr Wong first worked with the Hongkong Oratorio Society, itself in its 31st year.

His departure will certainly sadden members of the Hongkong Oratorio Society, who will lose both a fine conductor and great friend.

Sunday's concert will be a useful warm-up for the Society's Korean tour and the program will be the same as that which will be sung in Seoul on April 2, in the 4,000-seat Sejong Cultural Centre Main Hall, except that in Seoul the encore will be the 23rd Psalm, sung in Korean.

The program consists of three motets by Bruckner, three Negro spirituals, Puccini's *Gloria* and the glorious Easter-tide music of Parts II and III of Handel's *Messiah* — this section of Sunday's concert will be accompanied by members of the Hongkong Philharmonic orchestra.

Soloists will be Ella Kiang, Sylvia Chen, David Lui and Chan Wai-chiu, with pianist Cindy Chik, harpsichordist Larry Schipull and organist John Wilson.

Tickets are available at all URBTIX outlets, priced from $20 to $50. The concert is presented by the Oratorio Society, supported by the Urban Council and the Council for the Performing Arts of Hongkong.

Dr Wong Wing-hee ... will conduct his final concert in Hongkong.

《南華早報》

**首屆香港 -
日本聯合慈善音樂會**

**貝多芬《合唱幻想曲》、
《第九交響曲》**

指揮：
福村芳一

獨唱：
松本美和子[s]、嚴仙霞[a]、
吳文修[t]、Michael Rippon[b]

伴奏：
香港管弦樂團

地點：
香港大會堂音樂廳

黃安倫《詩篇廿二篇》

指揮：
黃飛立

獨唱：
任蓉 [s]、張蓮 [s]、林偉林 [b]

伴奏：
黃健瑜

地點：
沙田大會堂演奏廳

THE HONG KONG ORATORIO SOCIETY
CHORAL CONCERT
A Far-east premiere of Huang An Lun's
"Psalm 22"
A special Presentation for the 9th Convention of the
World Association of Chinese Church Music

Conductor : Huang Fei Lih Professor, Central Conservatory
of Music, Beijing, China.
Sopranos : Jenny Ren – Famous Taiwan vocalist
residing in Rome, Italy.
Helen Chang
Baritone : William Lim   Organist : Wong Kin Yu

Tickets: $10, 20, 30   Concession tickets are available to students and the
27th July, 1988   elderly over 65. Tickets are now available at Sha Tin
(Wednesday) 8:00 p.m.   Town Hall, Tuen Mun Town Hall, Tsuen Wan Town Hall
Auditorium, Shatin Town Hall and all Urbtix outlets. Telephone Booking: 5-739595
                             Enquiries: 0-6942556 (Sha Tin Town Hall)
➤ Jointly presented by the Regional Council
Supported by the Council for the Performing Arts

香港聖樂團演唱會
THE HONG KONG ORATORIO SOCIETY
CHORAL CONCERT

遠東首次演唱黃安倫作品
"詩篇廿二篇"
A Far-east premiere of Huang An Lun's
"Psalm 22"

指揮　黃飛立   Conductor : Huang Fei Lih
女高音　任蓉   Sopranos : Jenny Ren
　　　　張蓮   Helen Chang
男中音　林偉林   Baritone : William Lim
風琴伴奏　黃健瑜   Organist : Wong Kin Yu

任蓉女士之演出由
國泰航空公司贊助

Miss Jenny Ren's Performance
Supported by Cathay Pacific Airways Ltd.

一九八八年七月廿七日（星期三） 下午八時
沙田大會堂演奏廳

27th July, 1988 (Wednesday) 8:00 p.m.
Auditorium, Shatin Town Hall

1988 年 10 月 2 日

**韋華第《榮耀頌》、
蕭士塔高維奇《森林之歌》**

指揮：
陳晃相

獨唱：
潘若芙[s]、朱慧堅[a]、
呂國璋[t]、程路禹[bb]

客席演出：
香港兒童合唱團

伴奏：
蘇明村、黃健瑜、湯芷怡

地點：
香港大會堂音樂廳

1988 年 12 月 18 日

韓德爾《彌賽亞》

指揮：
黃飛然

獨唱：
江樺[s]、陳之霞[m]、王帆[t]、
李建真[b]

伴奏：
管弦樂隊、黃健瑜、
John Wilson

地點：
沙田大會堂演奏廳

「黃飛然自一九六一年至一九六八年擔任香港聖樂團指揮，為本團初期的發展工作打下良好基礎……經過二十多年後，香港聖樂團能使多年的夢想成真，再次有機會邀請到黃飛然先生擔任今晚演唱會的指揮，實在是十分有意義及難能可貴的。」

（場刊）

"Veteran Hongkong Oratorio Society maestro Frank Huang returned from Vancouver to conduct this performance and deserves high praise for the general success of the evening...The 100-strong chorus was exceptionally fine."

《南華早報》

1988 年 12 月 27 日

[澳門] 韓德爾《彌賽亞》

指揮：
Veiga Jardim

獨唱：
江樺[s]、陳之霞[m]、王帆[t]、
李建真[b]

伴奏：
澳門室樂團、黃健瑜

地點：
澳門主教大堂

1989 年 3 月 5 日

埃爾加《耶穌門徒》

指揮：
陳晃相

獨唱：
馮志麗 [s]、王帆 [t]、趙麗坤 [m]、
楊允田 [b]、李建真 [b]、朱承恩 [b]

伴奏：
管弦樂隊、黃健瑜

地點：
香港大會堂音樂廳

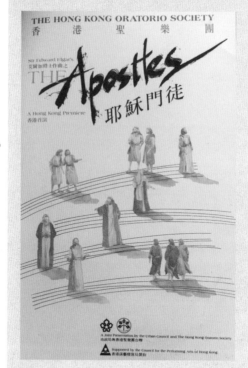

"The performance on Sunday, by the Oratorio Society, was
an enterprising undertaking, and credit must surely go to the
artistic director for introducing the work to Hong Kong, thereby
increasing further the singers' already extensive repertoire."

《南華早報》

第二屆香港 - 日本聯合慈善音樂會

海頓
《瑪麗亞·特蕾莎彌撒曲》、
佛瑞《安魂曲》

香港演藝學院

[澳門] 佛瑞《安魂曲》

指揮：
Veiga Jardim

獨唱：
錢迪勵 [s]、陳晃相 [b]

伴奏：
澳門室樂團

與香港中樂團合作演出普及中外合唱曲

指揮：
于粦

獨唱：
陳嘉璐 [a]、呂國璋 [t]

地點：
香港大會堂音樂廳

1989 年 6 月 10 日

《中華頌》

聯同三十個本地合唱團演出

指揮：
黃永熙等

地點：
香港伊利沙伯體育館

1989 年 8 月 26-27 日

《創世記》、《彌賽亞》、《以利亞》選曲

指揮：
黃永熙

獨唱：
Mary Poulter[s]、王漪璇[s]、
陳少君[s]、朱慧堅[a]、
曾永耀[t]、呂國璋[t]、
黎列剛[t]、楊允田[b]、
陳晃相[bb]

伴奏：
蘇明村、黃健瀚

地點：
北區大會堂、元朗聿修堂

1989 年 12 月 2 日

香港文化中心開幕獻禮

馬勒《第二交響曲》

指揮：
Stuart Challender

聯合演出：
雅詞合唱團、香港巴赫合唱
團、香港管弦樂團合唱團

伴奏：
波士頓交響樂團

地點：
香港文化中心音樂廳

5 November – 6 December, 1989　一八八九年十一月五日至十二月六日
INTERNATIONAL
CELEBRATION OF THE ARTS
TO OPEN THE HONG KONG CULTURAL CENTRE
香港文化中心開幕獻禮
國　際　演　藝　菁　華
BOSTON SYMPHONY ORCHESTRA
波士頓交響樂團
香港文化中心
HONG KONG CULTURAL CENTRE
An Urban Council Presentation

1989 年 12 月 16 日

佛漢 • 威廉斯
《基督今日降生》及
聖誕曲 （香港兒童合唱團）

指揮：
黃永熙

獨唱：
Ruth Wilcox[s]、
Philip Brink[t]、
Hugh Phillipson[b]

伴奏：
澳門室樂團、余必達、
黃健瑜

地點：
荃灣大會堂演奏廳

1989 年 12 月 26 日

[澳門]（重複以上節目）

1990-1999 年

導讀：

1990 年代是香港歷史重要時期，尤其是 1997 年主權移交，自此回歸中國管治。這十年也是香港聖樂團六十五年歷史中演出場數最多的十年，首次走出亞洲進行巡演，同時唱遍兩岸四地。

據不完全統計，聖樂團在這十年有不少於七十五場演出，那是 1970 年代演出數目的兩倍。其中有相當一部份是與其他藝團合作演出，1997 年「七一」回歸前後演出數目達二十一場次，為歷年之冠。到內地演出的次數亦增多，先後到廈門、上海、北京演出。

進入「不惑」之年的聖樂團經歷幾項重要發展。首先是陳永華教授 1995 年出任音樂總監至今。聖樂團亦出版發行首張唱片，由陳教授指揮他為聖樂團創作的《第四交響曲 - 謝恩讚美頌》。在香港回歸系列音樂會上，他創作、指揮《九州同頌》作慶賀。

此外，這十年甚為突出的是聖樂團幾代成員的多元和國際化，可謂相識滿天下。1991-92 年間由指揮前輩黃飛然牽頭成立溫哥華聖樂團，亦創造條件讓香港聖樂團到當地聯袂演出，兩年後溫哥華聖樂團回訪，在港、滬演出。1998 年再一次走出大中華地區，前往以色列演出，由蘇明村指揮，同樣創造歷史。

這段時期另一個重要發展是香港小交響樂團的創立，由聖樂團主席余漢翁同時兼任主席，兩個團多次合作演出，成為香港九十年代一個重要音樂現象。兩團搭檔亦成就了兩岸三地頂級指揮來港合作，包括嚴良堃、陳澄雄、陳佐湟、葉聰等，演出多首中西名曲，其中嚴良堃、陳澄雄分別指揮二團錄製《長恨歌》、《彌賽亞》兩張唱片，留下音樂瑰寶。

唱片以外，1997 年開始亦推出聖樂團團訊季刊《讚頌》，以中英文介紹樂團資訊及活動，鼓勵團員提筆參與，凝聚歸屬感，亦為籌組「聖樂團之友」作準備。

1990 年 3 月 17 日

第三屆香港 - 日本聯合慈善音樂會

G Sendo《故鄉の四季》、韓德爾《彌賽亞》

地點：
香港演藝學院

1990 年 5 月 20 日

威爾第《安魂曲》

指揮：
Veiga Jardim

獨唱：
任蓉[s]、譚天眷[a]、劉維維[t]、
陳晃相[b]

伴奏：
香港小交響樂團

地點：
香港大會堂音樂廳

「香港小交響樂團是一個不牟利的團體，於一九九〇年由一群本地青年樂手組成，以期推廣香港的音樂活動。除了定期舉行音樂會來提高樂手水準外，更為本港各演藝團體伴奏。」

（場刊）

周凡夫：「演出後，台上台下歷久不止的掌聲，便可知道具有良知血性的心靈，都在這首安魂曲的演出中獲得了共鳴！」

《信報》

114

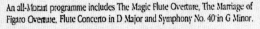

The Magic of
Mozart

**Debut Concert by
the Hong Kong Sinfonietta**

Conductor: Richard Tsang

Flute soloist: Chan Kwok Chiu

An all-Mozart programme includes The Magic Flute Overture, The Marriage of Figaro Overture, Flute Concerto in D Major and Symphony No. 40 in G Minor.

8pm 8 Sept. 90 (Sat) Auditorium, Sha Tin Town Hall
8pm 15 Sept. 90 (Sat) Auditorium, Tsuen Wan Town Hall
$20, 30, 40

Choral Concert by
The Hong Kong Oratorio Society

Conductor: **Jimmy Chan**

Orchestra: **Hong Kong Sinfonietta**

Soloists: Mieko Nakajima, Cecilia Chu, Oliver Lo, Bosco Chan
Justina Wong, Cynthia Luff, David Lui, Malcolm Barnett

Programme includes Kodaly's Matra Picture, Mozart's Vesperae Solennes de Confessore and Rossini's Stabat Mater.

8pm 29 Sept. 90 (Sat) Auditorium, Sha Tin Town Hall
$20, 30, 40

△ Supported by the Council for the Performing Arts of Hong Kong

Half-price tickets are available for full-time students and senior citizens aged 60 or above
Tickets are now available at all URBTIX outlets
Telephone Bookings: 734 9009
Enquiries: 691 2536 (Sha Tin)   414 0144 (Tsuen Wan)
Programme subject to alteration with Regional Council's announcement as final.
Presented by Regional Council

"A rare treat for choir lovers" "

《南華早報》

1990 年 9 月 29 日

高大宜《馬耳他景色》、
莫扎特《莊嚴晚禱曲》[1]、
羅西尼《聖母悼歌》

指揮：
陳晃相

獨唱：
中嶋美枝子 [1s]、黃少萍 [s]、
朱慧堅 [1a]、嚴仙霞 [a]、
盧思彥 [1t]、呂國璋 [t]、
陳啟靈 [1b]、Malcolm Barnett [b]

伴奏：
香港小交響樂團

地點：
沙田大會堂演奏廳

1990 年 10 月 19-20 日

第十三屆亞洲藝術節

關迺忠《白石道人詞意組曲》

指揮：
關迺忠

獨唱：
錢迪勵[s]、呂國璋[t]

伴奏：
香港中樂團

地點：
香港文化中心音樂廳

HONG KONG CHINESE ORCHESTRA
The 13th Festival of Asian Arts Concert Series

❀ An Urban Council Presentation

"Breezes from the Eastern Sea"

Featuring Shakuhachi end-blown flute virtuoso Sakata Seizan specially invited from Japan

Principal Conductor : *KUAN Nai-chung*
Shakuhachi Solo : *SAKATA Seizan*
Soprano Solo : *Delia CHIEN*　　Tenor Solo : *David LUI*
Chorus : *Hong Kong Oratorio Society*

Works by Japanese and Chinese composers, inspired by music tastes of China's Tang and Song dynasties:

- The Mask of Sakya (Premiere) (Shakuhachi & Chinese Orchestra)
- Haru No Umi
- Suite of the Taoist Priest Baishi
- Rhapsody for Orchestra
- The Moon Over Guan Shan
- Ancient Melodies of Dunhuang

Hong Kong Cultural Centre Concert Hall
19 and 20. 10. 1990 (8 pm)
Ticket Prices: $75, $55, $40, $30
Tickets available at all URBTIX outlets

Ticket Reservation: 7349009

香港醫學會音樂會

**帕里、馬洛特、
韓德爾聲樂作品，
韋華第《榮耀頌》**

指揮：
陳晃相、汪西三（韋華第）

獨唱：
潘若芙 s

伴奏：
香港醫學會樂團、黃健翮、
余必達

地點：
香港大會堂音樂廳

1990 年 12 月 16 日

聖誕音樂會

夏龐蒂埃《聖誕小彌撒曲》、
聖桑《聖誕神曲》、
聖誕頌歌

指揮：
陳晃相、黃天榮

眾獨唱

伴奏：
香港小交響樂團

地點：
香港文化中心音樂廳

1991 年 3 月 10 日

第四屆香港 -
日本聯合慈善音樂會

莫扎特《C 大調加冕彌撒曲》

地點：
香港大會堂音樂廳

16 December, 1990 (Sunday) 8pm
Hong Kong Cultural Centre Concert Hall

XIANG GANG SHENG
YUE TUAN
香港聖樂團

HP003919

一九九〇年十二月十六日（星期日）晚上八時
香港文化中心音樂廳

Christmas Concert by Hong Kong Oratorio Society
香港聖樂團聖誕音樂會

An Urban Council Presentation
市政局主辦

Supported by the Council for the
Performing Arts of Hong Kong
香港演藝發展局贊助

1991 年 4 月 7 日

**[澳門] 紀念莫扎特逝世
二百周年音樂會**

莫扎特《C 大調加冕彌撒曲》

指揮：
Veiga Jardim

獨唱：
Mary Poulter[s]、鄺翠霞 [m]、
Michael Ryan[t]、楊允田 [bb]

伴奏：
澳門交響樂團

地點：
聖老楞佐教堂

1991 年 5 月 4 日

**樂團三十五周年
紀念音樂會**

**歌劇選段 [1]，
莫扎特《C 小調彌撒曲》等**

指揮：
Stephen Layton

獨唱：
江樺 [1s]、馮志麗 [s]、嚴仙霞 [m]、
王帆 [t]、陳晃相 [bb]

伴奏：
香港小交響樂團

地點：
香港大會堂音樂廳

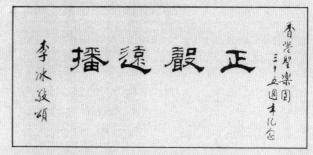

"Full-blooded choir sparkles in Mozart's grand choruses"

《南華早報》

120

1991 年 10 月 27 日

樂團三十五周年
紀念音樂會

孟德爾遜《以利亞》

指揮：
黃永熙

獨唱：
任蓉 s、Jane Dunstan a、
王帆 t、Ralf Döring b、
唐恒偉（童聲）

伴奏：
香港小交響樂團

地點：
香港文化中心音樂廳

黃永熙：「自 1956 年成立以來，聖樂團在各方面都取得相當的進展，相信這不是自詡之詞……最重要的，是我們肯作出承擔，並願意付出時間和努力。」

江樺：「香港聖樂團像是一個龐大的家庭。」

王帆：「每當我踏入聖樂團的時候，我好像回到自己的家。」

陳浩才：「香港聖樂團能夠維持三十五年，且不斷將合唱水平提高，有關負責人及團員所付出的精神、人力及物力實在難以數算，不過這是絕對值得的。」

陳供生："When the Hong Kong Oratorio Society was founded 35 years ago, we knew then it was going to make history. It did."

Joan Jasper: "The cohesive spirit that prevails in [HKO] Society makes for a feeling of love in interpreting the notes of the scores."

曹繼業：「我和內子在香港聖樂團廿三年……每星期二可以『拍拖』去練習，練完可以『拍拖』去『宵夜』，可以說是人生一樂也。」

（場刊）

奇幻聖誕音樂會

指揮：
張毓君

客席演出：
香港浸會學院手鈴隊

伴奏：
香港小交響樂團、
黃健瑜、蘇明村、
戚明儀

地點：
香港大會堂音樂廳

1991 年 12 月 29 日

[澳門] 奇幻聖誕音樂會

1992 年 3 月 8 日

**第五屆香港 -
日本聯合慈善音樂會**

歌劇合唱

地點：
香港大會堂音樂廳

1992 年 4 月 12 日

**紀念《彌賽亞》演出
二百五十週年音樂會**

韓德爾《彌賽亞》

指揮：
Veiga Jardim

獨唱：
江樺 s、嚴仙霞 m、王帆 t、
陳晃相 bb

伴奏：
香港小交響樂團

地點：
沙田大會堂演奏廳

PRE-CANADIAN TOUR CONCERT BY
HONG KONG ORATORIO SOCIETY
Haydn's Seasons

香港聖樂團
加拿大演唱前音樂會
海頓之「四季頌」

11 July 92 (Sat) 8pm
Hong Kong Cultural Centre Concert Hall
九二年七月十一日（星期六）
晚上八時　香港文化中心音樂廳

Accompanied by Hong Kong Sinfonietta
香港小交響樂團伴奏

HONG KONG
CULTURAL CENTRE
香港文化中心

Supported by the Council for
Performing Arts
香港演藝發展局贊助

加拿大巡演預演

海頓《四季頌》

指揮：
陳晃相

獨唱：
黃少萍 s、王帆 t、關傑明 bb

伴奏：
香港小交響樂團

地點：
香港文化中心音樂廳

樂團主席余漢翁：「加拿大旅行演唱會是香港聖樂團首次在亞洲以外的地區演出，將會是本團歷史上的一個重要里程碑。」

（場刊）

1992 年 7 月 24 日 **

[溫哥華]

海頓《四季頌》

指揮：
陳晃相

獨唱：
黃少萍 s、王帆 t、關傑明 bb

伴奏：
曾華琛、John Wilson

地點：
Richmond Gateway Theatre

1992 年 7 月 25 日

[溫哥華]

韓德爾《彌賽亞》

指揮：
黃飛然

獨唱：
江樺 s、譚天眷 m、王帆 t、
楊允田 bb

伴奏：
管弦樂隊
（領奏：Bill Walley）

地點：
Glad Tidings Christian
Fellowship

1992 年 7 月 31 日

[多倫多]

海頓《四季頌》

指揮：
陳晃相

獨唱：
黃少萍 s、王帆 t、關傑明 bb

伴奏：
曾華琛、John Wilson

地點：
Roy Thomson Hall

124

匯唱九二

**陳永華《第四交響曲 –
謝恩讚美頌》（委約作品）**

指揮：
陳永華

獨唱：
葉綺娟[s]、呂國璋[t]

伴奏：
香港小交響樂團

地點：
香港大會堂音樂廳

1992 年 12 月 19 日

舒茲《聖誕故事》及
聖誕曲

指揮：
張毓君

獨唱：
陳愛堅 s 、楊允田 bb 、
（朗誦）招肇琦、馮智恒

伴奏：
香港小交響樂團、
黃健瑜

地點：
沙田大會堂演奏廳

1993 年 3 月 7 日

第六屆香港 -
日本聯合慈善音樂會

韋華第《榮耀頌》

地點：
香港大會堂音樂廳

126

Anita Wilson: "I remember a very different concert in China-
-in the stifling heat of an August summer on the island of
Gulangyu, off Xiamen, when we sang to an attentive and
appreciative audience, some of whom had travelled for several
hours just to be there. Our conductor on that occasion was Dr
Chan Wing-wah who said as we left the stage that the only
thing that was still dry was his bow tie! "

《讚頌》

1993 年 7 月 31 日 *

1993 香港聖樂團廈門演唱會：香港預演

浦賽爾《小號與弦樂奏鳴曲》、
莫扎特《聖體頌》、
韋華第《榮耀頌》、
韓德爾《彌賽亞》選曲

指揮：
陳永華

獨唱：
葉綺娟 [s]、陳愛堅 [s]、
朱慧堅 [a]、Arlis Hiebert [t]、
楊允田 [bb]

伴奏：
香港小交響樂團、孔慶怡

地點：
香港堅道天主教座堂

1993 年 8 月 7-8 日 **

[廈門]

作品同上

指揮：
陳永華

伴奏：
香港小交響樂團

陳永華《第四交響曲 –
謝恩讚美頌》、
布拉姆斯《安魂曲》[1]

指揮：
陳永華、張美萍 [1]

獨唱：
江樺 [s]、呂國璋 [t]、
Michael Rippon [1b]

伴奏：
香港小交響樂團、黃健瑜

地點：
香港文化中心音樂廳

佛漢 • 威廉斯
《基督今日降生》及
聖誕曲

指揮：
黃永熙

獨唱：
馮志麗 [s]、柯大衛 [t]、
Derek Anthony [b]

客席演出：
香港兒童合唱團

伴奏：
香港小交響樂團

地點：
香港文化中心音樂廳

Concert by

HONG KONG
ORATORIO
SOCIETY
香 港 聖 樂 團 音 樂 會

4.10.1993 (Mon 星期一) 8:00pm
Hong Kong Cultural Centre Concert Hall 香港文化中心音樂廳
A joint presentation by the Urban Council and the Hong Kong Oratorio Society
市政局與香港聖樂團合辦
Supported by the Council for the Performing Arts 演藝發展局贊助

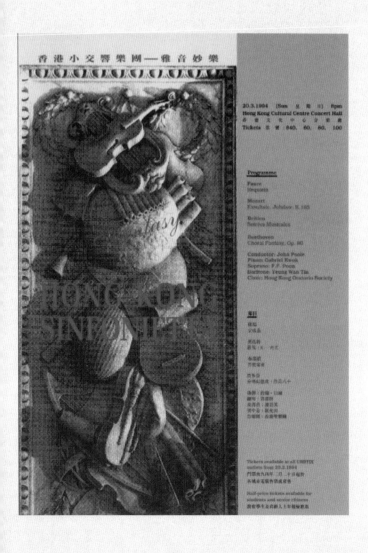

1994 年 3 月 13 日

第七屆香港 - 日本聯合慈善音樂會

佛瑞《安魂曲》

地點：
香港文化中心音樂廳

1994 年 3 月 20 日

香港小交響樂團音樂會

佛瑞《安魂曲》、貝多芬《合唱幻想曲》

指揮：
John Poole

獨唱：
潘若芙[s]、楊允田[b]

鋼琴獨奏：
郭嘉特

地點：
香港文化中心音樂廳

1994 年 8 月 6 日

香港聖樂團 · 溫哥華聖樂團聯合巡迴演唱會

韓德爾《彌賽亞》

指揮：
黃飛然

1994 年 8 月 7 日

陳永華《第四交響曲 –
謝恩讚美頌》[1]、
貝多芬《歡樂頌》

指揮：
陳永華[1]、曹丁

伴奏：
上海廣播電視交響樂團

地點：
上海商城劇院

1994 年 8 月 12 日

韓德爾《彌賽亞》

指揮：黃飛然

獨唱：
任蓉[s]、陳之霞[m]、陳容[t]、
楊允田[b]

1994 年 8 月 14 日

陳永華《第四交響曲 –
謝恩讚美頌》[1]、
貝多芬《歡樂頌》

指揮：
陳永華[1]、陳佐湟

獨唱：
葉綺娟[s]、陳之霞[m]、陳容[t]、
程路禹[bb]

伴奏：
香港小交響樂團

地點：
香港文化中心音樂廳

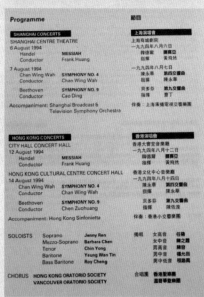

Society chairman Henry Yu: "The idea of organizing the series of concerts stems from Mr Stephen Sun, the chairman of Vancouver Oratorio Society, hoping there is another valuable chance for the collaboration between [us], after the success of the Canada tour concert two years ago."

（場刊）

陳偉光《交響詩篇三部》
（委約作品）[1]**、**
黃自《長恨歌》
（葉純之配器）

指揮：
陳偉光 [1]、蘇明村

獨唱：
葉綺娟 [s]、卓真 [1s]、劉森坪 [t]、
程路禹 [bb]

伴奏：
香港小交響樂團

地點：
沙田大會堂演奏廳

裴高賴西《聖母頌歌》及
聖誕曲

指揮：
蘇明村

獨唱：
陳愛堅 [s]、吳錦輝 [m]、
曾永耀 [t]、關傑明 [bb]

客席演出：
香港小天使合唱團

伴奏：
香港小交響樂團、
黃健瑜

地點：
香港文化中心音樂廳

第八屆香港 -
日本聯合慈善音樂會

貝多芬《第九交響曲》

地點：
香港大會堂音樂廳

**第二次世界大戰結束
五十周年紀念音樂會**

威爾第《安魂曲》

指揮：
Veiga Jardim

獨唱：
徐以琳[s]、陸蘋[a]、劉維維[t]、
李建真[b]

客席演出：
香港雅樂社合唱團、
廣州交響樂團

伴奏：
香港小交響樂團

地點：
香港大會堂音樂廳

**布魯克納《安魂曲》[1]、
陳永華《第四交響曲 –
謝恩讚美頌》**

指揮：
陳永華

獨唱：
葉綺娟[s]、戴俊彬[t]、
陳愛堅[1s]、嚴仙霞[a]、
劉森坪[t]、關傑明[b]

伴奏：
香港小交響樂團

地點：
香港演藝學院音樂廳

ENRICHING CITY LIFE

The Urban Council Presents

DECEMBER

1995

COMING ATTRACTIONS

HONG KONG CULTURAL CENTRE

8/12
(Fri)
8pm
Concert Hall

Organ Recital by Bernhard Gfrerer
First-prize winner of 'Outstanding Musicianship' from the State Ministry for Cultural Activities in Vienna
Programme includes works by Mozart, Mendelssohn, Bach, Bonnet, Guilmant, Gigout and Boëllmann.
$120, 80, 50
Enquiries: 2734 2926

17/12
(Sun)
8pm
Concert Hall

Hong Kong Oratorio Society Christmas Concert '95
Conductor : Dr. Chen Zuohaung
Choir : Hong Kong Oratorio Society
Guest Performer : The Hong Kong Children's Choir
Orchestra : Hong Kong Sinfonietta
Organ : Wong Kin Yu
Alto : Cecilia Chu
Tenor : Eric Cheung
Baritone : Petrus Cheung
$100, 80, 60
Enquiries: 2734 2929

巴赫《一嬰孩為我們誕生》
及聖誕曲

指揮：
陳佐湟

獨唱：
朱慧堅 [a]、張朝暉 [t]、
張健華 [b]

客席演出：
香港兒童合唱團

伴奏：
香港小交響樂團

地點：
香港文化中心音樂廳

第九屆香港 -
日本聯合慈善音樂會

莫扎特《安魂曲》

地點：
香港大會堂音樂廳

香港聖樂團四十周年紀念音樂會

孟德爾遜《以利亞》

指揮：
陳永華

獨唱：
陳芳齡 s、嚴仙霞 a、
朱慧堅 a、戴俊彬 t、張健
華 b、葉宇澄（童聲獨唱）

伴奏：
香港小交響樂團

地點：
香港大會堂音樂廳

香港聖樂團四十周年紀念音樂會

巴里
《他們宣告，我就喜悅》、
衛斯理《聖父賜福》、
艾爾蘭《謝恩讚美》

指揮：
蘇明村

獨唱：
葉宇澄

伴奏：
黃健羽

約翰 • 盧特
《美麗的世界》、
《榮耀頌 – 第一樂章》

指揮：
張毓君

伴奏：
香港小交響樂團、
黃健羽

香港聖樂團名譽會長朱文偉：「過去的四十寒暑充滿了挑戰和苦樂。然而，每次挑戰都帶來了新盼望和動力；經一事長一智，我們也在這種經驗和學習歷程中成長了。」

陳永華：「一個藝術團體或藝術家之成功並不在於模仿，而是開創及建立自己的特色。」

余漢翁：「在慶祝香港聖樂團成立四十周年紀念時，不應該沉醉於過去的成就，最好是展望將來，配合新計劃以期取得更大的進步。」

Joan Jasper："The unfailing dedication of the people in the choir and on the committee is truly something to hold precious in my many memories. They even coped with my Cantonese and made sure that I understood when the meetings lapsed into that language instead of English."

（場刊）

Laudate 讚頌

The HKOS Newsletter　香港聖樂團團訊　**January 1997** 一月號

Greetings from the Music Director p2

The Myth of Oratorios by Andrew Cheung p3

The Voice as an Instrument by Peter Au-Yeung p4

Special Photo Supplement from the Concerts p4, 5

Members Column p7

Friends' Column p8

Coming Events p8

Editorial Team

Chief Editor:
Peter Au-Yeung
Asst Editor (English):
Barry Anderton
Asst Editor (Chinese):
Amy Wong
Production Manager:
Martin Kwok
Co-ordinator:
Billy Cheung

WELCOME TO THE FIRST ISSUE OF *LAUDATE*, THE Society's newsletter, which will be published quarterly. We hope that this will encourage a stronger sense of identity amongst members, as well as enable us to keep in touch with those members who have become inactive for the time being. *Laudate* is first and foremost your newsletter, and as such your contribution is essential. Those who feel intimidated by the presence of experts in the Society would do well to remember that music experts will not be experts in everything that would have a place in the Society newsletter. The Editors will do their best to persuade our music experts to illuminate us in every issue. We will also carry news of coming activities and concerts. Anyone sending in a review of one of our performance would be held in gratitude by the editorial team. Similarly, reports on any Society events (especially any photos), news and views will also be most welcome. A Member's Column will also be included for those special items of news. The Society is setting up a Friends organization. *Laudate* would also serve to keep them informed. There is a Friends' Column for this purpose. The most difficult step in writing is to start. So pick up your pen now and write!

歡迎大家閱讀香港聖樂團團訊「讚頌」創刊號。「讚頌」將於每季出版。藉著這通訊，我們希望能增強團員的歸屬感，及維繫著暫時缺席的團員。「讚頌」正是我們的團訊，除刊登活動和音樂會消息外，相信編們們將盡力說服樂團裏的音樂專家每期撰寫專文以培養大家的音樂修養。但是音樂專家並非事事專長，沒有可能撰寫其他稿件以填滿其餘的篇幅；因此，很需要大家投稿支持。編輯部歡迎有關樂團活動消息（尤其是相片），個人意見的稿件。大家亦可將報章的樂評轉給編輯部。「讚頌」將設「團員專欄」報導團員動態。樂團現正籌組「聖樂團之友」；而「讚頌」亦設「聖樂團之友」欄為團友提供訊息。說起寫作，開始落筆最困難，現在就拿起筆來寫吧！

p1

**陳永華《第四交響曲 –
謝恩讚美頌 – 第一、三樂章》**

指揮：
陳永華

獨唱：
江樺[s]、戴俊彬[t]

**黃安倫《詩篇一百五十篇》、
海頓《納爾遜彌撒曲》**

指揮：
黃永熙

獨唱：
徐慧[s]、嚴仙霞[a]、曾永耀[t]、
楊允田[b]

伴奏：
香港小交響樂團、黃健瑜

地點：
沙田大會堂演奏廳

1996 年 12 月 22 日

韓德爾《彌賽亞》

指揮：
張毓君

獨唱（出場次序）：
劉森坪 [t]、楊健明 [b]、張皓 [a]、
楊允田 [b]、嚴偉 [s]、楊羅娜 [s]、
陳愛堅 [s]、江樺 [s]、車遠強 [b]、
呂國璋 [t]、張健華 [b]、
梁靜宜 [s]

伴奏：
香港小交響樂團、
黃健瑜、蔡麗安

地點：
香港文化中心音樂廳

1997 年 2 月 2 日

第十屆香港 -
日本聯合慈善音樂會

韓德爾《彌賽亞》

伴奏：
香港小交響樂團

地點：
香港文化中心音樂廳

1997 年 3 月 9 日

Hongcouver concert
for Elders

韓德爾《彌賽亞》選段

指揮：
黃飛然

獨唱：
江樺 [s]、王帆 [t]

伴奏：
黃健瑜、曾華琛

地點：
香港大會堂音樂廳

Laudate 讚頌

The HKOS Newsletter 香港聖樂團團訊 April 1997 四月號

And now abideth faith, hope, charity, these three: but the greatest of these is charity.
1 Corinthians 13:13

Sweet Charity by Henry Yu p2

The Myth of Oratorios II by Andrew Cheung p3

The Voice as an Instrument II by Peter Au-Yeung p4

Handel's Musical Piracy by Allison So p6

Photos from Hongcouver Concert p7

Members Column p5

Friends' Column p8

Coming Events p8

Editorial Team

Chief Editor:
Peter Au-Yeung
Asst Editor (English):
Barry Anderton
Asst Editor (Chinese):
Amy Wong
Production Manager:
Martin Kwok
Co-ordinator:
Billy Cheung

Joint Composition Celebrates 10 years of Charity Concerts

The 10th Hong Kong—Japan Joint Charity Concert began with the usual formalities, speeches and of course, the presentation of the cheque to the Community Chest. That the joint concerts have been held for ten successive years is a small occasion for celebration, and the performance of an extra piece of light music before the main programme summarizes the spirit of cooperation between the two participating organizations. It was not any old piece of light music but one written by Mr Fujimori of the Japanese Club chorus . The two lively outer orchestral sections provide a contrasting frame to the middle choral section, setting a couple of verses by John Wilson. This joint composition symbolizes the past efforts of both the Society and the Japanese Club chorus as well as recalling the "birth" of the Sinfonietta through this series of charity concerts.

Hongcouver Concert for Elders
The City Hall, Sunday 9 March 1997

Barry Anderton

The *Messiah* was written in 1742 and its first performance was for charity. Handel could little imagine that his most famous choral work would be performed some two hundred and fifty years later in South East Asia for the benefit of elderly Chinese citizens living in Vancouver, Canada. Nevertheless, I think that if it were possible for Handel to be aware of this concert, he would have approved of it! After all, he was a German living in a strange land and he was a man with a very charitable disposition.

Handel's *Messiah* is part of the standard repertoire of our Society, so much so that whenever it is announced that we will perform it at a future concert, quite a few members would say " not the *Messiah* again!". Never-

Continued on page 7
p1

Glimpses from the Hongcouver Concert

Continued from page 1
theless, it is such a great work that members really do enjoy repeating it. On this occasion, less than 50 members of the choir hurriedly rehearsed with Mr Frank Huang on the Saturday evening prior to the performance. It was very fortunate that this smaller choir turned out to be well balanced across all of the sections.

A single two-hour rehearsal on Saturday evening coupled with a one-hour dress rehearsal on the day was all the preparation time available. Although it was mainly exerpts from the second part of the *Messiah*, the performance was extremely polished and few in the appreciative audience could have imagined that the rehearsal time has been so brief.

The choir responded very well to the experienced and sensitive conducting of Mr Frank Huang in performing the second half of this charity concert before an audience of respectable size in the City Hall. The choir was accompanied by Miss Wong Kin Yu on the organ and Ms Ella Kiang and Mr Wong Fang sang well-appreciated solos accompanied by Mr Timmy Tsang.

The members who participated in the concert thought it a very worthwhile venture combining singing with a very good purpose.

p7

"The [Choral Fantasy] was a considerably more spirited rendition than our last performance of the work conducted by John Poole. So much so that the choral section was replayed for the encore!"

《讚頌》

貝多芬《合唱幻想曲》

指揮：
葉聰

獨唱：
朱小強 [s]、施熙德 [s]、張皓 [a]、
莫華倫 [t]、呂國璋 [t]、張健華 [b]

伴奏：
香港小交響樂團、羅乃新
（貝多芬）

地點：
香港大會堂音樂廳

韓德爾《出埃及記》

指揮：
蘇明村

獨唱：
陳芳齡 [s]、張皓 [a]、簡頌輝 [t]、
吳劍峰 [b]、余漢康 [b]

聯合演出：
雅樂社合唱團

伴奏：
香港小交響樂團、黃健瑜

地點：
香港大會堂音樂廳

黃永熙博士八十壽辰音樂會

黃永熙作品等

指揮：
黃永熙、陳永華、蘇明村

獨唱：
任蓉 [s]、陳芳齡 [s]、馮志麗 [s]、
嚴仙霞 [a]、王帆 [t]、陳晃相 [b]

客席演出：
德望女子中學合唱團、
中華基督教聖頌團、
香港國際音樂學校合唱團

伴奏：
香港小交響樂團、黃健翰、
蘇明村、黃衛明

地點：
香港大會堂音樂廳

"It was a memorable experience, which gave the [HK Oratorio] Society good exposure and doubled the membership of our Friends organization."

《讚頌》

Lavender Patten: "As we move into a new phase of Hong Kong's development, it is my earnest hope that the Hong Kong Oratorio Society will continue to make its unique contribution to Hong Kong's cultural life."

（場刊）

1997 年 6 月 27-29 日 ＊＊

慶祝回歸逍遙音樂會

指揮：
Barry Knight

獨唱：
Della Jonesm

伴奏：
香港小交響樂團

地點：
香港演藝學院歌劇院

Anita Wilson: "⋯at the Last Night of the Proms concerts at APA just before the change of sovereignty last year, I'd been dubious about the wisdom of this enterprise – could we really sing Land of Hope and Glory on such an occasion and in such a place? We could and we did and no-one who was there will ever forget it."

《讚頌》

九七回歸音樂節

陳永華《九州同頌》

指揮：
陳佐湟

獨唱：
莫華倫 [t]

聯合演出：
香港合唱團協會聯合合唱
團（九百人）

伴奏：
香港管弦樂團

地點：
香港體育館、
香港文化中心音樂廳

"Can anyone in the Oratorio Society remember performing
six times in as many days? The archives clearly show that
this is a record."

《讚頌》

Sam Lau: "It was gratifying to see the HK Oratorio Society organizing a Schubert evening, a welcome departure from its mainly sacred repertoire. There were many good things in the evening, a thoughtful programme, good mix of items and the presence of an ever eager choir."

《讚頌》

1997 年 10 月 18 日

為善寧會籌款音樂會

韓德爾《彌賽亞》 選段

香港大會堂音樂廳

1997 年 10 月 19 日

舒伯特之夜
（紀念舒伯特誕辰二百周年）

C 大調彌撒曲等

指揮：
蘇明村

獨唱：
陳愛堅[s]、洪黃順真[a]、
蔡邦懷[t]、朱贊生[b]

伴奏：
黃健翰、蘇明村

地點：
香港大會堂音樂廳

1997 年 11 月 2 日

朝聖者東方之旅音樂會：
慶祝道風山基督教叢林成立
七十五周年

Sigvald Tveit《朝聖者》
（世界首演）

指揮：
張美萍

獨唱：
陳芳齡[s]、Harald Olsen[t]

聯合演出：
欣樂詠團、亞洲聖禮及音樂學院
合唱團（菲律賓）

伴奏：
香港小交響樂團、中樂小組

地點：
香港文化中心音樂廳

1997 年 11 月 29 日

[澳門] 韋華第《榮耀頌》

指揮：Henrique Piloto

伴奏：
澳門室樂團

地點：
玫瑰堂

The Macau Tour

Group photo on sightseeing tour

The Choir with the conductor Mr Piloto and soloists in San Domingos Church

Participating in Sunday worship at the Macau Baptist Church

The choir in performing in the Church with the back of the head of the Governor of Macau in the foreground

1997 年 12 月 16-19 日

[台灣] 韓德爾《彌賽亞》

指揮：
陳澄雄

伴奏：
台灣省立交響樂團

地點：
基隆市基隆文化中心、
宜蘭縣省立蘭陽女中、
嘉義縣市國立中正大學、
台中市中興堂

「今日 [香港] 聖樂團已被公認為東南亞最佳合唱團之一。」

（引自台灣省立交響樂團 CD 小冊）

PANIS ANGELICUS

We premiered Doming Lam's setting of The 13th century Latin Prayer, Panis Angelicus at the last concert. The original text is by St Thomas Aquinas (1227 - 1274), and Panis Angelicus forms the last two verses of a prayer of seven verses. Whilst the first verse is quite familiar, especially through César Franck's setting, the second verse is also an integral part of the hymn. Modern research reveals that the last line of the first verse should be "Servus pauper et humilis". (Information and translations courtesy of Fr Peter Choi of the Catholic Cathedral)

Latin	English	中文
Panis angelicus fit panis hominum; dat panis coelicus figuris terminum. O res mirabilis: manducat Dominum pauper servus et humilis.	Farewell to types! henceforth We feed on angel's food: The slave, O wonder! eats the flesh Of his Incarnate God.	天神至甘之筵，成人糧日無間， 此糧乃降自天，除古禮棄舊典， 喜全能恩無邊，恭領主於心田， 罪人貧賤蒙主矜憐。
Te, trina Deitas unaque, poscimus; sic nos tu visitas sicut te colimus: per tuas semitas duc nos quo tendimus ad lucem quam inhabitas. Amen.	O blessed Three in One! Visit out hearts, we pray, And lead us on through Thine own paths To Thy eternal day. Amen.	至尊一體聖三，我眾敬禮朝參， 聊亦迴顧慈顏，懇賜神力平安， 導爾命勤行善，順爾引達天岸， 受享榮福以至永遠。

1997 年 12 月 21 日

聖誕音樂會 1997

巴赫《沉睡者醒來》、林樂培《天使之神糧》（世界首演）

指揮：
陳永華

獨唱：
劉辨琴 s、劉森坪 t、張健華 b

客席演出：
香港兒童合唱團

伴奏：
香港小交響樂團、黃健瑜、黃以明

地點：
香港文化中心音樂廳

1998 年 3 月 8 日

第十一屆香港 - 日本聯合慈善音樂會

貝多芬《第九交響曲》（第三、第四樂章）

指揮：
陳永華

客席獨唱

聯合演出：
香港日本人俱樂部合唱團

伴奏：
香港小交響樂團

地點：
香港文化中心音樂廳

1998 年 4 月 22 日

團員獨唱音樂會

地點：
香港大會堂劇院

1998 年 6 月 26 日

以色列巡迴演出前奏音樂會

舒曼《安魂曲》等

指揮：
官美如

獨唱：
施熙德[s]、嚴仙霞[m]、
劉森坪[t]、張健華[b]

伴奏：
香港小交響樂團

地點：
香港大會堂音樂廳

1998 年 8 月 10-20 日

以色列之旅 - 18th Zimriya World Assembly of Choirs

指揮：
蘇明村

伴奏：
黃以明

Sam Lau: "The HKOS scored a first in Hong Kong with the performance of Schumann's Requiem opus 148...The choral standard on this evening was good; the intonation was clean and there was a keen purpose of musical delivery. Most impressive of all, the choir sang with conviction ..."

《讚頌》

周凡夫：「截止一九九八年，香港聖樂團公開演唱《彌賽亞》已有三十三次了。」

（雨果唱片）

Barry Anderton: "Following a series of exhausting rehearsals terminating in an even more tiring recording session, the Oratorio Society gave a public concert of the Messiah...A very weary choir did its best to rise to the occasion and succeeded in the opinion of a very enthusiastic audience."

《讚頌》

以色列之旅匯報音樂會

黃安倫《詩篇一百五十篇》等中外合唱作品

指揮：
蘇明村

客席獨唱：
譚宇良 [t]

伴奏：
黃以明

敲擊：
錢國偉、何銘恩

地點：
香港大會堂劇院

1998 年 9 月 19 日

韓德爾《彌賽亞》

指揮：
陳澄雄

獨唱：
葉綺娟 [s]、嚴仙霞 [a]、
譚宇良 [t]、張健華 [b]

伴奏：
香港小交響樂團、
黃健翰、余必達

地點：
荃灣大會堂演奏廳

**孟德爾遜 《詩篇四十二 》
及聖誕歌**

指揮：
陳永華

獨唱：
江樺 [s]、簡頌輝 [t]、曾永耀 [t]、
孫永輝 [bb]、楊允田 [bb]

伴奏：
香港小交響樂團

地點：
香港文化中心音樂廳

**「華夏世紀情」
一九九九年新年音樂會**

[北京] 貝多芬《歡樂頌》

指揮：
陳佐湟

聯合演出：
明儀合唱團及國內合唱團、
香港小交響樂團

伴奏：
中國交響樂團

地點：
北京人民大會堂

周凡夫：「在進入千禧年來臨倒數的新一年，能夠通過音
樂演奏交流，加強兩岸四地的溝通、了解，提升樂師歌手
的合作性，確具實質與象徵意義。」

《星島日報》

**第十二屆香港 -
日本聯合慈善音樂會**

浦契尼《光榮彌撒》

指揮：
陳永華

聯合演出：
香港日本人俱樂部合唱團

伴奏：
香港小交響樂團

地點：
香港文化中心音樂廳

攜手創明天音樂會

**霍爾斯特《行星組曲》
海王星**

指揮：
葉聰

第一、二女高音和
女中音聲部

伴奏：
香港小交響樂團、
香港青年交響樂團

地點：
香港文化中心音樂廳

團員音樂會：聖樂頌賞

地點：
香港大會堂劇院

1999 年 5 月 8-9 日

「**香港合唱節九九**」

參演團體：
香港青年合唱團、
香港浸會大學女聲合唱團、
廣州少年宮合唱團、
香港巴赫合唱團、
德望學校女聲合唱團、
香港日本人俱樂部合唱團等

地點：
香港大會堂音樂廳

1999 年 7 月 10 日

威爾第《安魂曲》

指揮：
Veiga Jardim

獨唱：
阮妙芬 [s]、楊潔 [a]、柯大衛 [t]、
張健華 [b]

伴奏：
香港小交響樂團

地點：
香港大會堂音樂廳

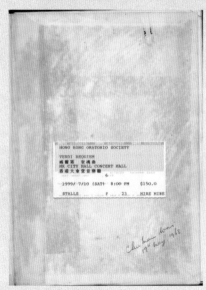

梁慧子：「香港聖樂團在大會堂舉行的音樂會，與一般演出有別，由於是次音樂會為紀念已故聖樂團的創辦人朱文偉，所以在開場前，席上觀眾均應邀起立靜默一分鐘。」

《大公報》

148

音樂慶典：
建國五十周年

朱踐耳《英雄的詩篇 –
交響大合唱》選曲

指揮：
葉聰

聯合演出：
明儀合唱團、
香港室內合唱團

伴奏：
香港小交響樂團

地點：
香港大會堂音樂廳

中華魂 - 長恨歌及
林聲翕聲樂作品演唱會

《萬福之門》[1]、
《海峽漁歌》[1]、
《可愛的香港》[1]，
《長恨歌》、《中華頌歌》
（第二樂章《文化藝術》、
第五樂章《頌讚》）

指揮：
張毓君[1]、嚴良堃

獨唱：
任蓉[s]、程路禹[b]、王帆[t]

聯合演出：
明儀合唱團

伴奏：
香港小交響樂團、黃健瑜

地點：
香港大會堂音樂廳

周文珊：「在嚴良堃的指揮棒下，唱出了很久未聽過如此動情的
《長恨歌》。」

《大公報》

黎鍵：「林聲翕教授這大型的《中華頌歌》全篇浸染了非常誠摯
的真感情，旋律極其動人，氣勢磅礡，音調鏗鏘。」

《文匯報》

九九聖誕音樂會

舒伯特《尊主頌》及聖誕曲選

指揮：
張毓君

獨唱：
鄭何美芳 s、許羨儀 s、
李冰 m、陳卓堅 t、
吳劍峰 bb

客席演出：
香港兒童合唱團

伴奏：
香港小交響樂團、黃健瑜

地點：
香港文化中心音樂廳

2000-2009 年

導讀：

進入二十一世紀的第一個十年，香港聖樂團迎來幾
項重要發展。首先是得到政府贊助，在上海街開設
多用途辦公室，幾十年的音樂會及會員資料得以集
中儲存。此外，聖樂團正式進入網絡世界，擁有自
己的網站。另外，沿用多年「香港聖樂團」這個中
文名字正式登記註冊。鑑於香港小交響樂團公司
化，聖樂團另覓伴奏樂隊，其中包括 2002 年的香
港弦樂團，一直合作至今。

演出方面，這個十年演出不少於六十四場次，數目
僅次於 1990 年代。2006 年幾乎全年演出金禧音樂
會系列，慶祝建團五十周年，壓軸是深圳聖誕音樂
會。在兩岸四地留下歌聲的同時，全團多次前往內
地城市與當地音樂家聯袂演出，例如 2006 年在北
京與中央芭蕾舞團管弦樂隊演出佛瑞《安魂曲》，
以及 2008 年在上海、蘇州巡演。2007 年在深圳與

深圳交響樂團演出孟德爾遜第二交響曲，客席指揮是聖樂團元老之一楊允田的
女兒楊焰嬅。

這十年間除了恆常聖誕演出和作曲家專題音樂會外，聖樂團亦多次參與慈善音
樂會。自 1988 年的港日音樂會連續舉行十七年後，2004 年在貝多芬《歡樂頌》
歌聲下落幕。2005 年參與聖安德烈教堂百年籌款，四年後更赴廣州市，為東
山堂籌款演出《彌賽亞》，同樣載入史冊。

這期間也有兩場別具意義的演出。首先是 2002 年由聖樂團主辦「樂韻春風 40
年」，慶賀江樺老師從事音樂教育四十周年音樂會。另一場是 2007 年由音樂
總監陳永華親自指揮香港中樂團和明儀合唱團聯袂首演新作品《第八交響曲 -
蒼茫大地》。

這段期間聖樂團與香港一道經歷傷感。首先 2003 年非典來襲，香港頓成悲情城
市。當疫情稍退，聖樂團在 6 月舉行「願世界和平」音樂會，以三首至愛神曲選
段慰藉社會。同一年，黃永熙博士息勞歸主，聖樂團以「光輝的樂章」音樂會作
悼念，指揮包括遠道從加拿大專程來港的黃安倫，親自指揮首演《安魂曲》。

2000 年 3 月 19 日

第十三屆香港 -
日本聯合慈善音樂會

約翰 • 盧特《安魂曲》

指揮：
陳永華

獨唱：
徐慧 [s]

聯合演出：
香港日本人俱樂部合唱團

伴奏：
香港城市室樂團

地點：
香港文化中心音樂廳

"The new format concert programmes have proven popular with our audience. The A4-size booklets were first used at the 'Soul of China' concert in memory of Lin Sheng-shih...the format was tried a second time with the Bach concert. There were less than 10 booklets left [in the hall after the concert]"

《讚頌》

團員音樂會

地點：
香港大會堂劇院

向巴赫致禮 （紀念巴赫逝世二百五十周年）

《第五十一清唱劇》、
《D 大調聖母頌歌》等

指揮：
陳永華

獨唱：
葉綺娟 [s]、梁思敏 [m]、
嚴仙霞 [a]、簡頌輝 [t]、
關傑明 [bb]

伴奏：
香港小交響樂團、
黃健瑜

地點：
香港文化中心音樂廳

四位作曲家

羅西尼《小莊嚴彌撒曲》

指揮：
蘇明村

獨唱：
阮妙芬 s、嚴仙霞 a、
萬建平 t、張健華 bb

聯合演出：
天主教香港教區聖樂團

伴奏：
黃健瑜、黃以明、
余必達

地點：
香港大會堂音樂廳

聖誕音樂會

貝多芬《歡樂頌》、
巴赫《第二十九清唱曲》等

指揮：
陳永華

獨唱：
陳嘉璐 s、嚴仙霞 a、
萬建平 t、張健華 bb

客席演出：
香港兒童合唱團

伴奏：
香港小交響樂團

地點：
香港文化中心音樂廳

Ouside Broadcast for Macau Messiah

The Society had its first ever simultaneous outside broadcast of a concert with the Holy Saturday evening performance of the Messiah at Sao Domingos Church in Macau. An estimated 200 or so people attended the performance outside the church after the inside was packed to capacity for the concert. The half a dozen or so rows of chairs, which had been put there for the outside audience, rapidly filled up before the concert. It was quieter on the Easter Sunday morning performance, with hardly another standing audience outside, but the church was still packed to capacity.

This concert tour was the first to Macau since its handover in 1999, our last tour being the performance of Vivaldi's Gloria at the end of November 1997. Our old friend, Maestro Veiga Jardim conducted the performance from the harpsichord again. Some 50 members gave up their Easter weekend to participate in two performance of the Messiah, at 8pm on Holy Saturday and 11am on Easter Sunday. The audience was very appreciative especially the head of ICM, who was quite taken by the performances. She attended with her husband on Saturday night and took her son along for the Sunday morning concert. Let's hope the ICM will remember the Society when they are looking for a performance of sacred choral music.

p4

Photos from the Macau Tour

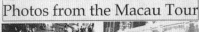

Look at the crowds and the queues!

A photo for the stars in the Treasury — Hallelujah, Hallelujah!

Another view of the Big Screen — Relaxing at the noodle party

As the Concert Tour took place over two days of the Easter weekend, it was a less coherent affair than usual. Due to Church commitments of many members, people arrived in a few parties and left in many more as some took the advantage of staying in Macau for the rest of the long holiday weekend. However, as the audience response showed, we put in two good performances, which were well received.

p5

周凡夫:「多年來未再踏足澳門的香港聖樂團,能和澳門室內樂團再度攜手,重續港澳兩個具代表性的音樂團體長期交流合作的傳統。」

《大公報》

2001 年 3 月 11 日

第十四屆香港 - 日本聯合慈善音樂會

巴赫 《聖馬太受難曲》

指揮:
陳永華

聯合演出:
香港日本人俱樂部合唱團

伴奏:
深圳交響樂團

地點:
香港文化中心音樂廳

2001 年 4 月 14-15 日

[澳門]

韓德爾《彌賽亞》

指揮:
Jeiga Jardim

獨唱:
林惠珍[s]、楊潔[a]、于吉星[t]、
Ian Cousins[b]

伴奏:
澳門室樂團

地點:
玫瑰堂

四十五周年紀念音樂會

海頓 《創世記》

指揮：
陳永華

獨唱：
阮妙芬[s]、嚴仙霞[a]、
戴俊彬[t]、關傑明[b]

伴奏：
深圳交響樂團、余必達

地點：
香港大會堂音樂廳

董趙洪娉："The Hong Kong Oratorio Society has stood the test of time and proven itself to be a robust amateur organization."

（場刊）

余漢翁：「慶祝成立四十五周年的香港聖樂團和慶祝成立二十周年的高雄市漢聲合唱團，兩團分別在自己的城市主辦一個音樂會……同時各自演唱多首體現各自文化特色的合唱歌曲。」

（場刊）

夏日和諧曲 - 香港

莫扎特《C 小調彌撒曲》及盧特《安樂窩》等合唱作品

指揮：
孫愛光（莫扎特）、蘇明村

聯合演出：
高雄市漢聲合唱團

伴奏：
深圳交響樂團

地點：
香港大會堂音樂廳

2001 年 8 月 13 日

夏日和諧曲 - 台灣：港台文化交流演唱會

節目同上

指揮：
蘇明村

聯合演出：
高雄市漢聲合唱團

伴奏：
高雄市交響樂團

地點：
高雄市中正文化中心至德堂

感恩讚美 香港聖樂團 四十五周年紀念音樂會

聖詩作品

指揮：
官美如、趙伯承

獨唱：
江樺 s、簡頌輝 t

伴奏：
黃健褕、黃以明、
余必達

地點：
香港文化中心音樂廳

音樂總監陳永華："In a world of uncertainty and anxiety, music helps to bring in peace of mind, religious music in particular. When technology is advancing at an uncontrollable speed, we should all be grateful that we could enjoy a moment of musical serenity and help to make this world less hostile and more human."

（場刊）

「香港聖樂團成立於一九五六年，團員超過百名，每年平均舉辦六場音樂會，可稱是香港歷史最悠久、團員最多和最活躍的合唱團。」

（香港政府新聞公報）

聖誕音樂會 2001

孟德爾遜《詩篇九十五》、佛漢 • 威廉斯《聖誕幻想曲》

指揮：
陳永華

獨唱：
黃少萍 s、陳愛堅 s、陳漢強 t、關傑明 b

客席演出：
香港兒童合唱團

伴奏：
香港小交響樂團、黃健翰

地點：
香港文化中心音樂廳

第十五屆香港 - 日本聯合慈善音樂會

莫扎特《安魂曲》

指揮：
陳永華

獨唱：
徐慧 s、史韶韻 m、鹿內芳仁 t、張宏恩 b

聯合演出：
香港日本人俱樂部合唱團等

伴奏：
深圳交響樂團

地點：
香港大會堂音樂廳

孟德爾遜 《以利亞》

指揮：
陳永華

獨唱：
徐慧[s]、嚴仙霞[a]、戴俊彬[t]、
張健華[b]、林浩恩
（童聲獨唱）

伴奏：
香港小交響樂團

地點：
香港大會堂音樂廳

深圳之旅演出

冼星海《黃河大合唱》

指揮：
俞峰

聯合演出：
廣州交響樂團合唱團、
深圳等合唱團

伴奏：
深圳交響樂團、
高雄市交響樂團、
澳門室樂團

地點：
深圳體育館

周凡夫：「今次參加深圳的《黃河》演唱，看來將會打開西方合唱藝術進入深圳的大門，有助填補中國這方面長期以來的空白。這可說是香港藝團適應政治環境轉變發揮存在價值的有效策略的例子。」

《信報》

2002 年 6 月 30 日

**江樺老師 -
樂韻春風四十年**

莫扎特《讚美上主》、
王世光《長江之歌》及
獨唱曲等

指揮：
陳永華

聯合演出：
江樺學生合唱團

地點：
香港大會堂音樂廳

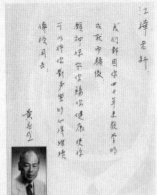

「據不完全統計，在香港聖樂團的演出中，由江樺或由她調教出來的高足擔任獨唱的音樂會，所佔比例高達百分之六十。」

《大公報》

2002 年 9 月 14 日

美樂頌主 - 巴洛克及
浪漫時期法國聖樂作品

夏龐蒂埃《謝恩讚美頌》、
拉莫《聖母頌》、
比才《羔羊頌》、
聖桑《稱頌主名》、
《阿利路亞》、
古諾《莊嚴彌撒曲》

指揮：
官美如

獨唱：
黃葉綺娟 s、趙慧德 s、
陳思光 ct、簡頌輝 t、
關傑明 bb

伴奏：
香港弦樂團、黃健瑜、
余必達、譚懷理

地點：
香港大會堂音樂廳

2002 年 12 月 15 日

樂韻愛心頌聖誕

夏龐蒂埃《子夜彌撒曲》
及聖誕歌曲

指揮：
蘇明村

獨唱：
陳愛堅 s、楊玉芬 s、
陳思光 ct、吳振輝 t、
楊允田 bb

客席演出：
香港兒童合唱團

伴奏：
澳門室樂團、黃健瑜、
戚明儀

地點：
香港大會堂音樂廳

2002 年 12 月 26 日

澳門聖誕音樂會

**重複香港節目，
加《彌賽亞》選曲**

指揮：
蘇明村

獨唱：
陳愛堅[s]、楊玉芬[s]、
陳思光[ct]、吳振輝[t]、
楊允田[bb]

聯合演出：
澳門演藝學院合唱團

伴奏：
澳門室樂團

地點：
澳門主教座堂

2003 年 3 月 16 日

第十六屆香港 - 日本聯合慈善音樂會

布拉姆斯《安魂曲》

指揮：
陳永華

聯合演出：
香港日本人俱樂部合唱團等

伴奏：
深圳交響樂團

地點：
香港大會堂音樂廳

2003 年 6 月 1 日 /7 日 */**

「願世界和平」音樂會

《彌賽亞》、《創世記》、《以利亞》選曲等

指揮：
陳永華

主持：
羅乃新

獨唱：
陳愛堅 [s]、歐陽慧文 [s]、
洪黃順真 [a]、譚宇良 [t]、
陳卓堅 [t]、楊健明 [b]

伴奏：
香港弦樂團、黃健瑜、
余必達

地點：
香港大會堂音樂廳、
荃灣大會堂演奏廳

「樂團希望藉音樂為氣餒的人帶來希望，為寂寞中奮戰的人帶來愛和溫暖，更盼望世界每一角落也不再面對肉體和心靈的戰爭，得享世界和平與內心的平安。」

（政府新聞公報）

166

**頌歌銅響 -
盧特及當代作品選**

指揮：
張毓君

獨唱：
陳愛堅 [s] 、楊允田 [bb] 、
馬冠華（童聲獨唱）

伴奏：
城市銅管樂團、黃健瑜、
戚明儀、黃士倫、樊麗華、
陳穎祺

地點：
香港大會堂音樂廳

團員音樂會

鋼琴伴奏獨唱、小組

地點：
香港科學館演講廳

Hong Kong Oratorio Society

Members' Concert 2003

Science Museum Lecture Hall
Sunday 30th November 2003, 7:30pm

Members' Concert 2003

Ensemble 1	Piano: Huang Yee Ming
O lovely peace	GF Handel
Hark! The goat-bells ringing	H Smart
Martin Cheung	Piano: Huang Yee Ming
The goodness of God	CPE Bach
The Lord is my Light	F Allitsen
Agnus Dei	G Bizet
Rita Lam	Piano: Paul Chong
Oh! Had I Jubal's lyre	GF Handel
Saper vorreste	G Verdi
Risa Wong	Piano: Huang Yee Ming
Non so piu	WA Mozart
Voi che sapete	WA Mozart
Ensemble 2	Piano: Chan Wing Man
Laudamus te	A Vivaldi
Abendlied	F Mendlessohn
Lilian Mak	Piano: Paul Chong
Solveig's Song	E Grieg
Ouvre ton Coeur	G Bizet
Wong Mi Lin	Piano: Cherry Chan
In quali eccessi, ...Mi tradi quell'alma ingrate	WA Mozart
Ave Maria	C Gounod
Andis Au-Yeung	Piano: Maureen Lim
Alleluia	WA Mozart
Quando mem vo	G Puccini
May Chan	Piano: Michael Cheung
Schließe mein Herze	JS Bach
Près des remparts de Seville	G Bizet
Allerseelen	R Strauss
Ensemble 1	Piano: Huang Yee Ming
I would that my love	F Mendlessohn
I feel pretty	L Bernstein

2003 年 12 月 21 日

聖誕音樂會 2003

**韓德爾《第四加冕曲》、
陳永華《第四交響曲 –
謝恩讚美頌》等**

指揮：
陳永華

主持：
羅乃新

獨唱：
梁頌儀 ˢ、戴俊彬 ᵗ

客席演出：
聖保羅書院合唱團

伴奏：
香港弦樂團、黃健瑜

地點：
香港文化中心音樂廳

董趙洪娉：「經歷了過去一年種種考驗，今年聖誕別具
意義，願大家借此節慶以愛心和活力重建這城市。」

（場刊）

2003年12月26日

澳門樂團
《聖母頌聖誕音樂會》

莫扎特《聖體頌》、
黃安倫《詩篇一百五十篇》

指揮：
黃安倫

聯合演出：
澳門演藝學院合唱團

地點：
澳門玫瑰堂

2004年1月11日

「騰歡聲徹、眾樂諧和」-
中文大學四十周年
校慶音樂會

貝多芬《歡樂頌》等

指揮：
陳永華

聯合演出：
中文大學崇基合唱團、
中文大學學生會合唱團

伴奏：
香港小交響樂團

地點：
香港文化中心音樂廳

The 17th
HONG KONG – JAPAN
JOINT CHARITY CONCERT
第17回港日連合慈善音楽会

Presented and sponsored by
The Hongkong Japanese Club
Supported by
Consulate-General of Japan
The Hong Kong Japanese Chamber of Commerce and Industry

第十七屆香港 -
日本聯合慈善音樂會

**貝多芬 《第九交響曲》
（第三、四樂章）**

指揮：
陳永華

獨唱：
增田 [s]、嚴仙霞 [m]、
鹿內芳仁 [t]、張健華 [b]

聯合演出：
香港日本人俱樂部合唱團等

伴奏：
深圳交響樂團

地點：
香港文化中心音樂廳

2004 年 4 月 10-11 日

澳門音樂會

舒伯特
《降 A 大調第五彌撒曲》

地點：
澳門玫瑰堂

2004 年 6 月 18 日

天音妙韻舒伯特

舒伯特
《降 A 大調第五彌撒曲》、
《聖母讚主曲》等

指揮：
陳永華

獨唱：
徐慧 s、史韶韻 m、簡頌輝 t、
林俊 b

伴奏：
澳門樂團、黃健瑜

地點：
香港文化中心音樂廳

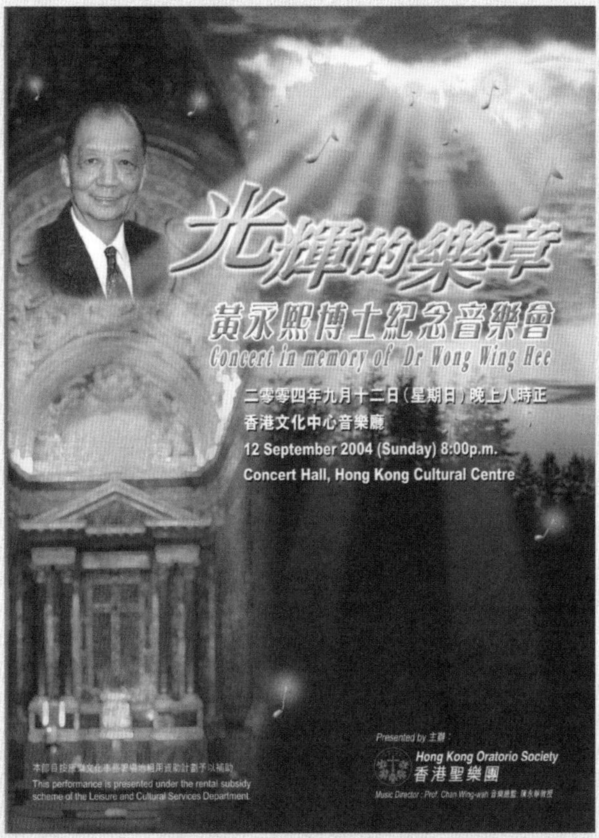

楊健明：「黃永熙博士在信仰和聖樂事工上的堅持與奉獻，感動和造就了很多後輩。」

（場刊）

2004 年 7 月 24 日

澳門音樂會

貝多芬《合唱幻想曲》、《第九交響曲》[1]

指揮：
邵恩

獨唱：
馬梅[1s]、劉華[s]、楊潔[1a]、魏松[1t]、唐衛平[t]、徐小明[t]、張峰[1b]

聯合演出：
上海歌劇院合唱團、
澳門演藝學院合唱團

地點：
澳門文化廣場

2004 年 9 月 12 日 **

「光輝的樂章」黃永熙博士紀念音樂會

孟德爾遜《以利亞》選段

指揮：
陳永華

獨唱：
陳愛堅[s]、許羨儀[a]、曾永耀[t]、楊允田[bb]

黃安倫《安魂曲》（無伴奏混聲合唱，香港聖樂團委約、世界首演）

指揮：
黃安倫

獨唱：
嚴仙霞[a]、簡頌輝[t]

聯合演出：
天主教香港教區聖樂團、
中華基督教聖頌團

伴奏：
黃健揄

地點：
香港文化中心音樂廳

2004 年 12 月 18 日

[深圳] 聖誕音樂會 2004

韓德爾《彌賽亞》選曲、聖誕歌曲等

主辦：
深圳交響樂團

地點：
深圳少年宮

2004 年 12 月 19 日

聖誕音樂會 2004

節目同上

指揮：
蘇明村

獨唱：
梁靜宜[s]、嚴仙霞[a]、
呂國璋[t]、朱承恩[bb]

客席聯合演出：
加拿大卡城華人聖樂團、
香港教育學院合唱團

伴奏：
深圳交響樂團、黃健瑜、
黃以明

地點：
香港文化中心音樂廳

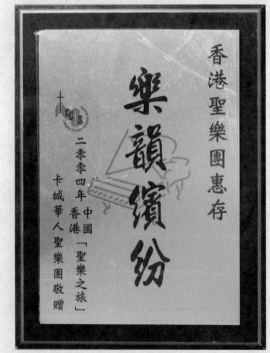

[澳門] 聖誕音樂會 2004

海頓 《創世記》

指揮：
Veiga Jardim

獨唱：
陳其蓮[s]、葛毅[t]、袁晨野[bb]

伴奏：
澳門樂團

地點：
澳門玫瑰堂

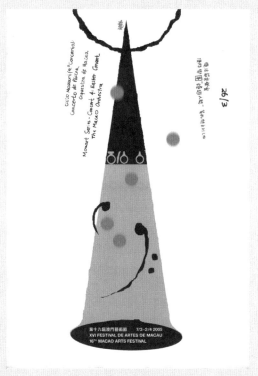

**[澳門] 第十六屆澳門
藝術節：復活節音樂會**

莫扎特《安魂曲》

指揮：
Michael Lloyd

獨唱：
陳小群[s]、楊潔[a]、宋波[t]、
張建魯[bb]

伴奏：
澳門樂團

地點：
澳門玫瑰堂

**大師沙利略與
天才莫扎特**

沙利略《榮譽頌》、
《謝恩讚美頌》、
莫扎特《安魂曲》

指揮：
官美如

獨唱：
梁頌儀[s]、林婉儀[a]、
戴俊彬[t]、關傑明[bb]

伴奏：
澳門樂團、黃健瑜

地點：
香港大會堂音樂廳

「是次音樂會的選曲能讓聽眾一窺甚少演奏的沙利略歌
劇、協奏曲和聖歌選段，全為香港首演作品。」

《大公報》

**天上人間滿載榮光 -
屯門、沙田**

指揮：
陳永華

獨唱：
葉葆菁[s]、羅月蟾[s]、
邵煥英[s]、陳德美[m]

伴奏：
香港弦樂團

地點：
屯門大會堂、
沙田大會堂演奏廳

「曾被形容為『用心靈歌頌，充滿說服力』的香港聖樂團
即將聯同香港弦樂團演出兩場音樂會。」

（政府新聞公報）

聖安德烈教堂百周年籌款音樂會

韋華第：《榮耀頌》等

指揮：
符潤光

地點：
九龍聖安德烈教堂

2005 年 12 月 18 日

金禧聖誕音樂會
花都浪漫聖誕夜

指揮：
陳永華

獨唱：
葉葆菁[s]、史韶韻[m]、
周珍妮[a]、柯大偉[t]、
張健華[b]

客席演出：
新加坡國際學校合唱團

伴奏：
香港弦樂團、黃健瑜

地點：
香港文化中心音樂廳

2006 年 4 月 7 日

[澳門] 安魂天音
布拉姆斯《安魂曲》

指揮：
邵恩

獨唱：
呂麗莉[s]、袁晨野[b]

聯合演出：
上海歌劇院合唱團

伴奏：
澳門樂團、
上海歌劇院交響樂團

地點：
澳門玫瑰堂

2006 年 5 月 7 日 **

金禧音樂會系列
海頓《四季頌》

地點：
香港文化中心音樂廳

中央芭蕾舞團團長趙汝蘅：「期待着中央芭蕾舞團交響樂團與香港聖樂團的合作，不僅僅是創先河，重要的是我們在不斷成長。寧靜的音樂感悟心靈，坦然釋放……」

香港聖樂團主席楊健明：「與『中巴』首度合作，為本團的歷史又寫下新的一頁……這次有新突破——我們的演出不再框在幾套大型作品之內，而能嘗試『另類』曲目。」

（場刊）

2006 年 7 月 15-16 日

北京之旅音樂會

佛瑞（福雷）《安魂曲》

指揮：
張藝

伴奏：
中央芭蕾舞團交響樂團、
余必達

地點：
北京大學百周年紀念講堂

2006 年 9 月 18 日 ＊＊

金禧音樂會系列：
三代同堂莫扎特

《安魂曲》選段、法蘭茲 •
莫扎特《節日合唱曲》
（亞洲首演）

指揮：
陳永華

獨唱：
陳愛堅 s、陳德美 m、
簡頌輝 t、張健華 b

伴奏：
香港弦樂團、黃健翔

地點：
香港大會堂音樂廳

「《節日合唱曲》……在亞洲還未公開演唱
過，今次音樂會將會為此曲作亞洲首演。」

《明報》

金禧音樂會系列

**聖誕頌歌：巴赫《尊主頌》
與聖誕歌**

指揮：
陳永華

獨唱：
陳愛堅[s]、施熙德[s]、
劉思敏[a]、簡頌輝[t]、
張健華[bb]

客席演出：
新加坡國際學校合唱團

伴奏：
深圳交響樂團

地點：
香港文化中心音樂廳

**[深圳] 金禧音樂會系列
（重複以上節目）**

地點：
深圳大劇院

陳永華
《第八交響曲：蒼茫大地》
（香港中樂團委約：
世界首演）

指揮：
陳永華

聯合演出：
明儀合唱團

伴奏：
香港中樂團、黃健羭

地點：
香港文化中心音樂廳

「選奏的作品皆可反映出陳永華熱愛和平，渴望世界大同
的理想，讓人在紛亂的世情中激發出奮發向上的心志。」

《大公報》

陳永華：「一件藝術品，如果要流傳下去，一定是充滿寬
恕和仁愛的，因為人類並非不朽，惟有透過寬恕和仁愛做
出來的事情才是不朽的。」

《經濟日報》

2007 年 4 月 15 日

威爾第《安魂曲》

指揮：
官美如

獨唱：
葉葆菁[s]、王宏堯[m]、謝天[t]、
廖聰文[bb]

聯合演出：
香港雅樂社合唱團

伴奏：
深圳交響樂團

地點：
香港大會堂音樂廳

官美如評論兩岸三地獨唱家："Their singing skills are of
a very high standard, and we also consider this a cultural
exchange."

《香港虎報》

2007 年 7 月 15 日

明儀合唱團四十三周年音樂會

陳永華
《第八交響曲 – 蒼茫大地》
（黃學揚改編）

指揮：
曹丁

聯合演出：
明儀合唱團、香港雅詠團

伴奏：
香港中樂團小組、黃健瑜、
梁珮珊

地點：
香港文化中心音樂廳

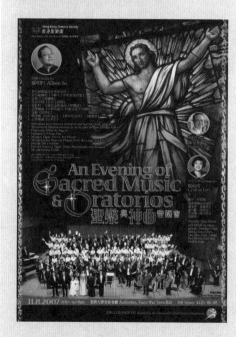

2007 年 8 月 11 日

聖樂與神曲音樂會

《創世記》、《出埃及記》、
《猶大馬加比》、
《以利亞》、《彌賽亞》
等選曲

指揮：
蘇明村

獨唱：
陳愛堅[s]、羅月蟾[s]、
嚴仙霞[a]、陳德美[a]、
許羨儀[a]、陳卓堅[t]、
陳晃相[b]、馮建成[b]

伴奏：
香港弦樂團、黃健瑜

地點：
荃灣大會堂演奏廳

大型合唱音樂會：
長征組歌

《長征組歌》及
中國合唱作品

指揮：
嚴良堃、蔣燮斌

聯合演出：
香港合唱團協會、
北京軍區戰友文工團合唱團

伴奏：
雙鋼琴（蘇明村、梁珮珊）、
北京軍區戰友文工團管弦樂團

地點：
香港文化中心大劇院

保羅 • 麥卡尼
《利物浦神劇》

指揮：
趙伯承

獨唱：
梁頌儀 [s]、吳凱珊 [m]、
柯大衛 [t]、張健華 [b]

聯合演出：
香港兒童合唱團

伴奏：
黃健瑜、賈那素

地點：
香港大會堂音樂廳

2007 年 12 月 15-16 日

[深圳] 與孟德爾遜歌頌聖誕

孟德爾遜第二交響曲《讚美之詩》、韋華第《榮耀頌》選段、聖誕歌等

指揮：
楊焜嬅

獨唱：
饒嵐 s、譚樂軒 s、簡頌輝 t

伴奏：
深圳交響樂團、
黃健瑜

地點：
深圳音樂廳、
香港文化中心音樂廳

「香港聖樂團將首次赴深圳音樂廳演出⋯⋯與深圳交響樂團聯同美國加州聖地亞哥大學音樂系主任兼管弦樂團總監楊焜嬅，為觀眾獻上美妙聖潔的讚美之詩。」

《大公報》

海頓《創世記》

指揮：
陳永華

獨唱：
阮妙芬 [s]、簡頌輝 [t]、張健華 [b]

合唱：
聖保羅男女中學合唱團、
學士合唱團

伴奏：
香港弦樂團、黃健瑜

地點：
香港文化中心音樂廳

[上海、蘇州] 2008 滬港蘇合唱音樂會

海頓《創世記》（選曲）等

指揮：
陳永華、呂東富

獨唱：
阮妙芬 s、簡頌輝 t、張健華 b

聯合演出：
上海大學研究生合唱團、
上海師範大學行知合唱團、
蘇州港大思培學院合唱團

伴奏：
上海師範大學萬方青年
交響樂團、黃健瑜、
和辰傑

地點：
上海師範大學
田家炳樓音樂廳、
上海大學偉長樓劇院、
蘇州高校區獨墅湖劇院

華東音樂之旅贊助人之一，
香港聖樂團榮譽會長陳大
枝、陳邱敏英伉儷。

2008 年 6 月 22 日

浪漫中的敬虔中的浪漫
布魯克納《謝恩讚美頌》、
羅西尼《聖母悼歌》

指揮：
官美如

獨唱：
葉葆菁 [s]、陳珮琪 [m]、
盧思彥 [t]、廖聰文 [bb]

合唱：
雅詞合唱團、
香港雅樂社合唱團

伴奏：
香港弦樂團、黃健瑜

地點：
香港文化中心音樂廳

「香港聖樂團將為樂迷獻上兩套作品……合唱團超過一百五十人
演奏，連同本港女高音葉葆菁、台北女中音陳珮琪、本港男高音
盧思彥及台北男低音廖聰文等多位海內外歌唱家同台演出，體現
香港作為一個國際城市的藝術面貌。」

《香港商報》

2008 年 10 月 5 日

巴赫《節慶妙韻》

指揮：
潘明倫

獨唱：
饒嵐 [s]、陳愛堅 [s]、嚴仙霞 [a]、
鍾偉開 [t]、關傑明 [bb]

伴奏：
香港弦樂團、黃健瑜

地點：
荃灣大會堂演奏廳

2008 年 12 月 14 日

歡樂 • 快樂 • 聖誕樂

布列頓《聖誕頌歌儀式》
選段、哈趙《歡樂·快樂·
聖誕樂》、聖誕頌禱、
聖誕歌等

指揮：
陳永華、趙伯承

獨唱：
陳愛堅 [s]

客席演出：
新加坡國際學校合唱團、
青協香港旋律、香港青年
協會李兆基小學手鈴隊

伴奏：
香港弦樂團、黃健瑜、賈
那素、孫尹婷

地點：
香港文化中心音樂廳

「聖樂團今次音樂會最吸引的地方，不是所選的康塔塔，
而是在原有班底上，邀得著名女高音饒嵐作為『外援』，
與團裏的砥柱人物如陳愛堅以及嚴仙霞等知名歌唱家，合
力呈獻巴赫的康塔塔。」

《大公報》

2009 年 4 月 26 日

孟德爾遜 《以利亞》

指揮：
陳永華

獨唱：
阮妙芬 s、吳凱珊 m、
簡頌輝 t、張健華 b

嘉賓演出：
聖公會林護紀念中學合唱團

伴奏：
香港弦樂團

地點：
香港文化中心音樂廳

2009 年 7 月 19 日

[廣州]

韓德爾《 彌賽亞》 –
暨天河堂籌款大型神劇聖樂會

指揮：
陳永華

獨唱：
陳愛堅 s、陳德美 m、
許羨儀 m、張健華 b

伴奏：
廣州市東山堂聖樂團
（管弦樂隊）

地點：
廣州市基督教東山堂

「[林護中學混聲]合唱團 2008 年 7 月到北京參加第九屆中國國際合唱節，並且取得金獎，成績令人鼓舞。」

（場刊）

2009 年 9 月 13 日

黃金閃爍巴洛克 - 韓德爾及友人

韋華第《D 大調榮耀經》、巴赫《D 大調聖母讚主曲》、韓德爾《彌賽亞》選段

指揮：
陳永華

獨唱：
陳愛堅 s、陸堅智 ct、
簡頌輝 t、張健華 b

客席演出：
聖公會林護紀念中學合唱團

伴奏：
香港弦樂團、黃健瑜、
孫尹婷、余必達

地點：
荃灣大會堂演奏廳

2009 年 12 月 17 日

繽繽紛紛平安夜

巴赫清唱劇第一百零四首《醒來吧》、佛漢 • 威廉斯《聖誕幻想曲》、《繽繽紛紛平安夜》等

指揮：
陳永華

獨唱：
張健華 b

客席演出：
香港兒童合唱團、
新加坡國際學校合唱團、
香港青年協會
李兆基小學手鈴隊

伴奏：
香港弦樂團、黃健瑜

地點：
香港文化中心音樂廳

香港聖樂團主席楊健明：「香港聖樂團自五十三年前成立以來，每年均舉辦聖誕音樂會，為成千上萬的聽眾帶來聖誕的祝福與喜樂。」

（場刊）

2010-2021 年

導讀：

進入新千禧年第二個十年，香港聖樂團迎來六十鑽禧大慶，成為香港歷史最悠久而仍然活躍的藝團，較 1957 年改名的香港管弦樂團年長一歲。2016 年的甲子之慶也是聖樂團首訪美國之旅。一年後再接再厲，全團到美加為香港特區成立二十周年誌慶，在羅省地標迪士尼音樂廳演出。

這十年記錄聖樂團五十三演出場次，其中十二場在海外和內地進行，那是一項紀錄。除了上述 2016、17 年兩次海外巡演，聖樂團 2014 年重訪溫哥華，紀念一年前離世的黃飛然，也首訪卡加利，與「加拿大卡城華人聖樂團」合演。

至於內地演出，除了重訪深圳、廣州，2015 年首訪鎮江、南京，以香港作壓軸。2018 珠港澳合唱音樂會，在美輪美奐的珠海大劇院歌劇廳，演出陳永華第八交響曲《蒼茫大地》的首樂章。演出由黃學揚博士改編為弦樂和中樂小組合奏版本，2010 年「京港」慈善音樂會上演，也在 2017 年北美之行演出。2019年陳永華的《第九交響曲 - 仁愛大同》，先後在香港、加拿大安大略省首演，同年 10 月在香港文化中心《黃河大合唱》音樂會上，改以管風琴伴奏演出第一樂章。以上演出全部由陳永華指揮香港聖樂團，權威演繹。

這十年間，聖樂團邀請眾多合唱等藝術團體客席演出，包括 2012 年成立的合唱小組「聖樂聲揚」、聖公會林護紀念中學等演出巴洛克及浪漫時期神曲。聖誕音樂會更呈多樣化，請來眾童聲合唱團、手鈴隊等共樂。2018 年聖誕音樂會迎來 1967-1969 年男低音團員、香港中文大學校長段崇智，以聖樂團新任名譽贊助人身份客串指揮領唱。

鑽禧大慶的聖樂團與時並進，2011 年與創世電視結成媒體合作夥伴，在視頻播放音樂會等。2017 年樂團網站升級，採用專業網站設計，加入大量歷史檔案資料，在各主要社交媒體平台上分享和互動。

2020 年新冠疫情肆虐香江，聖樂團被迫取消全年音樂會，那是團史的首次。唯一亮相是參與梁建楓指揮「香港樂團」演出貝多芬《歡樂頌》，全程需戴着口罩與其他合唱團合演。所幸 2021 年演出有限度恢復，在母親節、安魂曲音樂會上，讓音樂治療心靈，歲末以聖誕感恩頌為聖樂團六十五年之旅畫上句號。✿

復活節音樂會

韓德爾《彌賽亞》選段

指揮：
陳永華

獨唱：
陳愛堅[s]、簡頌輝[t]、張健華[b]

客席演出：
香港威爾殊男聲合唱團、
聖公會林護紀念中學合唱團

伴奏：
香港弦樂團、黃健瑜、
鍾裕森

地點：
香港文化中心音樂廳

京港同心顯關懷 – 2010 年慈善音樂會 （支持香港紅十字會中國賑災金）

陳永華 《第八交響曲 – 蒼茫大地》（黃學揚改編）

指揮：
蓬勃

聯合演出：
北京音樂家協會合唱團、
黎草田紀念音樂協進會合
唱團

伴奏：
中樂小組、黃健瑜、
劉同杉

地點：
香港大會堂音樂廳

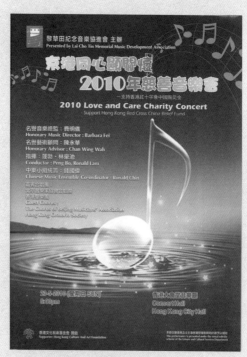

布拉姆斯與布魯克納

布拉姆斯《四重唱》四首、
布魯克納
《第三號 F 小調彌撒曲》

指揮：
官美如

獨唱：
葉葆菁 s、連皓忻 m、
盧思彥 t、車遠強 bb

伴奏：
香港弦樂團、黃健瑜、
賈那素

地點：
香港大會堂音樂廳

跨世代的安魂曲

莫扎特、布魯克納、佛瑞及盧特《安魂曲》選段

指揮：
陳永華

獨唱：
李秀暶 s、張健華 b

伴奏：
香港弦樂團、周文珊

地點：
荃灣大會堂演奏廳

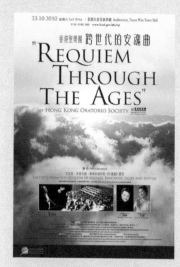

「一同演出的還有韓籍女高音李秀暶、男中音張健華和香港弦樂團，樂團主要透過小組示範音樂會，提高市民對音樂藝術的興趣。」

（政府新聞公報）

聖誕神曲匯

迺斯特胡特《親愛的聖徒歌頌主》清唱劇、夏龐蒂埃《D 大調謝恩讚美頌》、巴赫《聖誕神曲》、《彌賽亞》等選段

指揮：
陳永華

獨唱：
陳愛堅 s、張健華 b

客席演出：
香港童聲合唱團

伴奏：
香港弦樂團、黃健瑜、孫尹婷

地點：
香港文化中心音樂廳

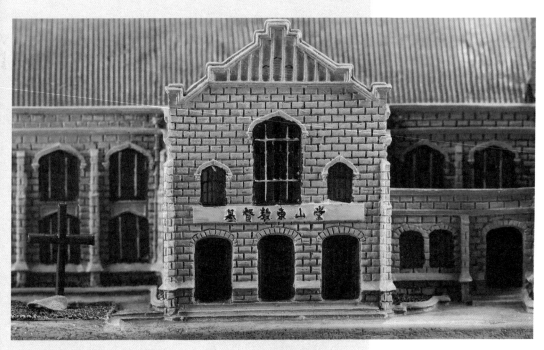

廣州基督教東山堂與香港聖樂團聖樂讚美會

巴赫
《耶穌，世人仰望的喜悦》、
韋華第《榮耀頌》、
莫扎特《聖體頌》等

指揮：
陳永華

地點：
廣州市基督教東山堂

巴赫《聖約翰受難曲》

指揮：
趙伯承

獨唱：
饒嵐 [s]、鄺勵齡 [m]、吳智誠 [t]、
林俊 [bb]、黃日珩 [bb]

伴奏：
香港城市室樂團

地點：
香港文化中心音樂廳

**孟德爾遜與孟德爾遜：
姊弟情深**

**芬妮 • 孟德爾遜：
《聖經故事》、
菲力斯 • 孟德爾遜
《以利亞》選曲**

指揮：
陳永華、梁卓偉

獨唱：
饒嵐 [s]、潘藝敏 [s]、劉思敏 [a]、
簡頌輝 [t]、張健華 [b]

聯合演出：
聖公會林護紀念中學合唱團

伴奏：
香港弦樂團

地點：
荃灣大會堂演奏廳

「[梁卓偉]上周六任客席指揮……見他功架十
足，令小妹聽出耳油。」

《頭條日報》

2011 年 12 月 18 日

感恩聖誕夜

韓德爾：德汀根《謝恩讚美
頌》、《彌賽亞》（選段）
及聖誕歌等

指揮：
陳永華

獨唱：
陳愛堅 s、劉思敏 a、
簡頌輝 t、張健華 b

客席演出：
香港童聲合唱團

伴奏：
香港弦樂團、黃健瑜

地點：
香港文化中心音樂廳

香港聖樂團主席楊健明：「這次成功演出，有賴超
過 200 位演出者，過去數月的努力排練的成果。」

（場刊）

2012 年 4 月 9 日

**伯樂 • 千里馬 -
布拉姆斯與德伏扎克**

布拉姆斯
《德意志安魂曲》、
德伏扎克《謝恩讚美頌》

指揮：
官美如

獨唱：
李蕙妍 s、錢深銘 b

聯合演出：
香港中文大學崇基合唱團、
香港和聲

伴奏：
香港弦樂團

地點：
香港文化中心音樂廳

2012 年 9 月 15 日

戰爭與和平 - 海頓和布列頓

《戰爭彌撒曲》、布列頓《聖靈的世界》

指揮：
陳永華、葉詠媛

旁白：
李嘉盈、Jonathan Douglas

獨唱：
阮妙芬 [s]、鄺勵齡 [a]、
簡頌輝 [t]、陳國堅 [bb]

聯合演出：
聖公會林護紀念中學合唱團

伴奏：
香港弦樂團

地點：
荃灣大會堂演奏廳

「歷史上有些戰爭是為正義與和平而戰的，但有更多開戰的原因只是出於侵略與自私。作家記錄下人們所思所想，宣之為文。作曲家則藉音符表達自己的感受。」

《信報》

2012 年 11 月 11 日

韋華第《榮耀頌》- 講座音樂會「聖樂聲揚」

指揮：
趙伯承

伴奏：
香港城市室樂團

地點：
香港聖公會諸聖座堂

2012 年 12 月 16 日

聖誕音樂會 2012

巴赫《第一四零清唱劇》、
《彌賽亞》、《創世記》
等選段及聖誕歌

指揮：
陳永華

獨唱：
羅月蟾 s、歐陽志剛 t、
吳劍峰 bb

客席演出：
香港童聲合唱團、
香港青年協會
李兆基小學手鈴隊

伴奏：
香港弦樂團、黃健瑜

地點：
香港文化中心音樂廳

香港聖樂團主席楊健明：「我們的演出也包括剛由香港聖樂團成立的青年聖樂合唱團『聖樂聲揚』及由團員施熙德和家人組織的『施歌班』。」

（場刊）

[深圳] 2012
聖誕音樂會 《彌賽亞》

地點：
深圳音樂廳

巴赫《尊主頌》
母親節獻禮

《聖母頌》巡禮、巴赫
《尊主頌》等

指揮：
趙伯承

獨唱：
陳愛堅[s]、林頌騫[s]、阮妙芬[s]、
張吟晶[m]、陳倬熙[t]、林俊廷[b]

客席演出：
HKOS 聖樂聲揚、
青協香港旋律

伴奏：
香港城市室樂團、周文珊

地點：
香港文化中心音樂廳

香港聖樂團主席楊健明：「今次音樂會是香港聖樂團首次在母親節特意將美妙音樂獻給所有母親。」

（場刊）

2013 年 9 月 29 日 *

音樂神童 - 孟德爾遜

《第一個沃普爾吉斯之夜》、
《聖保羅：第一部份》

指揮：
陳永華、葉詠媛

獨唱：
蔣頌恩 s、劉韻 a、梁路安 t、
張健華 b、林俊廷 bb、
顏星豪 bb、楊迅凌 bb

聯合演出：
聖公會林護紀念中學合唱團

伴奏：
香港弦樂團

地點：
荃灣大會堂演奏廳

2013 年 10 月 19 日

黃永熙博士逝世十周年紀念音樂會

《普天頌讚》、
《榮耀主頌》、《歡欣歌》、
《稱謝歌》、《奇妙主宰歌》、
《收成歌》、
《耶和華是我的牧者》、
《聖法蘭西斯禱文》、
《詩篇一百五十篇》等

詩班：
香港聖樂團、
循道衛理聯合教會
九龍堂詩班、
香港聖公會諸聖座堂詩班、
中華基督教聖頌團、
基督教香港崇真會
救恩堂聖詠團

地點：
循道衛理教會九龍堂

2013 年 12 月 15 日

聖誕幻想曲

佛漢 • 威廉斯
《聖誕幻想曲》等

指揮：
陳永華

獨唱：
施熙嘉

客席演出：
基督教國際學校合唱團、
HKOS 聖樂聲揚、
香港童聲合唱團、
香港青年協會李兆基小學
手鈴隊

伴奏：
香港弦樂團、黃健翊

地點：
香港文化中心音樂廳

貝多芬的平安與喜樂

貝多芬《第九交響曲》
第三、第四樂章、
舒伯特《歡樂頌》、
古諾《加利亞》

指揮：
梁卓偉

獨唱：
阮妙芬 [s]、張吟晶 [a]、
譚天樂 [t]、黃日珩 [b]

合唱：
Good Hope Singers、
聖公會林護紀念中學
舊生合唱團

伴奏：
香港弦樂團、
香港大學學生會管弦樂團成員

地點：
香港大會堂音樂廳

2014 年 5 月 25 日 **

[溫哥華]
從亙古到永遠 - 祢是神
（與溫哥華聖樂團合辦）

《創世記》、《以利亞》、
《詩篇一百五十篇》、
《第四交響曲 –
謝恩讚美頌》等

指揮：
陳永華、黃國豐

獨唱：
施熙德[s]、陳卓堅[t]、
楊允田[bb]、蕭葉葆荵[s]、
林葉鳳冰[a]、關業壯[t]、
涂道揚[bb]

伴奏：
管弦樂隊

地點：
溫哥華 Westside Church

2014 年 5 月 31 日

[卡加利]
節目同上

溫哥華聖樂團駐團指揮陳慧中：「[香港、溫哥華聖樂團] 這兩個分處太平洋東西兩岸的聖樂團，都是由信仰涵養與音樂素養兼備、受人尊敬的黃飛然老師擔任創團指揮⋯⋯今年香港聖樂團再度訪加，這不僅是再續二十年前緣，而是富涵一個世代傳承的意義。」

（場刊）

Hong Kong Oratorio Society

音樂神童莫扎特與
孟德爾遜

莫扎特《降 E 大調至
聖聖體聖事禱文》、
孟德爾遜
《聖保羅：第二部份》

指揮：
陳永華、葉詠媛

獨唱：
蔣頌恩 [s]、劉韻 [a]、簡頌輝 [t]、
張健華 [b]

合唱：
聖公會林護紀念中學合唱團

伴奏：
香港弦樂團

地點：
荃灣大會堂演奏廳

普世歡騰聖誕音樂會

聖桑《聖誕神曲》及
齊唱聖誕歌等

指揮：
陳永華

獨唱：
陳愛堅 [s]、羅月蟾 [m]、
今村有里 [a]、許碧茵 [m]、
范安智 [a]、陳卓堅 [t]、
馮建成 [b]

客席演出：
香港童聲合唱團、
國際基督教學校合唱團

伴奏：
香港弦樂團、黃健瑜

地點：
香港文化中心音樂廳

2015 年 4 月 6 日

讚美頌

海頓《C 大調感恩頌歌》、
韓德爾《D 大調烏得勒支
讚美頌德》、
莫扎特《慶幸─歡喜》、
陳永華《第四交響曲－
謝恩讚美頌》

指揮：
陳永華、韓進豐

獨唱：
阮妙芬[s]、陳愛堅[s]、
楊啟恩[s]、陳德美[a]、
今村有里[a]、蘇哲[t]、
陳卓堅[t]、楊知行[bb]

聯合演出：
天主教香港教區聖樂團

伴奏：
香港弦樂團、黃健瑜

地點：
香港大會堂音樂廳

2015 年 5 月 25 日

聲動 - 2015 香港青年
交響樂團年度音樂會

陳永華《聲動》（首演）、
柯夫《布蘭詩歌》選段等

指揮：
陳永華

聯合演出：
天主教香港教區聖樂團

伴奏：
香港青年管樂團

地點：
香港大會堂音樂廳

香港聖樂團主席楊健明：「是次音樂會以『讚美頌』為主題，欣然步入第六十年。」

（場刊）

2015 年 8 月 22 日

**廣州市基督教東山堂與
香港聖樂團音樂會**

巴赫《耶穌，
世人仰望的喜悦》、
韋華第《榮耀頌》、
韓德爾《彌賽亞》選曲等

指揮：
陳永華

獨唱：
陳愛堅 [s]、洪黃順真 [a]、
陳卓堅 [t]

地點：
廣州市基督教東山堂

奇妙巴赫

清唱劇《堅固保障》、
《尊主頌》、
《聖馬太受難曲》、
《B 小調彌撒曲》選段

指揮：
陳永華、黃國豐

獨唱：
蔣頌恩 s、林佩頤 a、
張健華 bb

聯合演出：
聖公會林護紀念中學
混聲合唱團

伴奏：
香港弦樂團

地點：
荃灣大會堂演奏廳

2015 年 12 月 12-13 日 /21 日

[南京 / 鎮江]
在至高之處
榮耀歸與神音樂會

貝多芬《C 大調彌撒曲》、
莫扎特《C 小調彌撒曲》、
莫扎特《屬天之后》、
韓德爾《上主説》、
韓德爾《彌賽亞》選段

指揮：
朱承恩

獨唱：
江樺 s、馮志麗 s、陳愛堅 s、
陳嘉璐 a、嚴仙霞 a、
蔣雅琴、陳卓堅 t、楊展奇、
楊健明 b

合唱：
加拿大卡城華人聖樂團、
江樺合唱團、加京聖樂團、
多倫多聯合詩班

伴奏：
管弦樂隊

地點：
南京市基督教莫愁路堂、
鎮江市宣德教堂、
循道衛理聯合教會香港堂

2015 年 12 月 26 日

聖誕禮讚

沙邦提爾《讚美頌》、
德伏扎克《讚美頌》、
趙學文《節日號曲》、
《光榮頌》（首演）

指揮：
陳永華

獨唱：
張健華 bb

合唱：
香港童聲合唱團、
加拿大卡城華人聖樂團

伴奏：
香港弦樂團、黃健翰

地點：
香港文化中心音樂廳

香港聖樂團主席楊健明：「回顧 2015，我們非常感恩，
因這是一個非常活躍和成功的一年：我們在香港、廣州、
南京共舉辦了五場音樂會。」

（場刊）

團員音樂會
MEMBERS' RECITAL

1956-2016

香港聖樂團六十周年
Hong Kong Oratorio Society 60th Anniversary

15 April 2016 | 8:00pm

Lecture Hall

HK Science Museum

九龍尖沙咀東部科學館道二號

香港聖樂團
Hong Kong Oratorio Society

音樂總監：陳永華教授 Music Director: Prof. CHAN Wing-wah, JP

www.Oratorio.org.hk

六十周年鑽禧音樂會 - 團員音樂會

地點：
香港科學館演講廳

[聖地牙哥] 六十周年 鑽禧音樂會

地點：
路德會教會 、
加州聖地牙哥大學
Shiley Theatre、
Camino Hall

Music Coterie

2016 Pre-Tour Joint Concert with Hong Kong Oratorio Society

Dr. Angela Yeung, conductor

A musical preview of the Coterie Tour to Honolulu & Hong Kong, joined by members of the Hong Kong Oratorio Soc
Free Admission with free-will donation at the door.

Program: CHAN Wing Wah, The Lord is My Shepherd • César Franck, Alleluia • Charles Gounod, Gallia; Saint Cecilia Mass • Gustav Holst, Hymn to the Waters; Hymn to the Travellers • Gwyneth Walker, Followers of the Lamb.

Saturday, May 14, at 2:30 p.m
Penasquitos Lutheran Church
14484 Penasquitos Dr, San Dieg
CA 92129

Sunday, May 15 at 2:30 p.m.
Shiley Theatre, Camino Hall,
University of San Diego

Soloists:
Irene Marie Patton, soprano
Dana Worden, soprano
Jonathan Cebreros, tenor
YEUNG Wan Tin, bass

[檀香山] 六十周年
鑽禧音樂會

地點：
Sacred Hearts Academy
Chapel

六十周年鑽禧音樂會

陳永華《耶和華是我的牧者》、
格溫妮絲．沃克
《羔羊的追隨者》、
貝多芬《合唱幻想曲》

指揮：
楊炤嬅

獨唱：

Irene Marie Patton[s]/Dana
Worden[s]、陳德美[a]、
Jonathan Cebreros[t]/
陳卓堅[t]、張健華[bb]

聯合演出：
美國大聖地牙哥室樂合唱團

伴奏：
美國大聖地牙哥室樂團、
香港弦樂團、
Sandra Wright Shen、
黃健翰

地點：
香港大會堂音樂廳

2016 年 9 月 10 日 **

**六十周年鑽禧音樂會
- 天籟之音**

**布列頓《天國的良伴》、
陳浩貽《讚美上主》、
孟德爾遜
《以利亞：第二部份》**

指揮：
陳永華、楊欣諾

獨唱：
劉卓昕 [s]、蔣頌恩 [s]、
陳皓琬 [m]、簡頌輝 [t]、
宋狄樟 [t]、張健華 [b]

聯合演出：
聖公會林護紀念中學合唱團

伴奏：
香港弦樂團、黃健瑜

地點：
荃灣大會堂演奏廳

資深男低音楊允田

2016 年 12 月 11 日

六十周年鑽禧
聖誕音樂會 -
聖誕感恩頌

黃學揚《詩篇一零四篇》、
陳永華《感恩頌》
（詩篇六十五篇）、
比才《謝恩讚美頌》及
聖誕歌等

指揮：
陳永華

獨唱：
阮妙芬 s、林俊傑 t

客席演出：
香港童聲合唱團、
維多利亞幼稚園及
滬江維多利亞學校合唱團

伴奏：
香港弦樂團、黃健翰

地點：
香港文化中心音樂廳

香港聖樂團主席歐陽志剛：「香港聖樂團相信音樂能夠為歌者和聆聽者帶來喜樂，同時也能豐富人的心靈。」

（場刊）

2017 年 5 月 1 日

跨世紀頌讚

**浦朗克《榮耀頌》、
盧特《榮耀頌》、
陳永華《耶和華是我的牧者》**

指揮：
鄭智山

獨唱：
曾麗婷 [s]、陳愛堅 [s]、
今村有里 [a]、陳卓堅 [t]

聯合演出：
香港新青年合唱團

伴奏：
香港弦樂團、唐展煌

地點：
香港大會堂音樂廳

[三藩市]
「港美音樂文化之旅」
音樂會 - 慶祝香港回歸
二十周年

**陳永華 《第八交響曲 –
蒼茫大地》（黃學揚改編）**

聯合演出：
清韻合唱團

伴奏：
香港特區 20A 樂隊
（領奏：陳永堅）、
香港聖樂團中樂組、
黃健翰

地點：
赫伯斯特劇院

HKOS Chinese Music Ensemble is newly established in 2016 for this meaningful Musical Journey in Celebration of the 20th Anniversary of the Establishment of the HKSAR.

香港聖樂團中樂組於2016年為是次極具意義的音樂文化之旅 暨慶祝香港回歸20周年而成立.

香港聖樂團主席歐陽志剛："HKOS is pleased to bring over 60 members to USA for a new chapter of our choral journey after celebrating its own 60th anniversary...we are grateful that this cultural exchange brings us together for the love of music."

清韻合唱團主席蔡振中："In the 20 years since [1997], Hong Kong continues to flourish as a unique and vibrant city...we honor the HKSAR in maintaining its heritage and diversity, while exhibiting great courage to break new cultural, political and economic grounds."

（場刊）

周凡夫：「香港聖樂團訪問美國西岸兩大名城的香港回歸音樂會，第一場在三藩市可説是『打響頭炮』，第二場在洛杉磯則可用『圓滿成功』來形容……樂團的六、七十位歌手大部份仍是在職人士，除了要自付旅費，還要放下工作；三藩市的清韻合唱團與樂隊合共三、四十人，在三藩市演出後，同樣要驅車南下洛杉磯，各人追求……音樂藝術上的美好感覺，與台下台上無數人分享，而這種美好感覺會長留在每一個人的人生回憶中，那是香港回歸二十周年的最佳慶典禮物。」

《大公報》

2017 年 6 月 25 日

[洛杉磯]
「港美音樂文化之旅」
音樂會 - 慶祝香港回歸
二十周年

節目同上

地點：
華特‧迪士尼音樂廳

首席伴奏黃健瑜
於迪士尼音樂廳管風琴

創世的喜悅

佛漢・威廉斯《祝福》、
丹・福雷斯特
《歡欣讚美主》、
海頓《創世記》

指揮：
陳永華、梁承恩

獨唱：
鄺勵齡[s]、今村有里[a]、
陳晨[t]、關傑明[bb]

合唱：
聖保羅書院童聲合唱團、
庇理羅士女子中學合唱團、
聖公會林護紀念中學合唱團

伴奏：
香港弦樂團、黃健瑜

地點：
荃灣大會堂演奏廳

2017 年 12 月 17 日

《聖誕感恩頌》

斯坦福《A 大調尊主頌》、
霍華斯《謝恩讚美頌》、
帕赫貝爾《G 大調尊主頌》、
伍卓賢《愛是不遙遠》
（首演）、
莫扎特《C 大調謝恩讚美頌》、
舒伯特《尊主頌》

指揮：
陳永華

獨唱：
羅曉晴[s]、今村有里[a]、黃耀德[t]、
韓元聲[bb]

客席演出：
香港童聲合唱團

伴奏：
香港弦樂團、黃健瑜

地點：
香港文化中心音樂廳

孟德爾遜及布魯克納的頌讚

布魯克納《謝恩讚美頌》、
孟德爾遜《讚美頌》、
陳永華《豎琴及樂隊：鳳舞》
（首演）

指揮：
Kristian Alexander

獨唱：
阮妙芬 [s]、張吟晶 [m]、宋狄樟 [t]、
陳俊堯 [bb]

聯合演出：
聖公會林護紀念中學
混聲合唱團

伴奏：
香港弦樂團、黃健瑜、
孫尹婷

地點：
香港大會堂音樂廳

香港聖樂團主席歐陽志剛：「香港首演是由本團音樂總
監陳永華教授特別為豎琴獨奏家孫韻婷及加拿大 Kindred
Spirits Orchestra 作曲的《鳳舞》，願此曲使聽眾啟迪出鳳
鳳其中一個象徵 —— 天下太平。此作品於上月在多倫多世
界首演。」

（場刊）

西洋合唱經典

**巴赫《D 大調尊主頌》、
海頓《創世記》、
孟德爾遜《以利亞》（選曲）、
帕萊斯特里那
《永恒的恩賜彌撒曲－垂憐頌、
羔羊頌》**

指揮 / 導賞：
陳永華

獨唱：
林俊傑[t]、張健華[b]、藍楚恩[a]、
吳綺琳（童聲）

合唱：
聖公會林護紀念中學合唱團

伴奏：
香港弦樂團、黃健翔

地點：
荃灣大會堂演奏廳

2018 聖誕音樂會

韓德爾《彌賽亞》

指揮：
陳永華

獨唱：
饒嵐 [s]、吳美智 [a]、
盧柏年 [ct]、黃加恩 [t]、
胡永正 [b]、陳晃相 [bb]

客席演出：
香港新青年合唱團、
聖公會林護紀念
中學合唱團

伴奏：
香港弦樂團、黃健瑜、
余必達

地點：
香港文化中心音樂廳

周凡夫：「香港聖樂團……邀請了香港新青年合唱團等助
陣，再加上香港弦樂團三十位樂師、六位獨唱家和執棒的
陳永華，合共便有二百七十六人！這未知會否是在香港演
唱《彌賽亞》的一個紀錄……接着從合唱團中走出來指揮
《齊來，宗主聖徒》的是香港中文大學校長段崇智教授。
段校長是香港聖樂團一九六六年至一九六九年的團員，後
赴笈美國……看來今日他對音樂的熱情初心仍在。」

《星島日報》

2018 年 12 月 28 日

[珠海] 2018 珠港澳
合唱音樂會
陳永華第八交響曲
《蒼茫大地》（第一樂章）

指揮：
陳永華

伴奏：
香港弦樂團成員

地點：
珠海大劇院歌劇廳

岑逸飛：「逾百人的［香港聖樂團］成員在合唱團唱逾四十年之久，最年長的也超過八十歲……陳永華作曲的《蒼茫大地》……不是有足夠人生的閱歷，很難表達其韻味。」

《信報》

**美樂大同 -
多倫多之旅預演**

**斯克里亞賓
《第一交響曲，第六樂章》、
德伏扎克《讚美頌》、
陳永華《第九交響曲 –
仁愛大同》[1]（首演）**

指揮：
陳永華

獨唱：
郭婉玲 [s]、林俊傑 [t]、
莫華倫 [1t]、陳俊堯 [b]

伴奏：
香港弦樂團、楊偉傑（笛子）、
沙涇珊（琵琶）、
劉瑞中（古箏）、王景松（笙）

地點：
香港大會堂音樂廳

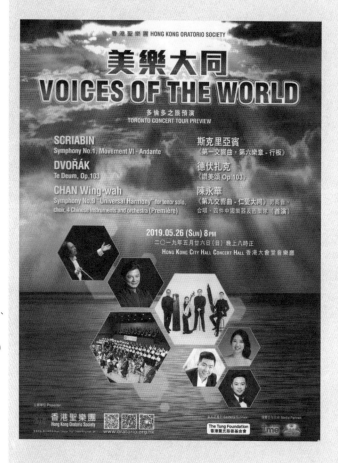

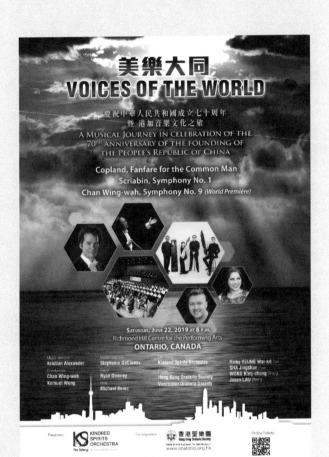

[多倫多]「慶祝中華人民
共和國成立七十周年暨
港加音樂文化之旅」

陳永華《第九交響曲 –
仁愛大同》[1]、
斯克里亞賓《第一交響曲》

指揮：
陳永華 [1]、Kristian Alexander

獨唱：
Stephanie DeCiantism[m]、
Ryan Downey[t]

聯合演出：
溫哥華聖樂團

伴奏：
Kindred Spirits Orchestra、
楊偉傑（笛子）、
沙涇珊（琵琶）、
劉瑞中（古箏）、王景松（笙）

地點：
安大略省列治文山表演
藝術中心

周凡夫：「陳永華這首作品不僅有很高的陳義……演出見出更為圓熟飽滿的效果；這在表達人類共同的崇高理想，以仁愛追求大同的題材上，可說正好能相互切合；為此，當晚演出後，不少觀眾都起立鼓掌，反映了當晚演出的感染力。」

《大公報》

君王與先知

韓德爾《加冕禮頌》、
莫扎特《加冕彌撒曲》、
孟德爾遜《以利亞》選曲

指揮：
林屴汧

獨唱：
阮妙芬[s]、劉韻[m]、林俊傑[t]、
張健華[b]

客席演出：
Ponte Singers

伴奏：
香港弦樂團、何穎姍

地點：
荃灣大會堂演奏廳

香港聖樂團主席歐陽志剛：「在香港這動盪時刻，讓我們盼望
新的黎明來臨和得到快速的醫治。」

（場刊）

2019 年 10 月 13 日

黃河大合唱

陳永華《第九交響曲 –
仁愛大同》[1]（首樂章）、
冼星海《黃河大合唱》

指揮：
陳永華[1]、曹丁

獨唱：
鄺勵齡[s]、張健華[b]

聯合演出
四百人合唱團

伴奏：
香港弦樂團、黃健瑜

地點：
香港文化中心音樂廳

2019 年 12 月 15 日

聖誕音樂會

韓德爾《彌賽亞》（選段）及聖誕歌

指揮：
陳永華

獨唱：
饒嵐 [s]、盧柏年 [ct]、黃加恩 [t]、胡永正 [b]

客席演出：
香港日本人合唱團

伴奏：
香港弦樂團、黃健瑜、余必達

地點：
香港文化中心音樂廳

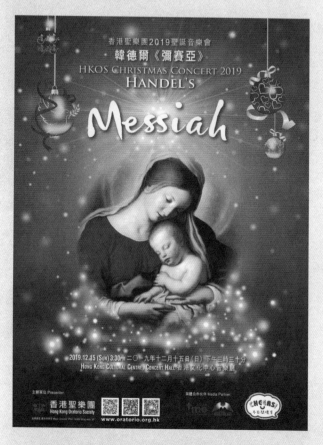

香港聖樂團主席歐陽志剛：「近月以來，香港經歷着許多挑戰，使得《彌賽亞》的內容，顯得更有意義和更為重要，因為它帶來了和平與盼望的信息。」

（場刊）

「香港樂團音樂總監梁建楓告訴記者：『70 多人的樂團和逾百人的合唱團，加起來有近 200 位演奏者，這是疫情以來在香港首次較大規模的演出。』」

《文匯報》

2020 年 11 月 16-18 日

天空交響曲 -
紀念貝多芬誕辰
二百五十周年演奏會

第九交響曲《歡樂頌》

指揮：
梁建楓

獨唱：
鄺勵齡 [s]、連皓忻 [a]、
莫華倫 [t]、黃日珩 [bb]

聯合演出：
香港歌劇院合唱團、
香港新青年合唱團、
明儀合唱團、Ponte
Singers

伴奏：
香港樂團

地點：
香港文化中心音樂廳

2021 年 5 月 9 日

母親節音樂會

比才《榮耀頌》、
海頓《創世記》（選段）等

指揮：
陳永華

獨唱：
阮妙芬[s]、林俊傑[t]、林國浩[b]

伴奏：
香港弦樂團、黃健瑜

地點：
香港大會堂音樂廳

香港聖樂團主席歐陽志剛：「由於新冠肺炎疫情，我們取消了 2020 年的所有音樂會。今天，我們興奮地重踏台板，與我們的聽眾重聚。」

（場刊）

2021 年 9 月 11 日

讓音樂治療心靈

莫扎特、佛瑞《安魂曲》

指揮：
陳永華

獨唱：
阮妙芬 [s]、陳珮珊 [m]、
曾鈺棋 [t]、張健華 [b]

伴奏：
香港弦樂團、黃健瑜

地點：
荃灣大會堂演奏廳

香港聖樂團主席歐陽志剛：「安魂曲可以簡單指向一種紀念的行動。我們的世界被瘟疫肆虐已逾一年半之久，而我們確實感受到亡者的離去，以及昔日生活方式轉變所帶來的哀愁⋯⋯我們期盼今天晚上的音樂會，能夠讓我們進一步邁向復元和重建。」

（場刊）

歐陽志剛（左）與段崇智（右）

聖誕感恩頌

韋爾第《榮耀頌》（選段）、
巴赫《尊主頌》（選段）、
莫扎特《聖母喜樂經》、
馬洛特《主禱文》、
比才《羔羊頌》、
德伏扎克《謝恩讚美頌》及
聖誕歌

指揮：
陳永華

獨唱：
阮妙芬[s]、林俊傑[t]、
張健華[b]

客席演出：
滬江維多利亞學校合唱團、
銅鑼灣維多利亞幼稚園合唱團

伴奏：
香港弦樂團、黃健翰

地點：
香港文化中心音樂廳

香港聖樂團駐團教牧蘇以葆主教：「兩年多了，我們對一切生活都有頹喪的感覺。因為社會運動及疫情緣故，要面對示威、暴動、封城、社交及各項限制⋯⋯香港聖樂團也曾停止練習及取消音樂會⋯⋯我們是否仍要在頹喪中等待？我們正在黑暗裏行走，我們那裏可有快樂及休憩？上主呀，我們在頹喪中，請來救我們！」

香港聖樂團主席歐陽志剛：「在過去的一段日子裏，雖然我們的世界經歷了巨大的挑戰，我們知道還有許多值得感恩的事情－包括歌唱和有機會以音樂來慶祝聖誕。」

（場刊）

HONG KONG ORATORIO SOCIETY

————————

EVENING OF CHRISTMAS MUSIC

at Morse House Auditorium, Cox's Road,
Kowloon, Hong Kong

Tuesday, 17th December, 1957,
8.30 p.m.

Conductor: Mr. THEODORE HUANG

————————

Programme

* 以上是香港聖樂團現存記錄中最早期的節目單封面

THE HONG KONG ORATORIO SOCIETY

presents

Elijah

An Oratorio

Composed by

F. MENDELSSOHN-BARTHOLDY

Friday, 11th May, 1962, 8.30 p.m.
City Hall, Concert Auditorium
Hong Kong.

TENORS

Mr. David Bartow	Mr. Paul Leon
Mr. Peter Beale	Mr. Lin Yuen Yang
Mr. Elzevior Chan	Mr. Ling Chu Ki
Mr. Chen Tsang Han	Rev. Donald O. Nelson
Mr. Thomas Cheng	Lt. Keith Ryding
Mr. Lee Tak Chuen	Dr. So Tsi Kuen
Mr. Ernest Chun	Mr. Philip Ting
Mr. Timothy Lee	Mr. Kent P. Yun

BASSES

Mr. Andrew M. S. Chan	Mr. Peter Liang
Mr. Chan Kung Sang	Mr. David Loo
Mr. Chan Ming Ching	Mr. Ernest Meier
Mr. Chan Tick Tsi	Mr. K. H. Poon
Mr. Chu Man Wai	Mr. R. W. Riley
Mr. Chu Tai Wo	Mr. Gerald Stryker
Rev. Walter de Velder	Mr. Andrew Wong
Capt. M. J. Hales	Mr. Daniel Wong
Mr. Wilfred Lee	Dr. S. C. Wong
Mr. William Lee	Mr. Tackway Wong
Mr. Leung Yuk Chan	

PATRONS AND COMMITTEE

Patrons:

Rev. J. BECHTEL   Mr. ROBERT K. C. LI

Director:

Rev. L. G. McKINNEY

Committee:

Mr. Chu Man Wai — *Chairman*

Mr. Thomas Cheng — *Vice-Chairman*

Miss Ruth Proft — *Hon. Secretary*

Mr. Cheng Tsung Heng — *Hon. Treasurer*

Mrs. Pola Lee — *Librarian*

Mrs. Delbert Anderson — *Attendance Secretary*

Rev. Walter de Velder — *Public Relation Office*

Mrs. Ruth Galster — *Accompanist*

Mrs. Evelyn Kwong — *Accompanist*

Miss Betty Chan — *Accompanist (Rehearsals)*

Guest Conductor: Mr. Frank Huang

Soloists: Rev. L. G. Mckinney — Bass
Miss Elizabeth Lee — Soprano
Mr. Frank Wiens — Boy Soprano
Mrs. Maureen Clark — Alto
Mr. Peter Beale — Tenor
Mr. Thomas Cheng — Tenor

Organist: Mrs. Evelyn Kwong

Pianist: Mrs. Ruth Galster

SOPRANOS

Mrs. Manfred Berndt
Miss Dolores Chan
Miss Rebecca Chan
Miss Diana Cheung
Miss Elizabeth Lee
Mrs. Pola Lee
Miss Jane Leung
Miss Sabrina Li
Miss Lillian Mark
Miss Ardis Nelson
Miss Susan Shaw
Miss Terry Stryker
Miss Ann Wong
Miss Ellen Wong
Miss Regina Wong
Miss Vivian Woo

ALTOS

Mrs. Delbert Anderson
Miss Carolyn Belote
Mrs. Maureen Clark
Miss Myra Downie
Mrs. Lenard Galster
Miss Sandra Holden
Mrs. Delia M. Kendall
Mrs. L. G. McKinney
Mrs. Daniel Nelson
Miss Ruth Proft
Mrs. Gerald Stryker
Miss Hannah Tan
Miss Rebecca Tan
Miss Anna Tse

THE HONG KONG CHINESE CHRISTIAN CHURCHES UNION

GOLD JUBILEE CONCERT

THE HONG KONG ORATORIO SOCIETY

presents

"JUDAS MACCABAEUS"

ORATORIO
BY
G. F. HANDEL

Friday, 9th July, 1965. 8:30 p.m.
Saturday, 10th July, 1965. 8:30 p.m.

CITY HALL, CONCERT AUDITORIUM
HONG KONG

「猶 大 瑪 喀 比」

韓 德 爾

主 席：黃作牧師
指 揮：黃飛然先生

獨 唱：糧雅南小姐—女高音
　　　周宏俊小姐—女低音
　　　田鳴恩先生—男高音
　　　陳供生先生—男低音

二重唱：陳劉沐蘭女士
　　　林朵慧堅女士

鋼 琴：聶玉琪小姐
管絃樂：普歌管絃樂團

香 港 聖 樂 團 團 員

·女高音·
陳　惠　庭
靈　順　瑜
洪　燕　溫
郭　潔　平
林　嘉　芳
李　呂　寶
潘　志　寧
邵　次　清
戴　致　茶
杜　玉　安
溫　可　屏
王　芷　容
黃　霜　凝
胡　五　英

·男高音·
陳　惠　庭
陳　宗　漢
朱　彥　卿
何　君　靜
凌　遠　揚
龍　惠　霜
蘇　白　檀

·男低音·
朱　文　偉
傅　忠　誠
林　鴻　圍
梁　耀　揚
廖　達　觀
梅　雅　禮
潘　園　崑
薛　洪　邁
鄧　鵬　懷
黃　傳

·女低音·
尋　慕　愛
朵　霈　然
朱　美　達
朱　慧　齡
林　慧　芳
邢　桂　丹

普 歌 管 絃 樂 團

·第一小提琴·
鄧　植　沛 (首席)
陳　泰　華
余　仕　綿
凌　錦　耀
謝　爱　暉
謝　文　達

·第二小提琴·
陳　克　勝
胡　炳　基
王　景　祥
張　樹　榮
方　建　民
梁　國　偉

·中提琴·
鄧　孫　慧琴
張　魏　清
鍾　耀　文
夏　桂　英

·大提琴·
王　友　健
詹　鍼　邦
Epifanio Despa

低音大提琴·
Thomas Inarzio

·單簧管·
J. Salonga
文　顏　力

·長笛·
陳　仲　賢
陳　玉　麟

·雙簧管·
張　乘　壽
周　卓　邦

·小號·
陳　元　帥

·伸縮喇叭·
李　夫　勞

·巴松管·
王　安　瀾
黃　蔭　傳

·定音鼓·
凌　池

HANDEL'S
MESSIAH

THE HONG KONG ORATORIO SOCIETY

Hon. President: Mr. Chu Man Wai
Conductors: Mr. Frank Huang
Dr. Wong Wing Hee
Accompanist: Mrs. Evelyn Kwong

COMMITTEE

Chairman: Mr. Peter Liang
Vice Chairman: Mr. Donald P. McComb
Hon. Secretary: Mrs. Joan Jasper
Hon. Treasurer: Mr. Chen Tsung Han
Public Relations Officer: Mrs. Milly Ko Lew
Concert Manager: Miss Li Ka Po
Librarian & General Affairs Officer: Miss Emilie Mahler
Mr. Chau Kung Sang

CONCERT SUB-COMMITTEE

Chairman: Miss Li Ka Po (Concert Manager)

Members: Mr. Donald P. McComb (Concert Programme Editor)
Mr. Nathan Ma (Hon. Secretary)
Miss Ella Yung (Ticket Officer)
Mr. Henry Yu (Stage Manager)

PUBLIC RELATIONS SUB-COMMITTEE

Chairman: Mrs. Milly Ko Lew

Members: The Reverend David C. P. Lew
Mr. Mervyn Loie
The Reverend Thomas Lung
The Reverend Herbert H. Pommerenke

SECTION LEADERS

Soprano Section: Mrs. Milly Ko Lew
Contralto Section: Mrs. Joan Jasper
Tenor Section: The Reverend David C. P. Lew
Bass Section: The Reverend Walter de Velder

The Urban Council and the Hong Kong Oratorio Society wish to express their appreciation and gratefulness to all those who made this performance possible.

— 19 —

THE HONG KONG ORATORIO SOCIETY
MEMBERS OF THE CHORUS

Sopranos	Contraltos	Tenors
Vera Au Yeung	Au Yoong Mu Jean	Chen Tsung Han
Betty Blakney	Alison Bell	Alex Cheung
Christina Chan	Judy J. Butler	Galahad Cheung
Helen Chan	Barbara Chen	Ho Kwan Ching
Ingrid Chan Yin	Iris Chen	Hung Cheung Kwing
Maria Chan	Sophia Cheng	James Hong
Chan Pak-Chun	Jean Day	Lee Tak Chuen
Diana Chen	Eglin Hanny	David C. P. Lew
Ingrid Y. K. Chen	Daisy Fong	Mervyn Loie
Stella Chen	Lorna Grant	Thomas W. Lung
Betty Cheng	Josephine Hong	Nathan H. Ma
Frances Chong	Linda F. Bey	Donald P. McComb
Kenny Choy	Joan H. Jasper	Ng Sui Pang
Kimmy Choy	Anita Jutzi	Rodger Singer
Rosita Chu Sau Man	Marion Langworthy	So Tsi Kuen
Fok Wing Yue	Grace Lee Chiu Yee	William Sung Chi Cheung
Veronica Fong Oi Kwan	Lee Wai Tsun	To Kwan Wing
Esther Fung Che Lai	Inge Liell	Kenneth Tsang
Nancy Han	Emilie Mahler	Rennie Tsang Lap Wah
Ho Wai Sze	Margaret Metzler	Marlon Wang
Jean Hong	Helen Smith	Lincoln Wu
Wendy Hsu	Sophia So	Henry Yu Hung-yung
Rachael Lam	Esther Tsui	Peter Yue
Violet Lam	Margaret Walls	
Eliza Yu Ping Lau	Melina Wong	**Basses**
Virginia Lee	Anita Yu	
Alice Leung Hei Ling		Au Siu Wing
Leung Wai Ching		Richard Blakney
Milly Ko Lew		Henry Chan
Li Ka Po		Jimmy Chan Foon Sheung
Joan Lo		Chau Kung Sang
Susie Shun-sui Lum		Moses H. W. Chan
Brenda Milson		Ramsey Chan
Anne Picking		Chang Siu Hay
Susan Poon		Dennis Cheng
Anne Wang Pauev		Benjamin Chong
Elke Schrander		Chu Man Wai
Melissa Singer		Paul Fu
Tan Yuk Ling		Colin D. B. Green
Doris To Yuk Ping		Paul S. Hong
Iris To		Lau Shun Yin
Tso Ho Fung Yee		Leonard Lee
Gisela Wolfram		Peter Liang
Janet Wong		Loren E. Noren
Josephine Wong Chun Mee		Herbert Pommerenke
Regina Wong		Walter de Velder
Wong Man Or		Taetway Wong
Amy Yip		Wallace Wong Tao-Cheong
Ella Yung		Wesley Yang
		Caleb Yau
		Young Chun Kwan
		E. C. M. Young
		James Yuen
		David Zorey

Instrumentalists

Trumpet — John Cheng
Tympani — Sheila Lai

— 20 —

THE URBAN COUNCIL AND THE HONG KONG ORATORIO SOCIETY

JOINTLY PRESENT

市 政 局 與 香 港 聖 樂 團 聯 合 主 辦

HANDEL'S ISRAEL IN EGYPT

演唱韓德爾作品：出埃及記

Conductor: Wong Wing Hee

指揮：黃永熙

Soloists

獨　唱

Sopranos	SUSAN POON	女 高 音：	潘 志 清
	PENELOPE CHAN		陳 愛 堅
Mezzo soprano	BARBARA CHEN	女 中 音：	陳 之 霞
Tenor	ALEX CHEUNG MAN	男 高 音：	張 汶

Accompanists

伴　奏

Pianist	CINDY CHIK	鋼琴：	戚 明 儀
Organist	WONG KIN YU	風琴：	黃 健 瑜

1 October 1978　8:00 p.m.　　一九七八年十月一日
CITY HALL CONCERT HALL　　下午八時正大會堂音樂廳

THE HONG KONG ORATORIO SOCIETY

Patrons:	Mr. WELLINGTON WONG	黃 天 樂
	Dr. P. C. WONG	貿 品 華
Hon. President:	Mr. CHU MAN WAI	朱 文 偉
Conductor:	Dr. WONG WING HEE	黃 永 熙
Accompanists:	Miss EVELYN LEE	李 淑 嫻
	Miss CYNTHIA YIM	嚴 仙 霞

COMMITTEE

Chairman:	Dr. CHARLES CHENG	鄭 棠 五 光
Vice-Chairman:	Mr. MERVYN LOIE	雷 耀 光
Hon. Secretary:	Mr. PETER LIANG	梁 耀 楯
Deputy Secretary:	Miss INGRID CHAN	陳 賢
Hon. Treasurer:	Mr. RAMSAY CHAN	陳 啟 堂
Concert Manager:	Mr. BENJAMIN CHONG	莊 純 道
Asst. Concert Manager:	Miss DOROTHY LEE	李 秀 華
Public Relations Officer:	Dr. ENOCH C. M. YOUNG	楊 啟 輝
Project Manager:	Dr. YEUNG KAI KIN	楊 啟 健
Librarian:	Dr. CHENG KIN FAI	鄭 健 輝
General Affairs Officers:	Mr. CLEMENT AU	區 紹 棠
	Miss PENELOPE CHAN	陳 愛 堅

CONCERT SUB-COMMITTEE

Chairman:	Mr. BENJAMIN CHONG	莊 純 道
Members:	Miss DOROTHY LEE	李 秀 華
	Mr. MERVYN LOIE	雷 耀 光
	Miss PENELOPE CHAN	陳 愛 堅
	Mr. CLEMENT AU	區 紹 棠

SECTION LEADERS

Soprano Section:	Mrs. GLORIA REID	李 嘉 蓮
Contralto Section:	Mrs. SONIA ARCHER	歐 白 永 貞
Tenor Section:	Mr. TSO KAI YIP	曹 繼 業
Bass Section:	Rev. LOREN E. NOREN	藍 仁

THE CHORUS

Female Voices

SONIA ARCHER	REBECCA FUNG	PEARL MA
KITTY AU KIT LING	MAVIS GRAY	ELIZABETH MACDONALD
PRISCILLA AU	DELIA HARRIS	THIVIAM NAVARATNARAJA
VERA AU-YEUNG	MAY HO	ALYANEE PEACOCK
AU YOUNG MU JEAN	JEAN HOLDEN	GLORIA REID
KATHLEEN E. BARKER	BELINDA HSU	SO YAN LAP
NICOLA CANNING	LILIAN HUI	ANGELA TAM
BEATRICE CHAN	HEATHER IP	CONNIE TAM
BELINDA CHAN	DOROTHY JONES	LUCETTE TAM
CHRISTINA CHAN	MILLY KO LEW	WINNIE TAM
GRACE CHAN	LOUISE KUO	TSO HO FUNG YEE
INGRID CHAN	GRACE KWONG	ALICE WONG
LILY CHAN	JULIANA LAM	ELIZA WONG
CHAN LAW YUK LIN	RACHEL LAM	WONG MI LIN
EPPIE CHENG	LAM SI SI	WU LO LANG MUI
STELLA CHENG	VIOLET LAM	PATRICIA YAP
CHENG TING WEI	DIANA LEE	YEUNG CHAN PUI WAI
JOSEPHINE CHU	DOROTHY LEE	YEUNG CHIU WAH
TERESA CHU	JACQUALINE LEE	NANCY YUEN
KATHLEEN DUNCAN	OLINA LIN	JANE YUNG
SUE DYSON	BRENDA LO	
BETTY FUNG	VIRGINIA LOO	

THE CHORUS

Male Voices

CLEMENT AU	ALFRED LEUNG CHUNG YENG
WALLY BROCKWAY	LEUNG YUN TING
RICHARD CANNING	DAVID C. P. LEW
BRUCE CHAN	PETER LIANG
PETER CHAN	MERVYN LOIE
RAMSAY CHAN	LUK CHI KIN
CHAN SAU SHUN	THOMAS W. LUNG
CHAN YAN CHI	FRANKEN MAN
CHARLES CHENG	ROGER MAXWELL
CHRISTOPHER CHENG	THOMAS SOO
CHENG KIN FAI	TAM WING PONG
RAYMOND CHEUNG	TANG KWAI LOK
TONY CHIANG WAI MAN	PETER TONG
BENJAMIN CHONG	TSO HUNG FAI
CHU MAN WAI	TSO KAI YIP
PAUL FU	WONG FANG
JOSEPH FIZZELL	YEUNG KAI KIN
DANIEL HO	YEUNG WAN TIN
IP CHAN LAM	ENOCH C. M. YOUNG
DANIEL KAO	HENRY YU
KONG CHI KWAN	YUEN CHUN PANG
FRANK KWOK HIN YEUNG	YUEN TIM CHUNG
KWOK YIU ON	YUEN WAI KWOK
LAU SAM PING	

冬春秋夏

香港圣乐团
北京演唱会
海顿"四季颂"
指挥：黄永熙
独唱：女高音•冯志丽
男高音•王 帆
男中音•杨洪基
合唱：
香港圣乐团北京演唱团
伴奏：
戚明仪 严贺洁

HAYDN'S ORATORIO
THE SEASONS
BY HONG KONG ORATORIO SOCIETY

日期：一九八四年四月二十一日及二十二日
地点：北京民族宫

香港圣乐团
一九八四年度职员表

赞助人	黄天柔
首席指挥	张有兴
指挥	黄永熙
伴奏	戚诚君
	严贺洁

委员会

主席	杨健明
副主席	谢北蒸 (J.H.Jasper)
秘书	高兰诗 (N.Goff)
司库	白婿雅 (K.E.Barker)
音乐会经理	庄纯道
公共关系经理	阮品强
乐器管理主任	黄美莲
总务主任	俞汉韵
特别事务主任	邓少云

北京演唱筹备委员会

主席	梁耀扬
秘书	黄美莲
司库	庄纯道
委员	阮品俪
	严贺洁
	马佩希
	俞汉韵
	熊忠诚

指挥	黄永熙
伴奏	严贺洁
独唱	女高音•冯志丽
	男高音•王帆
	男中音•杨洪基

合唱团员

女高音：L. BALLARD
陈贤
张敬仁
邓安妮
N. GOFF
M. HOWARTH
何凤仪(组长)
林铃秀
走课慧
D. NAVARATNARAJAH
A.M. PATTON
M. SCHMIDT
徐思恩
谢凤文
王芷芳
A. WILSON
黄美莲
黄福娴
丘凤娇
杨雯雯
原玉枝

女低音：A.B. DAY
A. HODGSON
D.E. JONES
V.L. JONES
J.H. JASPER
周思彰
马佩希
P.M. O'DWYER
J.G. TAYLOR
谭维拉(组长)

香港圣乐团
北京演唱团员

男高音：陈绍泉
曾继业(唱长)
F. DOYLE
何瑞雄
W.P. KARSEN
J.A. LUFF
T. LUNG
梁敏开
W. THOMSON
涛炳生
余汉韵
袁添松
黄飞然

男低音：朱家恩
庄纯道
L.J. ENDICOTT
傅忠诚
N.R. HOWARTH
梁耀扬
苏惠生
R.D. TAYLOR(组长)
J.F. WILSON
B. WHALEY
王志信
阮品强
欧阳鹏
杨健明

1985

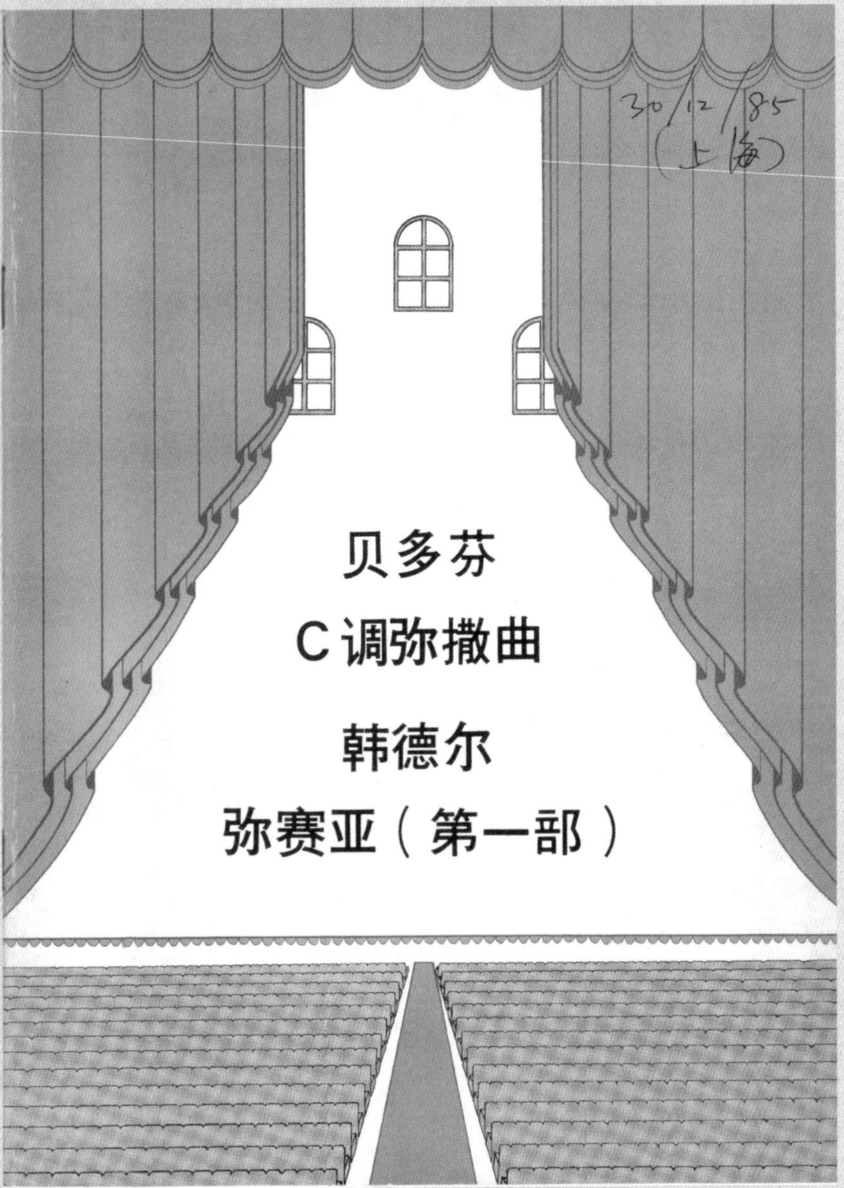
30/12/85
(上海)
贝多芬
C调弥撒曲
韩德尔
弥赛亚（第一部）

香港圣乐团
上海演唱会

贝多芬　　C调弥撒曲
BEETHOVEN　　MASS IN C

韩德尔　　弥赛亚(第一部)
HANDEL　MESSIAH (PART ONE)

独唱：女高音　　江　桦·冯志丽
　　　女低音　　严仙霞
　　　男高音　　吕国璋
　　　男低音　　温可铮·杨允田

合唱：
香港圣乐团上海演唱团

伴奏：上海乐团
　　　钢琴　严贺洁

指挥：黄永熙

香港圣乐团
一九八五年度职员表

赞助人	黄天莱
	张有兴
顾问	杨健明
首席指挥	黄永熙
指挥	张端君
伴奏	严贺洁

委员会
主席	谢忠匡（J. H. Jasper）
副主席	荘纯道
秘书	高兰诗（N. Goff）
司库	泰珍妮（J. Taylor）
音乐会经理	阮品强
公共关系主任	勒约翰（J. Luff）
乐谱管理主任	黄美莲
总务主任	余汉病

上海旅行演唱会委员会
顾问	杨健明
主席	梁福协
副主席	阮品强
秘书	王芷芳
司库	荘纯道
委员	汤润生
	朱承恩

－12－

香港圣乐团
上海演唱会团员

女声：王芷芳
丘凤娇
伍惠珍
杜小芝
林穗芬
胡爱珠
覃玉枝
麥珠晖
陈淑娟
傅淑香
陈雪青
冯亦丽
黄慧瑜
戴凤娥
吴惠恩
FORESTAL, Gillian Pauline
GOFF, Nancy Carol（高兰诗）
WILSON, Anita
朱懋曼
李毓绮
谭宪芝
陈曜佳
BARKER, Kathleen Esther（白匹雅）
JASPER, Joan Helen（谢忠匡）
JONES, Dorothy Emma
O'DWYER, Patricia
SALISBURY, Patricia Mary
SANTWAN, Darnayanthi
STEAD, Sheila Mary
TULLY, Gabrielle

男声：朱蕃攵
吴连顺
黄祖熙
黄丽松
马宁根
汤润生
郑汉光
欧阳忠明
LUFF, John Alfred
LUNG, Thomas W.
TEDBURY, George Ernest
朱承恩
阮品强
梁耀焕
杨允田
苏鲁生
杨健明

上海乐团
管弦乐队名单

乐队首席：陶宏然
第一小提琴：徐影望、陶然泉、黄永焸、邓翠蕾、萧丽娟、陈玛莉
　　　　　　王凌群、何永昌
第二小提琴：马明淑、庄蕊缪、朱堂碞、黄天珠、毛小春、张翼勇、韩大川
　　　　　　苗莉莉、施易璋、杨成泰
中提琴：魏先生、吴玛平、金人风、王桂煇、朱贤浩、孙昌道
大提琴：曹仁山、顾晶、高建约、倪咏真、陆金虎、何为真
低音提琴：梅宏焘、张志明、毛煜琴、高贺勇
长笛：朱工艾、沈玲、潘音
双簧管：孙明红、宋祥林、李国文
单簧管：洪宝立、岑建华、孙绵斌
大管：尹宪武、金宝龙
小号：徐顺超、黎天旭、施安词
圆号：赵昱、沈宪平、吴宗年
打击乐：范正和、宇宝宝、张顺康
钢琴：朱忠勤、王金弥
竖琴：参有健
特邀（长笛）：赵文海
圆号：许建军、郜永清
大管：陈杰
大提：陆金虎

Hong Kong Oratorio Society 30th Anniversary Concerts
香港聖樂團卅週年紀念音樂會

Handel's "ISRAEL IN EGYPT"
韓德爾「出埃及記」

Conductor: Andrew Cheung　指揮：張毓君
Soloists of this concert are members of The Hong Kong Oratorio Society.
本次音樂會之獨唱部份全由本團團員担任。
Accompanists: Cindy Chik　　戚明儀
伴　奏：　Agnes Marie Wu　鄔賈那素
　　　　　John Wilson　　　韋立新
25th May, 1986.　Hong Kong City Hall Concert Hall
一九八六年五月廿五日　香港大會堂音樂廳

Mendelssohn's "ELIJAH""
孟德爾遜 「以利亞」

Conductor:　Wong Wing Hee　　指揮：黃永熙
Soloists:　Esther Fung　　　獨唱：馮志麗
　　　　　Cynthia Luff　　　嚴仙霞
　　　　　Wong Fang　　　　王　帆
　　　　　Chen Rong Kwei　陳榮貴
With Orchestral accompaniment　樂隊伴奏

12 & 16 November, 1986. 一九八六年十一月十二及十六日
City Hall Concert Hall　　大會堂音樂廳

Handel's "MESSIAH"
韓德爾「彌賽亞」

Conductor:　Andrew Cheung　指揮：張毓君
Soloists:　Ella Kiang　　　獨唱：江　樺
　　　　　Lily Leung　　　　梁麗麗
　　　　　Arlis Hiebert　　施熙柏
　　　　　Hugh Phillipson　傳立新
With Orchestral Accompaniment　樂隊伴奏

21st March, 1987.　一九八七年三月廿一日
SHATIN TOWN HALL CONCERT HALL
沙田大會堂音樂廳

"GREAT ORATORIO FAVOURITES"
"聖樂精選"

Conductor: Wong Wing Hee　指揮：黃永熙
Soloists:　Ella Kiang　　　江　樺
　　　　　Esther Fung　　馮志麗
　　　　　Lee Bing　　　　李　冰
　　　　　Wong Fang　　　王　帆
　　　　　David Lui　　　　呂國璋
　　　　　Jimmy Chan　　陳晃相
　　　　　Enoch Young　　楊健明
Accompanists: Cindy Chik　　戚明儀
　　　　　Sandra Tong　　唐燕玉
　　　　　John Wilson　　韋立新
24 August, 1986.　Auditorium, Tsuen Wan Town Hall
31 August, 1986.　Auditorium Lut Sau Hall
一九八六年八月廿四日　荃灣大會堂演奏廳
一九八六年八月卅一日　元朗聿修堂演奏廳

CHRISTMAS CONCERT
聖誕音樂會

Conductor:　Wong Wing Hee　指揮：黃永熙
Soloists:　F.F.Poon　　　獨唱：潘若芙
　　　　　Barbara Chen　　陳之霞
　　　　　Michael Ryan　　米高頓恩
　　　　　Lee Kin Chun　　李建眞
Accompanists: Cindy Chik　伴奏：戚明儀
　　　　　John Wilson　　韋立新
22 December 1986　一九八六年十二月二十二日
City Hall Concert Hall　大會堂音樂廳

Beethoven's "MISSA SOLEMENIS"
貝多芬「莊嚴彌撒曲」

Conductor: Dr. Wong Wing Hee　指揮：黃永熙博士
With Orchestral Accompaniment.　樂隊伴奏
10th May, 1987.　一九八七年五月十日
City Hall Concert Hall　香港大會堂音樂廳

247

THE HONG KONG ORATORIO SOCIETY　香港聖樂團

Patrons:	Mr. Wellington Wong Tin Wing, JP	贊 助 人：黃 天 榮
	Mr. Hilton Cheong-leen, OBE, JP	張 有 興
	Mr. Nathan Ma	馬 寧 熙
Hon. President:	Mr. Chu Man Wai	名 譽 會 長：朱 文 偉
Adviser:	Dr. Enoch Young	顧 問：楊 健 明
Principal Conductor:	Dr. Wong Wing Hee	首 席 指 揮：黃 永 熙
Conductor:	Mr. Andrew Cheung	指 揮：張 毓 君
Principal Accompanist:	Miss Sandra Yong	首 席 伴 奏：唐 燕 玉
Accompanist:	Miss Cindy Chik	伴 奏：戚 明 儀

GENERAL COMMITTEE　執行委員會

Chairman:	Mrs. Joan Jasper	主 席：謝 忠 蓮
Vice-Chairman:	Rev. Thomas W. Lung	副 主 席：龍 惠 霖
Hon. Secretary:	Mrs. Patricia Salisbury	義 務 秘 書：施 樂 珥
Hon. Treasurer:	Miss Wong Mi Lin	義 務 司 庫：黃 美 蓮
Concert Manager:	Mr. Henry Yu	計 樂 會 經 理：余 漢 翁
Promotion Manager:	Mr. Wilson So	宣 傳 經 理：蘇 惠 生
General Affairs Officers:	Mr. Daniel Ho	總 務 主 任：何 雄 雄
	Mr. John Luff	盧 義 輝
Librarian:	Miss Jo Chan	圖 書 主 任：陳 早

SECTION LEADERS　聲部部長

Soprano Section Leader:	Mrs. Anita Wilson	女高音部部長：韋 安 蒂
Asst. Leader:	Miss Helena Yeung	副 部 長：楊 營 嬅
Alto Section Leader:	Mrs. Lucette Black	女低音部部長：黑譚繼往
Asst. Leader:	Miss Kay Barker	副 部 長：白 同 雅
Tenor Section Leader:	Mr. Tso Kai Yip	男高音部部長：曹繼業
Asst. Leader:	Mr. Daniel Ho	副 部 長：何 瑞 雄
Bass Section Leader:	Mr. Yeung Wan Tin	男低音部部長：楊 允 田
Asst. Leader:	Mr. Frank Kwok	副 部 長：郭 顯 揚

GENERAL AFFAIRS SUB-COMMITTEE　總務小組

Miss Kathleen Barker	白 居 雄
Mrs. Milly Ko-Lew	劉高妙玲
Mr. Simon Chu	朱 承 恩
Mr. Pau Fu	傳 忠 誠
Mr. Simon Lo	勞 德 恩

12

Female Voices	女聲			Male Voices	男聲
Vera Au Yeung	歐陽詠緹	Monica Mok	莫尼嘉	Eric Au Yeung	歐陽念頌
Lucette Black	黑譚繼往	Dodwell Mon'el		Chan Shou Shun	陳守信
Angel Chan	陳慈恩	Amy Ng	吳少智	Chan Wing Kin	陳永堅
Ingrid Chan	陳智	Serena Ng	吳卌霞	Chan Yan Chi	陳恩賜
Jo Chan	陳早	Elizabeth Ngan	顏佩萱仁	Benjamin Chong	莊純通
Chan Pak Chan	陳伯珍	Pat O'Dwyer		Joseph Chu	朱寀發
Sylvia Cheng	鄭慧思	Margaret Perrior		Simon Chu	朱承生
Chee Wan Yee	支讀怡	Patricia Salisbury	施樂珥	Sydney Chu	諸志明
Cher Chung	鍾雪璜	Damayanthi Santwan		Aetos Chung	鍾藹澄
Gladys Chung	鍾福慧	Sue Simon		Chung Ting Ting	鍾霆霆
Nancy Goff	葛蘭詩	Helena Tai	戴慧儀	Fan Yiu Ki	范耀基
Ruth Fan	范鳳鄒	Tang Yuen Suk Mei	鄧袁淑美	Paul Fu	馮志滿
Fu Suk Kee	符淑姬	Janet Taylor	泰珍妮	David Fung	馮炳暉
Polly Ho	何月平	Betty To	杜秀瓊仁	Daniel Ho	何瑞雄
Belinda Hsu	丘文珩	Sandra Tong	唐燕玉	Norman Howarth	侯偉夫
Joan Jasper	謝忠蓮	Tso Ho Fung Yee	曹何鳳儀	Patrick Huang	黃祖民
Dorothy Jones	章慧斯	Gay Tully		Billy Kwok	郭耀富
Ruby Jor-Choi	左鈺貴冰	Anita Wilson	韋安蒂	Lai Pong Wai	黎邦維
Elisabeth Kenyon		Angela Woo	胡安琪	Anthony Lau	劉關基
Pauline Koo	古寶潔	Alice Simon		Peter Liang	梁樑權
Violet Lam	林國玲	Amy Wong	王采雪	Simon Lo	勞德恩
Lucia Lau	劉淑恩	Lydia Wong	王麗曼慈	James Mak	麥浮宏
Maureen Lau	劉雅麗	Wong Mi Lin	黃美蓮	John Moorshead	巫信華
Clara Law	羅倩雯	Shirley Wong		Patrick Ng	伍志平
Chiffon Lee	李芯仿	Wu Lo Lang Mui	胡羅令梅	Siu Shun Cheung	蕭信章
Lee Yik Fung	李亦峰	Olive Wu	胡森緯	Tang Pak Yick	鄧伯翊
Leung Ching Yee	梁靜而	Virginia Wu	伍倩婷	Bruce Taylor	泰偉基
Judy Lo	盧淑愛	Amy Yau	丘亭鳳	George Tedbury	戴喬琪
Mary Lo	盧美儀	Beracah Yeung	楊普榮	Hugh Thomas	譚安暉
Loo Fo She	盧盧海彤	Monita Yeung	楊慧明	Stephen Tong	唐惠生
Judy Luk	陸喜慧	Stevie Yeung	楊縉兒	Tsang Wing Yiu	曾詠瑤
Clara Ma	馬麗新	Julia Yip	葉寶麗	Tso Kai Yip	曹繼業
Maisie Mark	麥靜雲	Yu Wong Chiu May	余黃超梅	Kent Wan	尹卍熾
Mok Miu Wah	莫妙華	Magdalene Yuen	翁玉玲	Eric A. Winckler	
		Mary Yuen	黃惠娟	Douglas S. Whyte	白德立
				Wong Yun Chee	王潤培
				Lincoln Wu	胡志明
				Henry Yu	余漢翁
				Yuen Chun Pang	袁竹彭
				Patrick Yuen	袁栢陶
				Yuen Tim Chung	袁添松
				Yuen Wai Kwok	袁偉國

13

VERDI'S REQUIEM
安 魂 曲

20 May, 1990 (Sunday) City Hall Concert Hall, 8 pm

一九九〇年五月二十日（星期日）
香港大會堂音樂廳晚上八時正

香 港 聖 樂 團

香 港 小 交 響 樂 團

執行委員會

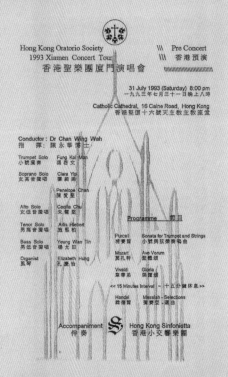

Hong Kong Oratorio Society
1993 Xiamen Concert Tour

\\\ Pre Concert
\\\ 香港預演

香港聖樂團廈門演唱會

31 July 1993 (Saturday) 8:00 pm
一九九三年七月三十一日晚上八時
Catholic Cathedral, 16 Caine Road, Hong Kong
香港堅道十六號天主教主教座堂

Conductor : Dr Chan Wing Wah
指　揮：陳永華博士

Trumpet Solo 小號獨奏	Fung Kai Man 馮啟文
Soprano Solo 女高音獨唱	Clara Yip 葉綺雨
	Penelope Chan 陳愛堅
Alto Solo 女低音獨唱	Cecilia Chu 朱雅麗
Tenor Solo 男高音獨唱	Artis Hiebert 西恩柏
Bass Solo 男低音獨唱	Yeung Wan Tin 楊允田
Organist 風琴	Elizabeth Hung 孔慶怡

Programme　節目

Purcell 浦賽爾	Sonata for Trumpet and Strings 小號與弦樂奏鳴曲
Mozart 莫扎特	Ave Verum 聖體頌
Vivaldi 華華弟	Gloria 榮耀頌

<< 15 Minutes Interval － 十五分鐘休息 >>

Handel 韓德爾	Messiah - Selections 彌賽亞 - 選曲

Accompaniment
伴奏

Hong Kong Sinfonietta
香港小交響樂團

香港聖樂團

女高音	女低音	男高音	男低音
布玉蓮	何樂丹	歐陽志剛	朱文偉
周友梅	李慧敏	曾永耀	葉振聲
鍾鳳屏	李佩玲	吳連強	高勤群
許樹儀	戴玉玲	會源輝	關係明
林泳怡	黃燦英	林仲明	梁耀揚
羅月繪	甄麗嫻	余漢戚	溫兆昌
梁翠娥	楊慧兒		王潤慈
莫妙華	盧瑋倩		
伍群兒	袁惠梅		
韋安蒂	胡羅冷梅		
王芷芳	曾樂懿		
王惠文			
顏張敬仁			
邵煥英			

香港小交響樂團

第一小提琴	中提琴	雙簧管
黃翎明 (團長)	顏星安 (首席)	邱嘉祺 (首席)
陳祖建	錢江	
陳華	戴嘉倩	小號
許健亞	黎家聯	馮啟文 (首席)
李金華		勞恆力
汪加		
	大提琴	定音鼓
第二小提琴	黃嘉輝 (首席)	錢國偉 (首席)
鄭慶 (首席)	馬國騮	
陳美妤		
陳冰		
何俊姓	倍大提琴	幹事
許賜來	吳子康 (首席)	吳紹強

香港聖樂團四十週年音樂會紀念特刊
Hong Kong Oratorio Society 40th Anniversary Souvenir Booklet

Programme:

Robert Plane
I Was Glad When They Said unto Me
Samuel Wesley
Blessed be the God and Father
John Rutter
To Dream Gentleman

My Soul Doth Magnify the Lord
Crescunto Absitae
Quest (Part I)
For the Beauty of the Earth
Chan Wing-wah
Sinfonia No. 4 Dean Brass Violin
Huang, Rubus

16th November, 1996 (Saturday) 8pm
Auditorium Shatin Town Hall
九九六年十一月十六日(星期六)下午八時
沙田大會堂演奏廳

Hong Kong Oratorio Society
香港聖樂團

Hon. Patron 樂譽贊助人		**Vice-Chairman** 副主席	
Mrs. Lavender Patten 彭定康夫人		Eric Au Yeung 歐陽志剛	
Hon. President 樂譽會長		**Membership Secretary** 會籍秘書	
Chu Man Wai 朱文暉		Violet Lam 林瑞芬	
Patrons 贊助人		**Recording Secretary** 記錄秘書	
Wellington Wong, J.P. 黃天賜		Anita Wilson 韋安帝	
Christina Ting Yuk Chu, J.P. 丁鈺珠		**Hon. Treasurer** 義務司庫	
Nathan Ma, M.B.E., J.P. 馬學熙		Wong Mei Lin 黃美蓮	
Simon Lee, M.B.E. 李國賢		**Concert Manager** 音樂會經理	
Hon. Auditor 義務核數師		Nelson Ip 葉؟聲	
Y.K. Wong & Co. 黃肇漿牌銀行		**Promotion Manager** 宣傳經理	
Conductor Emeritus 榮譽指揮		Cindy Lam 林珍芬	
Wong Wing Hee 黃永熙		**Librarian** 會籍秘書	
Music Director 音樂總監		Wong Wai Man 王惠文	
Chan Wing Wah 陳永華		**General Affairs Manager** 總務主任	
Conductors 指揮		Yue Hon Hong 余漢康	
Jimmy Chan 陳耀组		**Assistant Concert Manager** 音樂會副經理	
Andrew Cheung 張偉君		Veronica Chan 陳圖؟	
Allison So 蘇明村		**Assistant Promotion Manager** 宣傳副經理	
Accompanists 伴奏		Lovina Hui 許惠儀	
Wong Kin Yu 黃建驗		**Section Leaders** 聲部部長	
Cindy Chik 戚明迪		Virginia Siu 邵偉英	
Timmy Tsang 曾耀明		Christine Woo 胡志琪	
Peter Yue 余必達		Lucette Black 爲瑞維往	
Executive Committe 執行委員會		Tsang Wing Yiu 曾永耀	
Chairman 主席		Yeung Wan Tin 楊允田	
Henry Yu 余漢堯			

The Hong Kong Oratorio Society is recruiting new members. Interested persons please call Ms. Violet Lam 72836829 for audition details

香港聖樂團現招收新團員，有意者請致電
林瑞芬女士 (72836829) 安排試音。

Hong Kong Oratorio Society
香港聖樂團

Soprano 女高音		Alto 女低音		Tenors 男高音	
Andis Au Yeung 歐陽慧文	Mabel Wong 黃步梅			Eric Au Yeung 歐陽志剛	
Vera Au Yeung 歐陽詠薇	Wong Mei Lin 黃美蓮	May Chan 陳倬英		Chan York Yuen 陳毓泰	
Helen Brooks 白海倫	Amy Wong Tze Fong 王芷芳	Lucette Black 爲瑞維往		Simon Chan 陳卓敏	
Beatrice Chan 陳美華	Vicki Wong 王頴琪	Dorothy Hung 洪德薇		Chan Chi Ling 陳子陵	
Betty Chan 陳李美	Wong Wai Man 王惠文	Camilla Chui 徐秀瓊		Fung Chi Ching 馮志清	
Joanne Chan 陳銘霞	Christine Woo 胡志琪	Katherine Kung 龔凱琳		Daniel Ho 何偉國	
Patsy Chan 陳沙思	Wu Man Fun 胡文芬	Karen Fong 方曉婷		Kiyoshi Inagaki 稻垣清	
Rose Chan 陳麗珍峰		Elsie Ho 何殷詩		Paul Kong 江伯欽	
Esther Chau 周瑞真		Philia Kong 梁文峰		Martin Kwok 郭史頓	
Sylvia Cheng 鄭煥燕		Wu Lo Lang Mui 胡羅冷梅		Tsang Wing Yiu 曾永耀	
Yanni Cheng 鄭可茵		Phoebe Tang 鄧評江		Tso Kai Yip 曹繼業	
Patsy Cheung 張慧思		Shirley Pau 鮑鳳儀		Samuel Wong 黃福滿	
Gladys Chung 鍾麗媚		Abigail Wright 黃雅卿		Lincoln Wu 吳鑑倫	
Gail Harban 夏琪兒		Gwynneth Wright 官莉英		Henry Yu 余漢堯	
Carmen Ho 何馥雯		Kitty Tai 戴玉均		Peter Yue 余必達	
Selina Kam 金志穎		Grace Wong 黃美倫			
Cynthia Lai 黎家穎		Eva Yan 甄麗婷		**Basses 男低音**	
Cindy Lam 林瑞芬		Esther Yeung 楊信真		Barry Anderton 安道騰	
Violet Lam 林瑞芬		Stella Groves 高黎雲		Peter Au Yeung 歐陽昌興	
Clara Law 利道婷		Yu Mei Yee 余滿宜		Sydney Chu 朱贊生	
Corinna Lee 利德婷		Virginia Yue 盧偉倩		Chu Man Wai 朱文暉	
Winnie Lee 李麗娜		Mary Yuen 袁惠珍		Paul Fu 傅志誠	
Bianca Li 李卻儀				Amos Ho 何紹滇	
Loo Fo-she 吳盧澤郎				Nelson Ip 葉؟聲	
Mok Miu Wah 莫玅華				Andrew Kong 江輝安	
Nora Ng 吳雨霞				Lau Ming Hok 梁信閣	
Tracey Pestridge 彭翠林				Lo Ming Hok 羅名峰	
Virginia Siu 邵偉英				Lee Wing Fai 李榮暉	
Edith Shih Sun 孫施玉德				Simon Lo 盧志輝	
Tsang Mei Kuen 曾美娟				Stephen Sun 孫永輝	
Anita Wilson 韋安帝				Ng Kim Fung 吳劍峰	
				Benny Wong 黃士毅	
				Yue Hon Hong 余漢康	
				Yeung Wan Tin 楊允田	

Hong Kong Sinfonietta
香港小交響樂團

1st Violin		**Oboe**	
△ Huang Wei Ming 寶如成		○ Yau Ka Kei 邱嘉琪	
Goh Ching 吳娜		Leanne Nicholls	郝莉文
Chan Chi Kin 陳祖健			
Chen Ping 陳平		**Clarinet**	
Fu Hoi Lai 符海麗		Cheung Lai 張生	
Yap Kit To 葉潔韜		Kenny Chau 鄒浩	
Hui Chi Loi 許植材			
Tsai Loo 蔡如		**Basson**	
Pang Hiu Wan 彭曉雲		○ Chu Hing Sang 朱慶生	
		Lau Chi Fai 劉志輝	
2nd Violin			
○ Goh Ching 吳娜		**Horn**	
Chan Chi Kin 陳祖健		○ Ku Kam Shing 古錦成	
Chee Hung 離隆		Kwan Shan Ming 關山明	
Chee Hung 離隆		Leung Yat For 梁日科	
Tong Xiao Huan 唐曉環		So Tak Ta 蘇德泰	
Wilson Chu 朱偉遜			
Cheung Wai Hei 張偉希		**Trumpet**	
Kathryn Templeman 凱莉予		○ Fung Kai Man 馮啓文	
Jimmy Kwong 鄺子平		Ngan Chi Kuen 顏其權	
Yeung Yuk Chai 楊玉齊		Ng King Chuen 吳景全	
Ho Tat Wai 何達偉			
		Trombone	
Viola		Pak Wing Fai 白榮暉	
△ Ngan Sing On 顏؟安		Lee Ka Cheong 李家昌	
Chin Kong 錢؟		Tse Luen Wah 謝聯華	
Fang Siu Mei 房小梅			
Raymond Han 韓雷蒙		**Tuba**	
Francis Kan 簡彰能		○ Tossaporn Vongshemrat 杜華彰	
Tin His Chung 田熙聰			
Francis Kan 簡彰能		**Timpani**	
		Simon Williams 衛志明	
Cello			
△ Lau Yee 劉儀		**Percussion**	
Sham Di 沈笛		Chau Chui Tong 周服彤	
Wong Ka Fai 黃؟輝		Rebecca Ng 吳؟؟	
Ngai Man Keung 倪文強			
Kwan Ching 關؟		**Organ**	
Kwok Tang Chuen 郭登全		Wong Kin Yu 黃建驗	
		Elizabeth Tsang 曾؟؟	
Double Bass			
○ Pichain Vonghemrat 陳金球		△ Guest Concertmaster 客座樂團首席	
△ Ng Tsz Hong 吳子康		○ Principal 首席	
Wong Wing Lok 黃詠樂		⊕ Assistant Principal 助理首席	
Yam King Lam 任؟林			
Flute			
○ Chan Kwok Chiu 陳國超			
Yu Wing Chun 余؟進			

香港聖樂團 Hong Kong Oratorio Society

贊助人 / 委員 / 職員 Patrons / Staff / Committee

榮譽贊助人	Hon. Patron	執行委員會	Executive Committee
董建華夫人	Mrs. Betty Tung	主席	Chairman
		楊盛明	Enoch Young
榮譽會長	Hon. President		
鄭慕智	Charles Cheng	副主席	Vice Chairman
		利蕴蓮	Corinna Lee
贊助人	Patrons		
黃天榮	Wellington Wong	義務秘書	Hon. Secretary
黃乾亨博士	Dr. Philip K. H. Wong	歐陽國禮	Peter Au Yeung
楊靈玲	Serena Yang		
孔美琪	Maggie Koong	義務司庫	Hon. Treasurer
		黃美蓮	Wong Mi-lin
	Hon. Auditor		
陳作輝會計師行	Francis Chan Chok Fai & Co.	音樂會經理	Concert Manager
		勞隆意	Simon Lo
榮譽指揮	Conductor Emeritus		
黃永熙	Wong Wing-hee	總務經理	General Affairs Manager
		陳誠彥	Chan York-yuen
音樂總監	Music Director		
陳永華	Chan Wing-wah	樂譜管理經理	Library Manager
		莫妙華	Mok Miu-wah
指揮	Conductors		
張駿傑	Andrew Cheung	會籍經理	Membership Manager
蘇明村	Allison So	王芷芳	Amy Wong
伴奏	Accompanists	宣傳經理	Promotion Manager
黃健怡	Wong Kin-yu	許喬儒	Lovina Hui
黃以明	Huang Yee-ming		
瞿明頤	Cindy Chik	聲部部長	Section Leaders
余必達	Peter Yue	陳寶貽	Penelope Chan
		胡巡珠	Christine Woo
助理伴奏	Assistant Accompanist	魏慧娟	Sharon Ngai
黃健鐘	Wong Kin-chung	曾永耀	Tsang Wing-yiu
		楊光田	Yeung Wan-tin

會員贊助人 Member Sponsor :

一團員	One Member	黎苑珠	Cynthia Lai	顏家軼仁	Elizabeth Ngan
利蕴蓮	Corinna Lee	楊光田	Yeung Wan-tin	陳家美真	Betty Chan
		麥譚麗任	Lucette Black	陳子健	Clement Chan
		王惠文	Wong Wai-man	黃美蓮	Wong Mi-lin
		魏慧娟	Sharon Ngai	官文蘭	Kung Man-ian
				周發梅	Helen Chow

指定捐款 Indicated donations from :

陳愛堅	Penelope Chan	曹繼業	Tao Kai-yip	一團員	One Member

17

香港聖樂團 Hong Kong Oratorio Society

第一女高音	1st Soprano	女低音	Alto	男低音	Bass
艾麗信	Allinson, Irene	麥譚麗任	Lucette Black	鄭泰高	Charles Cheng
歐陽溢文	Andis Au Yeung	陸曉美	May Lam	朱贊生	Sydney Chu
陳幸美貞	Betty Chan	魏桑姬	Raye Heather Chen	馮栢添	Patrick Fung
*陳愛堅	*Penelope Chan	鄭婉薇	Sylvia Cheng	何栢暖	Amos Ho
陳詩思	Patsy Chan	張楊子彥	May Cheung	葉鎮仁	Apollo Ip
鄭敬慈	Patsy Cheung	徐家淇	Cindy Chik	羅子平	David Lo
周發梅	Helen Chow	許靄儀	Teresa Hau	勞德基	Simon Lo
朱麥歆	Maria Chu	洪黃麗真	Lovina Hui	吳劍峰	Ng Kim-fung
後藤秀子	Goto Hideko	堂文薰	Dorothy Hung	王潤榮	Wong Yun-chee
黎綺兒	Pansy Lai		Phelia Kung	*楊光田	*Yeung Wan-tin
利蕴蓮	Corinna Lee		Ada Lam	楊盛明	Enoch Young
梁寶琼	Caroline Leung		Candy Lau		
劉慧敏	Adrienne Lew		Santa Lau	*聲部部長 Section Leader
麥莉莎	Lilian Mak		Chloe Lor	
黃美蓮	Wong Mi-lin	*魏慧娟	*Sharon Ngai	The Hong Kong Oratorio
王芷芳	Amy Wong	王子如	Risa Wong	Society is recruiting new
楊燕超	Aliena Yeung	王英明	Yvonne Wong	members. Interested
		胡羅玲梅	Wu Lo Lang-mui	persons please call Ms. Amy
		黃步梅	Mabel Wong	Wong (2546 4996).

第二女高音	2nd Soprano	男高音	Tenor	香港聖樂團現正招收新團員。有
陳端霞	Joanne Chan	歐陽嘉傑	Peter Au Yeung	意者請致電王子芳女士 (2546
陳詠雯	Chan Wing-man	陳亦堅	Simon Chan	4996) 安排試音。
黎月娟	Cynthia Lai	陳子健	Clement Chan	
陸月娟	Amanda Luk	陳誠彥	Chan York-yuen	
陸佩文	Koren Mitchell	葉信昌	Aurum Ip	
莫妙華	Mok Miu-wah	郭啟俊	Martin Kwok	
孫麗芳	Vivian Suen	李肇年	Li Hin-nin	
謝愛娟	Candy Tse	麥穎聲	Mak Wing-sing	
王惠文	Wong Wai-man	*曾永耀	*Tsang Wing-yiu	
*胡志珠	*Christine Woo	吳維倫	Lincoln Wu	

香港弦樂團 Hong Kong Strings

第一小提琴	Violin I	大提琴	Cello	雙簧管	Oboe
梁樂熙	Nicolas Leung	張明輝	Cheung Ming-fai	譚子輝	Victor Tam
蔡璐	Tsai Loo	陳顯欣	Joyce Chan	何加振	Karen Ho
林斯敏	Alan Lam	王喜瑩	Christy Wong		
鄭文景	Alice Cheng	黃家輝	David Wong	小號	Trumpet
陳培德	Penny Chen			顏智耀	Joseph Ngan
陳錫儀	Danny Chan			吳景絵	Ng King-chuen
雷麗雅	Lily Lui	大提琴	Bass		
		馬華傑	Wilfred Ma	圓號	Horn
第二小提琴	Violin II	譚誠忻	Harty Tam	關山鳴	Benny Kwan
一丸綾子	Ayako Ichimaru				Ansv Nanda Suprecti
羅家文	Alvin Chan	長笛	Flute	岑慶愛	Shum Hing-cheung
羅珮文	Michelle Law	莊恬華	Ivy Chong	黃堅	Wong Kin
彭鴻玥	Pang Hiu-wan	何仲宵	Angus Ho		
趙明華	Chong Ming-wai			長號	Trombone
		單簧管	Clarinet	Yuko Niitsuma	
中提琴	Viola	林美如	May Lam	劉詠欣	Belinda Lau
廖智超	Lui Chi-chiu	劉翠華	Fenny Lau	葉俊傑	Yip Chun-kit
韓年華	Raymond Hon				
馮小雯	Fung Siu-man	巴松管	Bassoon	定音鼓	Timpani
陳子信	Evis Chan	張煜綸	Cheung King-lun	周原同	Chan Chin-tung
		張安琪	Angel Cheung		

16

香港聖樂團
www.Oratorio.org.hk

音樂神童：孟德爾遜
Mendelssohn
the Music Prodigy
香港聖樂團 Hong Kong Oratorio Society

29.9.2013 (星期日 Sun) 8pm
荃灣大會堂演奏廳
Auditorium, Tsuen Wan Town Hall

康樂及文化事務署
Leisure and Cultural
Services Department

香港聖樂團 Hong Kong Oratorio Society 贊助人/委員 Patrons/Committee Members

榮譽贊助人	HON. PATRON	音樂總監	MUSIC DIRECTOR
梁唐青儀女士	Mrs. Regina LEUNG	陳永華	CHAN Wing Wah, JP
榮譽會長	HON. PRESIDENTS	指揮	CONDUCTORS
鄭崇孟	Charles CHENG	官樂如	Carmen KOON
陳大枝	Alvin CHAN	趙伯承	Patrick CHIU
陳耀斌堯先	Fidelia CHAN	伴奏	ACCOMPANISTS
贊助人	PATRONS	黃建瑜	WONG Kin Yu
吳天榮	Wellington WONG, JP	余必建	Peter YUE
楊宿嫻	Serena YANG	賈那新	Marie Agnes GIA
鄺乾宇	Philip K H WONG	黃以明	HUANG Yee Ming
孔美絬	Maggie KOONG		
義務法律顧問	HONORARY LEGAL ADVISOR		
譚惠珠	Maria TAM, GBS, JP		
執行委員會	EXECUTIVE COMMITTEE	助理音樂會經理	ASSISTANT CONCERT MANAGER
主 席	CHAIRMAN	梁華纓	Caroline LEUNG
楊健明	Enoch YOUNG, BBS	張維鴻	Ringo CHEUNG
副主席	VICE CHAIRMAN (External Affairs)	實理總務經理	GENERAL AFFAIRS MANAGER (Acting)
時笑良	Joy SHI	張維鴻	Ringo CHEUNG
副主席	VICE CHAIRMAN (Internal Affairs)	樂譜管理經理	LIBRARY MANAGER
歐陽志剛	Eric AU-YEUNG	朱美娜	Maria CHU
義務秘書	HON. SECRETARY	會員經理	MEMBERSHIP MANAGER
郭柏明	Paul KWOK	黃美蓮	WONG Mi Lit
義務司庫	HON. TREASURER	宣傳經理	PROMOTION MANAGER
柳月娥	Emily LAU	林藹玲	Anita LAM
助理司庫	ASSISTANT TREASURER	聲部長	SECTION LEADERS
謝寶嫻	Candy TSE	陳愛堅	Penelope CHAN (S1)
音樂會經理	CONCERT MANAGER	胡志珊	Christine WOO (S2)
吳劍峰	NG Kin Fung	曾永蘭	TSANG Wing Yiu (T)
		馮建成	Patrick FUNG (B)

香港聖樂團鳴謝以下人士及機構
Hong Kong Oratorio Society wishes to acknowledge the following individuals and organisations

葉詩婷女士	Ms Vivian IP
蔣頌恩女士	Ms Grace CHIANG
劉靄宜女士	Ms Emily LIU
梁偉霖先生	Mr Christopher LEUNG
張健華先生	Mr Petrus CHEUNG
林偉廷先生	Mr Michael LAM
香港弦樂團	Hong Kong Strings
李少微老師	Ms LEE Siu Mei
聖公會林護紀念中學合唱團	SKH Lam Woo Memorial Secondary School Choir
創新電視	Cenmion TV
黃健瑜女士	Ms WONG Kin Yu
黃慧暉先生	Mr Alex WONG
唐展峰先生	Mr TONG Chin Fung
李建宏先生	Mr LI Kin Wang Peter
朱美娜女士	Ms Maria CHU
張倩儀女士	Ms Patsy CHEUNG

香港聖樂團 Hong Kong Oratorio Society

第一女高音 1st Soprano		女低音 Alto		男低音 Bass	
陳沛思	Patsy CHAN	學頌緹杜 *	Lucette BLACK	陳廷章	CHAN Ting-cheung
陳愛堅 *	Penelope CHAN	陳劭娟	Catherine CHAN	張健鴻	Ringo CHEUNG
陳秀嫻	Vivian CHAN	盧慧珣	Michelle CHAU	周東文	Ivan CHOW
周友梅	Helen CHOW	鄭紅惠	Sylvia CHENG	朱譽生	Sydney CHU
馮藍深	Mary FUNG	周文斌	Maggie CHOW	馮建成 *	Patrick FUNG
後藤芳子	Hideko GOTO	范安賀	Angie FRENCH	阿柏遜	Amos HO
何燕芬	Julianna HO	何雅詠	Catherina HO	戴元慶	Vincent HON
焦惠芳	Gabriela JIAU	洪黃姬美	Dorethy HUNG	林立政	Tony LAM
林毓玲	Anita LAM	龔杏芳	Fanny KUNG	李華龍	Lawrence LI
梁翠嫻	Caroline LEUNG	鄺慧妍	Natalie KWONG	勞德慈	Simon LO
盧玟	Fonda LO	黎宛璣	Cynthia LAI	吳劍峰	NG Kim-fung
羅旺平	LO Wong-ping	利娟珀	Corinna LEE	顏華富	Carlos NGAN
陳楚芬	Lynda TAN	梁慧青	Rebecca LEUNG	蘇以高	Thomas SOO
曾美鈞	TSANG Mei-Kuen	梁譽蘭	Veronica LEUNG	王潤森	WONG Yun-chee
黃美薇	WONG Mi-lin	大滝千作	Sharon NGAI	楊允田	YEUNG Wan-tin
		大滝千作	Chika OTAKI	楊建明	Enoch YOUNG
第二女高音 2nd Soprano		潘黎斯	Lindsey POON		
陳宋綾	Esther CHAN	黃惠娟	Annie WONG		
陳鎬程	Joanne CHAN	黃巧梅	Mabel WONG		
張少賢	CHEUNG Siu-yin	王笑芳	Yvonne WONG		
林瑞文	Bonnie LAM	胡蘆冷苗	WU LO Lang-miu		
柳月嬌	Emily LAU				
羅川嬿	Clara LAW	男高音 Tenor			
劉伊蕪	Jay LIU	歐陽志剛	Eric AU YEUNG		
馬美如	Ivy MA	歐陽嘉俊	Peter AU YEUNG		
繆瑤鈞	Miu MAU	陳卓堅	Simon CHAN		
蔡志明	Gillie TSOI	郭旺偉	Marcin KWOK		
胡志珊 *	Christine WOO	梁結華	LEUNG Kit-wing		
王巧芙	Agnes WONG	呂佳炘	Matthew LUI		
		齊永耀 *	TSANG Wing-yiu		
		黃賢德	Rio WONG		
		余杜文	Raymond YUE		
		袁廷松	YUEN Tim-chung		

* 聲部長 Section Leader

香港聖樂團
Hong Kong Oratorio Society

贊助人/委員 PATRONS / COMMITTEE MEMBERS

榮譽贊助人 HON. PATRON	段崇智教授 Prof. Rocky TUAN
會長 PRESIDENT	楊健明教授 Prof. Enoch YOUNG, BBS
榮譽會長 HON. PRESIDENTS	陳大枝先生 Mr. Alvin CHAN 陳邱敏英女士 Mrs. Fidelia CHAN
義務法律顧問 HON. LEGAL ADVISOR	譚惠珠女士 Ms. Maria TAM, GBM, GBS, JP
榮譽顧問 HON. ADVISOR	陳達文博士 Dr. Darwin CHEN, SBS
贊助人 PATRONS	孔美琪博士 Dr. Maggie KOONG, BBS, JP 楊章桂芝女士 Mrs. Cindy YOUNG
音樂總監 MUSIC DIRECTOR	陳永華教授 Prof. CHAN Wing-wah, JP
首席伴奏 PRINCIPAL ACCOMPANIST	黃健瑜女士 Ms. WONG Kin-yu
伴奏 ACCOMPANISTS	余必達先生 Mr. Peter YUE 黃以明女士 Ms. HUANG Yee-ming 何穎姍女士 Ms. Hilary HO
駐團牧師 SOCIETY CHAPLAIN	蘇以葆主教 The Rt Rev SOO Yee Po, Thomas, JP

執行委員會 EXECUTIVE COMMITTEE

主席 CHAIRMAN	歐陽志剛 Eric AU YEUNG
副主席 VICE CHAIRMAN	吳劍峰 NG Kim-fung
秘書及司庫 SECRETARY & TREASURER	王笑芳 Yvonne WONG
音樂會經理 CONCERT MANAGER	唐展峰 Tony TONG
總務經理 GENERAL AFFAIRS MANAGER	梁翠娥 Caroline LEUNG
樂譜管理經理 LIBRARY MANAGER	陶麗詩 Doris TAO
會籍經理 MEMBERSHIP MANAGER	范安智 Angie FRENCH
宣傳經理 PROMOTION MANAGER	張耀光 Jacky CHEUNG
聲部長 SECTION LEADERS	陳愛堅 Penelope CHAN (S1) 柳月娥 Emily LAU (S2) 墨譚鑾往 Lucette BLACK (A) 曾永耀 TSANG Wing-yiu (T) 馮建成 Patrick FUNG (B)

香港聖樂團
Hong Kong Oratorio Society

表演者名單 Performers List

第一女高音	1st Soprano
陳麗詩	CHAN Lai-sze
* 陳愛堅	Penelope CHAN
周燕祥	Irene CHAU
朱美歡	Maria CHU
徐晨淑	Maria CHUI
何燕芬	Julianna HO
焦惠芳	Gabriela JIAU
川瀨智子	Tomoko KAWASE
鄺蕙堯	KWONG Wai-yiu
黎穎敏	Cynthia LAI
林敏玲	Anita LAM
梁翠娥	Caroline LEUNG
盧 放	Fonda LO
施熙德	Edith SHIH
陳楚琴	TAN Lynda
陶麗詩	Doris TAO
曾美娟	TSANG Mei-kuen
韋靜嫻	Christine WAI
黃美蓮	WONG Mi-lin
翁思嘉	Scarlett YUNG

第二女高音	2nd Soprano
區麗和	Aileena AU
陳錦霞	Joanne CHAN
蔡詩韻	Swan CHOI
夏慧嫻	Catherine HAH
何卓會	Betty HO
韓月霞	Lillian HON
關嘉明	Mable KWAN
賴宇衛	Annie LAI
林婉文	Bonnie LAM
* 柳月娥	Emily LAU
羅月嬌	Clara LAW
劉聿臻	Jay LIU
馬美如	Ivy MA
宮松步美	Ayumi MIYAMATSU
莫妙華	MOK Miu-wah
黃朝華	Bonnie SHIH
沈慧華	Angela SHUM
孫麗芳	Vivian SUEN
蔡智明	Gillie TSOI
胡志琪	Christine WOO
葉嘉華	Bianca YIP

女低音	Alto
* 墨譚鑾往	Lucette BLACK
陳碧娟	Catherine CHAN
巢慧梅	Michelle CHAU
陳雅玲	Iris CHEN
鄭庭蕙	Sylvia CHENG
張浩年	Felix CHEUNG
周友梅	Helen CHOW
傅慧屏	Elcos FU
姬嘉柏	Tricia KRIEGER
龔杏芬	Fanny KUNG
林碧欣	Ada LAM
劉玉珠	Candy LAU
羅詠恩	Selina LAW
利順瓊	Corinna LEE
梁慧菁	Rebecca LEUNG
林婉琪	Janet LUM
魏慧娟	Sharon NGAI
溫穎雯	Windy WAN
王笑芳	Yvonne WONG
矢部真紀子	Makiko YABE
矢野優子	Yuko YANO
楊慧兒	Stevie YEUNG
嚴秀嫻	Agnes YIM

男高音	Tenor
歐陽志剛	Eric AU YEUNG
歐陽嘉傑	Peter AU YEUNG
陳卓堅	Simon CHAN
張耀光	Jacky CHEUNG
郭世傑	Martin KWOK
梁德楨	William LEUNG
內藤寧俊	Yasutoshi NAITO
吳政民	NG Ching-man
* 曾永耀	TSANG Wing-yiu
錢 豐	Johnny TSIN
黃志賢	William WONG
吳建強	Lincoln WU
余杜文	Raymond YUE

男低音	Bass
陳彧彥	CHAN York-yuen
張健鴻	Ringo CHEUNG
朱贊生	Sydney CHU
* 馮建成	Patrick FUNG
韓元聲	Vincent HON
林天星	Enoch LAM
李建宏	Peter LI
勞德恩	Simon LO
呂根榮	Vincent LUI
顏繼強	Carlos NGAN
蘇以葆	Thomas SOO
薛嘉翔	William SIT
孫永輝	Stephen SUN
唐展峰	Tony TONG
段崇智	Rocky TUAN
楊允田	YEUNG Wan-tin
楊健明	Enoch YOUNG

* 聲部長 Section Leader

香港聖樂團逢星期二晚上於香港文化中心均有排練，本團誠邀有合唱經驗及才華的人士參加試音，加入成為團員，有意者請詳閱刊於場刊第31頁之報名方法。
The rehearsals are held at the Hong Kong Cultural Centre each Tuesday evening. Experienced and talented singers are invited to audition as chorus members. If you are interested in joining us, please read the application details on page 31.

香港弦樂團
Hong Kong Strings

表演者名單 Performers List

First Violin	第一小提琴
** Nicholas LEUNG	梁 燊
Walter CHAN	陳清德
Samuel BIN	卞祉榣
Danny CHAN	陳揚儀
Pauline TANG	鄧沛玲
Andrew HSU	許銘境
King FUNG	馮紫竣
Shirley TANG	鄧慧婷

Second Violin	第二小提琴
* Terry CHAN	陳昌隆
Meg CHAN	陳綺怡
Steven LIAO	廖嘉智
TONG Sze Sze	唐詩詩
HUI Chi Kin	許智健
Davis YIU	姚漢林

Viola	中提琴
* LIU Chi Chiu	廖智超
Otto KWAN	關統洋
Ashton LAU	劉漢暉
POON Ngo Yeung	潘遨揚

Cello	大提琴
* CHEUNG Ming Fai	張明輝
Joyce CHAN	陳樂欣
CHONG Ling	莊 凌
Chole LING	凌卓妍

Double Bass	低音大提琴
* Eddie ZONG	宗小謙
Charlie WONG	王梓豪

Flute	長笛
* Mario SO	蘇家慶
Vanessa CHEUNG	張麗瑩

Oboe	雙簧管
* Rachel WONG	汪楚萍
Henry CHENG	鄭永健

Clarinet	單簧管
* Anthony WONG	黃智輝
Edwin KWONG	鄺彥聰

Bassoon	巴松管
* CHEUNG King Lun	張經綸
Vivian LEE	李瑋澄

Horn	圓號
* CHEUNG Sun Ming Sunny	張新名
WONG Kin	黃 堅
Ken YUEN	袁家麒

Trumpet	小號
* NG King Chuen	吳景銓
CHAN Yik Lok	陳亦樂

Alto Trombone	中音長號
* CHIU Hon Kuen	趙漢權

Tenor Trombone	次中音長號
* CHEUNG Po Yan	張溥甄

Bass Trombone	低音長號
* Donald CHOI	蔡秀賢

Timpani	定音鼓
* WAN Wai Wah	雲維華

Percussion	敲擊樂
* Carmen AU *	區家敏

1962

~~~~~~~~ ORATORIO SOCIETY ~~~~~~~~

"Elijah" Presented At City Hall

BY RUTH KIRBY

IT is just five years since "Elijah" was last heard in Hongkong, sung by the Hongkong Singers, conducted by Dr Ride, on a terrible wet night when the rain and thunder outside provided a noisy contrast to the singers praying for rain inside! Last night's performance was put on by the Hongkong Oratorio Society, its first City Hall production, and a fair and sincere effort. The conductor was Mr Frank Huang, who well knows how to control a choir and to elicit sweetness and tonal contrasts and effects.

However, I felt that the essential drama of the work had not quite been grasped. Mendelssohn conceived the story of "Elijah" as a drama, in which each actor has a very definite character as portrayed by the words—it is quite unlike "Messiah," where the excitement is all in the narrative. The handling was not sufficiently imaginative to hold one's interest all the time. Nevertheless, there were some very lovely moments and some very commendable singing.

THE long and exacting name part was sung by Rev L. G. McKinney, whose bass voice was always true except in one aria near the end ("For the mountains shall depart") when it was a little sharp. His delivery had much character, his words were mostly clear and when he allowed himself, he produced a fine resonance. He almost—but not quite—reached a splendidly mocking tone when deriding the Israelites who were calling upon Baal.

The tenor was Mr Peter Beale. His enunciation was perfectly clear at all times, and his intonation correct, but the voice itself is somewhat thin without much body to it.

Both the soprano (Miss Elizabeth Lee) and the alto (Mrs Maureen Clark) revealed rather too much vibrato. Miss Lee's soft and loud tones were pleasing, but the change from one to the other was usually too abrupt, and the crescendo on a rising note too sudden. Mrs Clark was also the alto in the performance five years ago, and if I remember aright, her voice was then more rounded and even than it was last night.

ALL four soloists sang with great sincerity and conviction, but the impact of the drama did not quite come across to the audience. Special mention must be made of young Frank Wiens, who sang the little solo of the child who espies the cloud "as big as a man's hand." The voice was perfect for the part, absolutely in tune and with the evanescent purity of the boy soprano.

The accompaniment was provided by a piano and a small organ, played respectively by Mrs Ruth Galster and Mrs Evelyn Kwong. As the choir was not a large one—about 70 in all—the accompaniment was fairly adequate, and in general very efficient. The greatest climax is, of course, when the rain comes, and the piano can never satisfactorily interpret "the waters gather, they rush along ... the stormy billows are high, their fury is mighty!" However, it was bravely done, and again in the chorus "Then did Elijah the prophet break forth like a fire," the piano part was excellently played.

IT was encouraging to see so many young singers—I discerned several school girls. One chorus, "Though thousands languish and fall beside thee and tens of thousands around thee perish" was sung in a rather too matter-of-fact and cheerful manner! But by the "Amen," the choir was singing really rousingly. Here I must go back to one of my hobby-horses; they sang best when they kept their heads up; so did the soloists. The more singers can dispense with music, the better they will sing, especially in dramatic works of this kind.

UNFORTUNATELY the opening part of this performance was very much disturbed by latecomers, who were allowed to enter by the too-obliging young usherettes and shown to their seats in the middle of the Introduction and first chorus. Indeed, there was such a gap between one chorus and recitative that the thread was lost. I would suggest that societies decide very firmly beforehand at what points to admit latecomers. Another noticeable factor was that though all seats were apparently sold, there were a good many empty places. And the hall was terribly cold!

After just over two months, the growing pains associated with getting accustomed to the City Hall are still with us. But I think that something is learned with every performance, and the Oratorio Society provides us with one more example of the liveliness of our local cultural organisations.

《南華早報》

255

Oratorio Society
SPIRIT OF 'CREATION' RE-CREATED
By CHARLES HARVEY

Throughout the realm of Christian unity the singing of Haydn's "Creation" is an eloquent testimony. On Friday night, in the City Hall Concert Hall, the spirit of "Creation" was re-created in The Hongkong Oratorio Society's performance.

This was no Huddersfield Choral Society nor Liverpool Philharmonic Choral Society epic—the incisive voices of Britain's northerners being a feature of its choirs; it succeeded because it was unpretentious, sincere and carefully-prepared. What is more, it made effective use of local resources.

Given the sensitive acoustics of the Concert Hall, a small but trained choir, soloists who had studied their subject material and a medium-size orchestra, a great deal can be achieved.

Young and keen

Professor Lin Sheng-shih, who can take pride in having a young and keen body of musicians within The South China Philharmonic Orchestra, had coached his players to favourable standards, before handing over the baton to the Rev L. G. McKinney, who conducted this performance.

The orchestra had been reinforced by several leading players from the Hongkong Philharmonic Orchestra, including Dr S. K. Wong and Dr S. M. Bard, whose gentle flutes produced a serene melodic line; and double-bass stalwart, A. Mannheim, who consistently is a pillar of strength in local performances.

Mr McKinney tends to accelerate the pace, as was evidenced in the soprano Air, "With Verdure Clad"; on the other hand, he never allowed the music to drag and finishes were trim and precise.

Well attuned

Intonation throughout was consistent and only occasionally were individual players off pitch. The singers — soloists and choir — were well attuned and this was especially evident in the duets and trios.

Of the soloists, the most favourable was Gordon Lockhart, whose rich bass has the merit of clarity. True intonation was a quality of the principals; the duets between Adam and Eve — Nancy Zi, soprano and Walter Wan, baritone, were gentle, but crystal-clear.

Lyrical quality

The tenor, Peter Beale, has a lyrical quality and he sang effectively and expressively; in the quiet passages, however, the words faded away and were lost.

The continuo part was taken on the piano by Ruth Galster. This was favourable. But for the next performance by the Society, it would be an advantage to have the harpsichord—and to invite Mr John Harley to play his self-made instrument.

Of Part I, the Chorus, "The Heavens are telling the glory of God" was very successful. Parts II and III were the best, Uriel's Air, "In Native worth and honour clad"; Uriel's Recitative, "O happy pair!", followed by the exultant Chorus, "Sing ye the Lord, ye voices all," being highlights.

《南華早報》

HONGKONG ORATORIO SOCIETY
Creditable Rendering Of St Paul
BY A GUEST CRITIC

ON Saturday evening in the City Hall Concert Hall, the Hongkong Oratorio Society continued what can fairly be called its tradition with a performance of St Paul by Mendelssohn, using a choir of some 45 people accompanied by the South China Sinfonietta orchestra nearly as strong. The combined forces came under the authoritative baton of Frank Huang.

St Paul, first performed in Dusseldorf in 1836 and, later the same year, in Liverpool, lacks the drama of Elijah and even approaches banality places, but is far from being mere choir fodder which was the case with many other oratorios of this period.

The choral writing is orthodox and the orchestration has the lyrical stamp of Mendelssohn, especially in the use of woodwinds, so that reasonably competent performers should give a pleasurable evening. In general terms this was the case.

In fact one could go further and say that it was a very creditable performance and, at the risk of sounding condescending—which is not intended, all the more so as most of the performers were Chinese and not steeped in the tradition of oratorio, as are numerous British choral societies.

I COUNTED five more men than women in the choir but it seemed to make a lot of difference. In the chorale, "To God on High," for example, the low tessitura of the soprano part was lost but when we got above C their brightness of tone came through to lighten the chording, as in "How lovely are the Messengers."

The men on the other hand, seldom faltered and the tenors especially reinforced their line on numerous occasions, but with discretion, to heighten the intensity of sound. Attack generally was good, which is not always the case in choral societies, and though entries are not difficult melodically they are often demanding rhythmically.

The orchestra was not over large, woodwind and brass being on the small side, so the odds against faulty intonation were lessened. More bite in the bowing would have enhanced the sometimes dull tone of the strings but we cannot leave the orchestra without mentioning the trumpet, singular.

This was seldom good, I am delighted to report—repeat delighted—simply because it was usually excellent. Time and time again John Cheng produced pristine clarity and "Sleepers, Wake," where he was skilfully aided by the horn, was only one example. The final chorus was well managed by all sections but, for me, the climax sparkled, due mainly to the trumpet.

OF the four soloists I would commend Nancy Zi, soprano, for beautiful diction (what is the point of standing up at all if we cannot understand the words?) and good tone but for an annoying wobble at the end of phrases. Ruth Chow, contralto, sounded majestic over a well controlled accompaniment in "But the Lord is mindful of his own." Ho Kwan-ching, tenor, never lacked sincerity but was careless with final consonants and baritone, Chan Kung-sang, was often drowned by the orchestra. This was so in his first aria, "Consume them all" and even though the accompaniment should have been more subdued a fuller and richer tone is required for the grandeur of St Paul.

Frank Huang demonstrated his musicianship, not for the first time, with a firm beat and the performance of the choir showed evidence of careful practice under his baton.

I look forward to next year and another oratorio.

《南華早報》

1956 — 1966

It is with great pleasure that the HONG KONG ORATORIO SOCIETY greets you at our concert this evening. We trust that you will enjoy listening to the singing of JOHANNES BRAHMS' "REQUIEM" accompanied by the Hong Kong Philharmonic Orchestra.

The Hong Kong Oratorio Society was founded just over ten years ago and the first concert was given in Queen Elizabeth School Auditorium, Kowloon, on October 26, 1956. Since that time some twenty oratorio concerts have been sung by the society in various halls, schools and churches, including Loke Yew Hall of the Hong Kong University, Wah Yan College, Kowloon, and the Christian Missionary Alliance Church in Kowloon Tong, Kowloon. Five concerts were sung in each of the last two mentioned places. Since May 11, 1962 the society has given seven concerts in the City Hall Concert Auditorium. To-night will mark our 8th performance in this fine music hall.

The chorus has sung such well-known oratorios as "Saint Paul", "St. John's Passion", "Elijah", "Creation", "Samson", "Judas Maccabeaus", Mozart's "Requiem". The "Messiah" has been sung twice, and parts of it several times. Selections from our oratorio for tonight, Brahm's "Requiem", have been given on two occasions.

We wish to pay tribute to our conductors, accompanists and soloists who have helped the society in such great measure during the past decade. Six conductors have responded to invitations to lead the chorus at various times. Theodore Huang, our first leader, conducted four concerts, followed by L. G. McKinney with four, George Wilson with three, Arrigo Foa with two, and John P. Muilenburg and D. E. Parker led us in one concert each. Our present leader, Frank Huang, has conducted the society in five concerts and tonight the chorus looks forward to singing under his guidance for the sixth time. Evelyn Kwong has been our faithful organ accompanist in nine concerts. At the piano we have had Lee Pak Fong for four concerts and our present piano accompanist, Irene Lo, will be in her fifth concert to-night. La Mae Mark accompanied the chorus at three presentations, Ruth Galster at two, and Tu Yuet Sin and Geoffrey Tankard played at one concert each. Fifteen women soloists have helped the society immensely throughout these years and we would mention those who have sung at four or more concerts, namely, Maureen Clark, Chen Lui Mu Lan, Nancy Zi and Ruth Chow. We are pleased that Nancy Zi is with us again this evening. In the early years of the society great help was given by soloists Edna Wong, Pauline Cheong-leen and Edna Chen. Of the men soloists, numbering twenty, who have sung with the society, this evening's soloist, Chan Kung Sang, has given eight performances. Robert Witcher has sung with us seven times. Other soloists who have performed with the society on three or more occasions are Ho Kwan Ching, Chan Ting Kwok and Solomon Young.

The society has been fortunate that in approximately one half of the concerts given in the past ten years it has been accompanied by orchestral instruments. We have been helped by the Poco Orchestra four times, the South China Philharmonic and the Hong Kong Philharmonic on two occasions each, and the South China Sinfonietta at one concert. We are delighted and priviideged to be singing with the Hong Kong Philharmonic Orchestra tonight.

The Hong Kong Oratorio Society was founded a decade ago by a few music lovers who believed that Hong Kong would appreciate good oratorio singing. From small beginnings, the chorus has grown to some seventy members, but we would wish for added strength and cordially invite singers to join us. Ten years of oratorio singing have enriched the lives of many members and there are those of us who have been with the society from its inception. We know also that thousands of people have enjoyed our concerts in the past years. We do not claim to be professional singers but we love to sing. We trust that you will have an enjoyable time to-night as the chorus and orchestra perform this timeless and magnificent music and that you will wish to attend our future concerts. We believe that oratorio singing is always a great delight.

— 1 —

（場刊）

十 年 努 力 （一九五六 / 一九六六）

香港聖樂團今晚歡迎閣下駕臨這個音樂會。在香港管絃樂團伴奏之下，我們謹以萬分的熱誠獻唱勃拉姆斯的「安靈曲」。

香港聖樂團遠在十年前創立。首次音樂會於一九五六年十月二十六日假座九龍伊利莎伯學校禮堂演出，迄今已舉行了大約二十個「神曲」的音樂會。地點皆在學校的大堂或禮拜堂，如香港大學的陸佑堂，九龍華仁書院禮堂，九龍塘宜道會禮拜堂。在後兩者曾舉行的音樂會，每處達五次之多。自從一九六二年五月十一日以來，聖樂團曾在設備完善的大會堂音樂廳舉行了七次音樂會，今晚已是第八次了。

聖樂團的合唱團曾整套地演唱過許多有名的「神曲」，例如巴哈的「約翰福音基督受難本紀」、韓德爾的「彌賽亞」、「參孫」和「猶大麥加保」、海頓的「創世紀」和「四季頌」、莫札特的「安靈曲」及孟德爾遜的「以利亞」和「聖保羅」，今晚所獻唱的勃拉姆斯「安靈曲」，多年前曾兩次選唱一部份。今晚則全部唱出。

我們值此機會向歷任的指揮、伴奏和獨唱者謹致謝忱。他們十年來給予本團的扶助至鉅。曾經接納本團的邀請而任本合唱團的指揮，共有六位。最初是黃明東先生，擔任音樂會共計四次；接著是麥堅理牧師擔任四次；威爾遜博士三次，富亞教授兩次；梅倫堡和柏嘉先生每位一次。現任指揮黃飛然先生領導本團演出的音樂會，已往達六次，今晚則是第七次上演了。鄺李淑嫻女士在已往的九個音樂會中，一直是本團忠誠的風琴伴奏者。至於鋼琴伴奏，李柏芳先生曾擔任四次。現任的伴奏者羅玉珙女士，則已是第五次擔任了。此外，麥雲嬋女士擔任伴奏三次；路德‧嘉爾絲達女士兩次；屠月仙和鄧嘉德女士各一次。在以往十年內，曾經幫助本團擔任獨唱的女歌唱家共十五位。其中演出四次或四次以上的有慕連、嘉勒、陳劉沐蘭、徐美芬和周宏俊女士。徐女士今晚再為我們演唱，我們十分欣慶和感謝。本團成立後最初幾年，曾經獲得如黃祉賢和周寶靈女士等獨唱者的寶貴幫助。男聲獨唱方面，十年來共有二十位，今晚演出的陳供生團員，業已擔任了八個音樂會的獨唱了。此外，擔任了七次的，有羅拔‧域查君；三次或三次以上的有何君靜、陳定國和楊毓智君。

聖樂團十年來舉行的音樂會中，約有一半是由樂隊伴奏的。在這方面，計普歌管絃樂團三次，華南管絃樂團和香港管絃樂團各兩次，華南小管絃樂團一次。今晚很高興和榮幸能在香港管絃樂團的伴奏下演唱。

聖樂團於十年前由一小撮愛好音樂人士創辦。他們相信本港市民喜歡「神曲」演唱。本團由微小的開端，發展為擁有數十位團員的合唱團。但是現在最急需的仍是增加人數，我們因此籲請全港的歌唱人士加入本團。十年的「神曲」演唱已令許多團員獲得豐富的經驗。由創辦迄今仍然出席演唱的團員大有人在。歷年以來已由盈千盈萬的人士欣賞過我們的音樂會。在技巧方面，我們不能自詡於職業歌唱家之林。我們只是愛好歌唱。並盼本團與樂隊今晚演出這首宏偉莊嚴，照耀古今的作品時，能予閣下深刻印象，從而樂於欣賞我們下次的音樂會。

我們深信「神曲」的美妙音樂常能帶給人們很大的喜悅。

— 2 —

（場刊）

香港合唱光輝一頁

陳浩才

前晚（星期二）香港聖樂團在大會堂，十五位樂隊隊員，兩位鍵盤樂器件奏者及四位獨唱者剛好超出一百的不朽傑作「彌賽亞」。為五月以來最熱鬧的一場音樂會打破了紀錄，不過論效果更大數字。論人數之多，這並不是一項的演出要好，因為每個人在指揮領導下，均在狀態中，正所謂貴情不貴多。就以伴奏樂隊為例，指揮著

香港聖樂團這次演出陣容相當大的階段，將成為本港樂壇史中光輝的一頁。

使香港合唱事業邁進到一個新和給留下最深的印象，當晚的演出往不得不到應有效果，反而影响本港樂隊在中穿聽到的細膩，而氣氛和整個演出，純用弦樂隊，加上電風琴和鋼琴（作古鍵琴用）補足容易控制而有把握得多。事實上當晚雖然器樂伴奏部份只有十五人，卻有

本港各合唱團體演唱「彌賽亞」不下數十次，就香港聖樂團本身已經是最大，但以這一次最令人滿意，往不只成為該聖樂團成立以來最勤人的一次演出，在本地合唱音樂會中像如此成功的亦屬罕見，足証本博士名下，在指揮方面的確有卓越的成績。

只選用弦樂隊（另加一必要的小號獨奏）而避免用銅管樂實屬明智之舉，過往樂隊伴奏，銅管樂部份往效能，就這首田園交响曲而論，是本港樂隊的襯托，加上電風氛圍的演奏。合唱部份是成績最突出，黃永熙的指揮熟練而有效，在技術上可以說沒有多大瑕疵。解決技份誇張，聽來不很自然。

，單就合唱團員已有八十人，另加十分均衡的音响效果和襯托出樂曲所需要的氣氛，為不常聽到的成功的器樂伴奏，這當然要歸功於指揮性，要達到這般境界，非有高深的安排和領導。

樂隊奏前奏曲，已給人一個清新的印象，管樂組的音响效果甚佳，可能是剛開始情緒未安定，在節奏方面還可以扣得較緊湊，這方面

其為欣賞他對「彌賽亞」的處理手細膩，含蓄，平淡中蘊藏動人的戲追求表面戲劇化效養是辦不到的。並不難，（過去幾年校際音樂節後請外來評判員客串指揮本港合唱團，那位先生都有製造緊張潮的本領，經具刺激性，而缺乏人力量）但要做到配合整首樂曲統一性就要講功夫了。

各聲部的發展輕重恰到好處，不同條不只清晰，且連接得優美，不妙的效果。比較上來說當晚四位獨情的樂句，巧妙地融和在一起，的成績顯得較弱，主要是音量不足不過伴奏方面有細緻的襯托，幫了不少忙，陳供生在唱這齣歌劇方面有出色的表現，但在演唱這類歌劇卻嫌

《星島晚報》

Ella Kiang, soprano

Lin Siang-yuen, tenor

Lee Bing, mezzo soprano

Malcolm Barnett, bass

The Requiem Mass in C Minor by Luigi Cheribini and Stabat Mater by Rossini will be sung by the Hong-kong Oratorio Society in a concert at City Hall next Saturday.

Seventy members of the society—now 13 years old —will take part in the concert (starting at 8 pm).

The works chosen have not been performed before in Hongkong.

Choir of 70 will present concert

Both are undisputed masterpieces and have been immensely popular with concertgoers for over a century.

In the words of Dr Noren, the society's vice-chairman: "It is good solid music—not Sunday school choir stuff and this choir is capable of it."

Wong Wing-hee will conduct and the soloists will be Ella Kiang (soprano), Lee Bing (mezzo soprano), Lin Siang-yuen (tenor) and Malcolm Barnett (bass).

The society is a non-profit-making organisation. It was founded by a group of music-lovers who believed that oratorio singing was both delightful to listen to and highly enjoyable to participate in.

Members come from all sections of the community — schoolteachers, civil servants, company executives, and social workers.

"Anyone" says Dr Noren "is welcome to join us, regardless of age, nationality or creed — the only qualification is to want to sing oratorios."

CITY HALL
Choral works applauded

BY S.C.M. POST MUSIC CRITIC

THE Hongkong Oratorio Society presented two choral works not previously performed in Hongkong and were warmly applauded by a large audience at the City Hall Concert Hall on Saturday.

Dr Wong Wing-hee, conductor, has been instrumental in not only improving the standard of the singing immensely but also has introduced new works of interest enlarging the repertoire rehearsed and performed in public. Dr Wong conducts with authority and precision, and his choice of tempi is good and he obtains from the choir and the accompanying orchestra a cleanness of attack and a co-ordination which indicates careful rehearsals together. This was evident in the two works presented — Cherubini's "Requiem in C major," and Rossini's "Stabat Mater."

THERE were many well played sections, and Mr Frank Huang leading the cellists played some attractive solo and accompanying passages.

The tone of the choir was for the most very good especially in the latter part of the "Dies Irae" and the concluding "Agnus Dei." Contrasts of tone and the range of dynamics were perhaps a little limited and influenced by the volume of tone of the accompanying orchestra. It was altogether a very creditable and enjoyable performance.

Rossini's dramatic and opera-like setting of the "Stabat Mater" featured Ella Kiang, soprano, Lee Bing, mezzo soprano, Lin Siang-yuen, tenor, and Malcolm Barnett, bass; a newcomer to the Hong-kong's concert stage.

Miss Kiang and Mr Lin star in opera productions each year and are fully experienced singers. They combine well together and give pleasure whenever they sing.

THE melodic settings of the soprano and tenor arias and the dramatic style of the solos suited these singers perfectly, although one could always quarrel with Rossini's approach to the religious text and his treatment of it as a composer.

Lee Bing's lovely mezzo voice was heard to advantage in the Cavatina and she and Miss Kiang sang beautifully the duet "Qui est homo."

Malcolm Barnett rose well to the demands of the solos. Although he did not, being an amateur and much less experienced than the other three fully trained and professional full-time musicians, match them in resonance or skilful projection, his voice nonetheless had an attractive quality.

The performance was a credit to our veteran Choral Society both for presenting new works and for reaching an over-all standard of merit for a local group of singers composed of very busy and active people of many professions and nationalities.

《南華早報》

1972

200 voices in Verdi mass

Times-Journal Nov. 23/72

Verdi's immortal masterpiece, the Manzoni Requiem, will be presented for the first time in the Philippines after almost a century of its last premiere in Italy.

This liturgical mass will be sung jointly by a chorus of 200 representing 33 church choirs from Chorale Philippines and complemented by the visiting Hongkong Oratorio Society. Gala performances will be on Nov. 25-26, at 6:30 p.m. at the Cultural Center of the Philippines.

Featured soloists are Conching Rosal, soprano; Kathy Sternberg, mezzo-soprano; Francisco Asenie-ro, tenor; and Noel Velasco, bass.

Dr. David Yap of Chorale Philippines and Dr. Wing-Hee Heyward Wong of Hongkong Oratorio Society will separately conduct the chorus under the accompaniment of the Manila Symphony Orchestra.

The 'Manzoni' Requiem is one of the most difficult and challenging pieces ever written by the renowned composer Verdi. Divided into seven parts, it opens with a suppliant Requiem and Kyrie into a tumultuous Tuba mirum, followed by a fugue for a double chorus in Sanctus, and ends with a melancholic Libera me.

Times Journal (Philippines)

1974

The voice of excellence

The Oratorio Society, one of our very active local choral groups, gave a performance of "The Seasons" by Haydn in the Concert Hall on Saturday evening, presented jointly with the Urban Council.

A large audience attested to the popularity of the society's performances and the large membership that it attracts. Performances have been given regularly, and many works have been presented. Rehearsals go on through the year.

Saturday's performance was conducted by Dr Wong Wing-hee. The large chorus has an international membership and although women members are in the majority, the male voices section was strong and balance was good.

The lovely melodies of "The Seasons" make it an attractive work of appeal to most tastes. The chorus, well trained and disciplined and very responsive to the conductor's direction, sang well throughout and with outstanding excellence in several selections.

The soloists were Lola Young, singing the part of "Jane," Michael Ryan the role of "Lucas", and Timothy Yung that of "Simon." The trio of soloists were heard to advantage in the concluding selection with the chorus of "Summer" – in "The gloomy clouds now fast disperse."

Michael Ryan was the outstanding soloist, singing with confidence and a good range of colour and with excellent diction.

Accompaniment was provided by Evelyn Lee at the piano, with the major burden of the exacting accompaniment for the chorus and soloists on Wong Kin-yu, at the organ, Richard Gamlen, Kim Kee-sun, Margaret Lynn and Peter Johnson, French horns and trumpets, and Sheila Lai, timpani. Lack of rehearsal time with the singers probably accounted for the insecurity of intonation and rhythmic co-ordination.

Some particularly enjoyable selections were the duet sung by Lola Young and Michael Ryan in "Autumn," the air by Timothy Yung in "Spring", and the air by Michael Ryan in "Winter." Soloists and chorus and accompanying musicians ended the evening's music with a triumphant outpouring of sound in the concluding Trio and Double Chorus. The Oratorio Society can list another performance that was attended and enjoyed by many members of the community.

《南華早報》

1975

EASTER SUNDAY, March 30, 1975 Page 15 創刊號 第十五版 一九七五年三月三十日復活節

歡迎香港聖樂團訪菲獻唱

香港聖樂團全體團員及樂隊合影，今明兩晚在菲文化中心獻唱

神曲「以利亞」獻唱秩序

引嗣（男中音）	站在以色列的主上帝前
序曲	
合唱	求主救助
女高音，女低音二重唱及合唱	求主垂聽
男高音誦詠	你們要革心改過
男高音獨唱	你們若誠心求我
合唱	但是主見不到你們悔改
女低音誦詠	以利亞，要離開這裡
女低音誦詠	藏在基立溪旁
女高音，男中音誦詠	我要怎樣做？
男中音誦詠	把妳兒子給我
男中音誦詠及合唱	我站在安息日的主前
合唱	巴力，我們呼喚你！
男中音誦詠	大聲求告吧，因爲他是神！
合唱	巴力，我們呼喚你！
男中音誦詠	大聲求告吧，因爲他是神！
合唱	巴力，我們呼喚你！
男中音誦詠及獨唱	你們到我這裡來
合唱	把重擔交給主
男中音誦詠	主呀，祢差遣天使
合唱	降下火來
男中音獨唱	祂所說的如火之熾熱
女低音獨唱	災禍降於捨棄祂的人們
男高音誦詠	衆人的上帝，助祢的子民！
男中音誦詠及青年及合唱	主呀，祢已把仇敵推倒
合唱	感謝上帝

——（休息）——

女高音獨唱	以色列呀，聽主所說
合唱	不用恐慌
男高音及男中音誦詠	神人哪
男中音獨唱	求取我命
男高音誦詠	看呀，他躺在羅騰樹下睡着了
女聲三重唱	舉目仰視
合唱	祂看顧着以色列
女低音誦詠	起來！以利亞
女低音獨唱	在主中休息
合唱	忍耐到底的必得救
男中音誦詠	循途而去
男中音獨唱	羣山將離去
合唱	以利亞於是如火般衝前
男高音獨唱	公義的人們必將顯照
合唱	祢的光輝必然照射

香港聖樂團組織百人合唱隊訪菲

今明晚在文化中心獻唱神曲『以利亞』

黃永熙博士指揮・星期一增加一場在靈惠基督教會與華僑青年合唱・

黃永熙博士

香港聖樂團（HONG KONG ORATORIO SOCIETY）創立於一九五六年，迄今廿載於茲。團員多係香港各教會聖樂團領導人物、宣教師、及各教會學校教師學生，經過嚴格的甄選和精密的訓練之後，始予錄取。因香港「華洋雜處」的特殊環境，團員的國籍和職業，頗爲複雜，國籍有英、美、加、瑞士、中國等，職業有教師、牧師、律師、醫生、牙醫、議士、會計師、工程師、政府人員、商人、學生……等；然而他們喜愛音樂，嗜好歌唱，近二十年來，每週舉行練習演唱，並積極攻研神曲（ORATORIO）從不中斷，每年至少舉行二次以上之公開演唱會，此外並常在電視，無線廣播電台，教堂，學校及其他公共場所爲公益事業舉行義唱。舉凡歷來名家所作名曲，幾乎皆經演唱，是以其精深嫻熟之程度，可想而知。

該團組織伊始，由黃明東擔任指揮，後黃君留美深造，先後由DR. GEORGE WILSON, 與JAMES McKINLEY擔任指揮，迨一九六七年黃永熙博士由美來港應聘擔任該團指揮，迄今幾經十載。查黃博士早年在滬，即已揚譽樂壇，且曾長期與陳明勳教授合作，負責歌劇配音指揮工作，並常客串指揮上海國際租界交響樂隊。其後留美，獲得哥倫比亞大學音樂博士學位。回港後主持普天頌讚改編事資，並創作樂曲多闋。除十年來義務指揮香港聖樂團外，並執教崇基學院（即香港中文大學），一九七二年膺任東南亞基督教聖樂促進會理事長，連任至今。同年復應菲律濱合唱團（CHORA-LE PHILIPPINES）之請，來岷客串指揮，由馬尼拉交響樂隊伴奏之一百五十人大合唱團，演唱凡第名歌「安之思曲」VERIS REQUIEM，極獲好評。

此次演唱「以利亞」神曲負責獨唱之菲籍歌唱家，皆係知名之仕，其中尤以CONSTATINO BERNARDEZ及FRANCISCO ASENIERO曾兩度應香港聖樂團之聘，前往香港，由香港政府主催該團公開演唱會，獻唱神曲「以利亞」及「參孫」之獨唱部份，博得香港人仕極高評價，是以此次香港聖樂團報聘菲島，仍請此二位歌唱家擔任男音獨唱節目，另請IRMA ENRILE及ER LINDA DALANAY ASCUNA擔任女音獨唱節目，配以文化中心交響樂隊之伴奏，藉謀促進港菲二埠之音樂界更形密切之交誼及合作。

鑒於此次演唱會規模之盛大，及陣容之強壯，係前所未見，菲華基督教會關心促進聖樂人仕，特此推擧由大岷區全體教會所支持之青年福音社，小雅歌合唱團，雅歌團契及東南亞基督教聖樂促進會菲島分會聯合主催此次一連二晚之獻唱會。

四月一日晚特別增加一場，在靈惠基督教會，該團與華僑各教會詩班青年合唱名歌三闋。

ACKNOWLEDGEMENT

The ECHOETTES acknowledge gratefully the generous contributions of the following advertisers which made the publication of this program possible:

THE GOSPEL PUBLICATIONS, INC. MALINTA STEEL PRODUCTS CORP.
Uy Se Kua Trading Ling Nam Wanton Parlor & Noodle Factory
Southern Sawmill, Inc. Jubilee Merchandising

《福音週報》

HONG KONG ORATORIO 100-VOICE CHOIR TO SING TONITE
Dr. Heyward Wong will conduct at CCP

4 RP SOLOISTS WILL TAKE PART

The Youth Gospel Center of the Philippine, the Echo Fellowship, South East Asia Sacred Music Promotion Society and the Echoettes are going to present the Hong Kong Oratorio Society Choir tonight at the Philippine Cultural Center. The visiting team is going to perform twice, March 30th and 31st, both to start at 7:30 p.m. Four outstanding Filipino soloists are also invited to take part in the program. Dr. Heyward Wong, an international well known conductor will direct the concert which will be accompanied by the Cultural Center Orchestra.

The Hong Kong Oratorio Society was formed in 1956. Its purpose has been to perform major choral works, primarily from the religious repertoire. International in character, the oratorio society numbers about 100 voices. Currently the membership has reached a total of 130 singers. These members meet every week throughout most of the year for regular rehearsals. Membership is determined by a simple audition with the conductor. Those who join the society represent many professions — students, church choir members, music teachers, pastors, medical personnel, solicitors, clerks and so forth. There are a number of couples in the choir, sometimes there are two generations of a family represented in the choir, showing that the common love of music is one effective bridge between the generations.

The Oratorio Society is governed by an annually elected committee of eight officers. The present committee officers are: Mr. Mervyn Loie — Chairman; Dr. Enoch C. M. Young — Vice chairman and Membership Secretary; Mr. Benjamin Chong — Treasurer; Miss Ingrid Chan — Secretary; Mr. Alex Cheung Man — Concert Manager; Mrs. Sara Brain — Public Relations officer; Rev. Thomas Lung — Librarian/Historian; and Mr. Peter Liang — General Affairs Officer. Honorary President, Mr. Chu Man Wai, the regular accompanist Miss Evelyn Lee, and the associate conductor Mr. Frank Huang are also members of the governing body.

Each year the Oratorio Society averages two major concerts. In addition there is a regular Christmas concert plus TV appearances at Easter and Christmas.

The Hong Kong Oratorio Society's first concert in 1956, conducted by Mr. Theodore Huang, featured compositions by Handel. Brahms and Beethoven. Since then the society has sung many of the familiar works of well known composers and introduced a number of lesser known composers and their compositions.

Contemporary music has also been represented in the Oratorio Society's concerts. They have presented Randall Thompson's "The Peaceable Kingdom," Alan Hohvahnes' "Transfiguration" and most recently, T.

Charles Lee's "Farewell Voyager."

In 1970, the Hong Kong Oratorio Society celebrated the bi-centenary of Beethoven by giving three performances of "Missa Solembis." These concerts were a joint presentation with the Hong Kong Philharmonic Orchestra.

The fifteenth anniversary of the formation of the Oratorio Society, celebrated in 1971, was celebrated by performing Handel's "Israel in Egypt." This was a joint presentation with the Chung Chi College Choir of the Chinese University of Hong Kong.

On the 27th of May 1972, for the first time in history of the Hong Kong Oratorio Society, it premiered a work by the contemporary American composer, Dr. T. Charles Lee.

The composer conducted the performances.

Late in 1972, the Oratorio Society's conductor, Dr. Heyward Wong, together with a delegation of its singers, joined the Chorale Philippines and their conductor Mr. David Yap in a presentation of Verdi's "Requiem." This was accompanied by the Manila Symphony Orchestra. Mr. David Yap conducted the first presentation and Dr. Heyward Wong conducted the second.

During 1975 the Hong Kong Oratorio Society is preparing to present three major works: Mendelssohn's "Elijah" in March, Haydn's "The Creation" in July, and Bach's "B Minor Mass" in October. The concert will be in Manila, while the July and October concerts will be in Hong Kong.

HONG KONG ORATORIO SOCIETY

OFFICERS AND SINGERS

Hon. President	Mr. Chu Man Wai
Conductors:	Dr. W. Heyward Wong
	Mr. Frank Huang
Accompanist:	Miss Evelyn Lee

EXECUTIVE COMMITTEE

Chairman:	Mr. Mervyn Y. K. Loie
Vice Chairman:	Dr. Enoch Young
Hon. Secretary:	Miss Ingrid Chan
Hon. Treasurer:	Mr. Benjamin Chong
Public Relations Officer:	Mrs. Sara Brain
Concert Manager:	Mr. Alex Cheung Man
Librarian & Historian:	Rev. Thomas W. Lung
General Affairs Officer:	Mr. Peter Liang

Sopranos

Chan, Christina
Chan, Ingrid
Chan, Linda Pi-wan
Chan, Pak Chun
Chan, Penelope
Cheng, Betty To Chuen
Cheng, Helen
Cheng, Pauline
Cheng, Stella
Chiu, Fausta Lai Kwan
Choi, Chi Lan
Chung, Esther
Fong, Yok Ying Grace
Ha, Lai Ying Katherine
Fung, Esther
Heisler, Mary Kaye
Holden, Jean
Hsu, Wen Ling Belinda
Hui, Lai Yue
Lee, Kwan Fong Miriam
*Lew Ko, Milly
Lin, Oi Che
Liu, Grace
Lo, Shiu Kwong Jean
Ng, May Yan
Tam, Wai Wah Elizabeth
Tso Ho, Fung Yee
Wang, Louisa
Wong, Alice
Wong, Doris
Yuen, Yuk Che

Contraltos

Au Yeung, Tung Yi
Brain, Sara
Chan, Yeuk Ying
Cockell, June
Craster, Olivia
Fung, Betty
Gates, Constance
Ho, Yue Sang Lorna
Jasper, Joan Helen
Lam, Kwok Heung Grace
Lee, Dorothy
Lee, Evelyn
Lee, Chiu Yee Grace
Leung, Patricia
Lo, Anita
Ma, Pearl
Ng, Cynthia
Tam, Connie
Wells, Cathy
Wilson, J.
Wong, Angela
Wong, Winnie
Wu Lo, Lang Mui
Yau, Fung Kiu
Yeung, Chan Pui Wah
Yeung, Chiu Wah
*Moberly, Sara

Tenors

Bonner, S. E.
Cheung, Man
Fu, Raymond
Ho, Wai Keung Daniel
Karsen, Wendell
Lew, C. P. David
Lung, Thomas S.
Po, Sum Cho
Tong, Peter
Tsang, Kenneth
*Tso, Kai Yip
Wang, Kenneth
Wong, Tit Foo
Yip, Chi Kwong Kenneth
Yu, Hung Yung Henry

Basses

Au, Clement
Chan, Shou Shun
Chan, Yam Yim Peter
Cheng, Charles
Cheng, Dennis
Cheng, Si Sing Samson
Chong, Benjamin
Chu, Man Wai
Chung, Daniel
Geisler, Herbert
Kwok, Hin Yeung Frank
Liang, Peter
Loie, Y. K. Mervyn
Man, Franken
Noren, Loren, E.
So, Shing Yit Eric
Yan, Timothy
Yeung, Wan Tin
Young, Enoch
Yung, Sit Tat Ricky

Four RP Outstanding Soloists

Constantino E. Bernadez
Baritone

Francisco C. Asienlero, Jr.
Tenor

Irma Ponce Enrile
Potenciano
Soprano

Erlinda Dacunay Ascuna
Contralto

Works presented by the HONG KONG ORATORIO SOCIETY from 1956-1974

1. J. S. BACH:
   St. John Passion
2. L. BEETHOVEN:
   Choral Fantasia
   Mass in C
   Mount of Olives
   Missa Solemnis in D
   Symphony No. 9
   "Choral"
3. J. BRAHMS:
   Requiem
   Song of Fate
4. L. CHERUBINI:
   Requiem in C Minor
5. A. R. GAUL:
   Holy City
6. G. F. HANDEL:
   The Messiah
   Samson
   Judas Maccabaeus
   Israel in Egypt
   Acis and Galatea
7. J. HAYD:
   The Seasons
   The Creation
8. A. HOHVAHNESS:
   Transfiguration
9. T. C. LEE:
   Farewell Voyager
10. F. MENDELSSOHN:
    St. Paul
    Elijah
    Hymn of Praise
11. W. A. MOZART:
    Requiem Mass
    Twelfth Mass
12. F. PFAUTSCH:
    A Time for Dancing
13. G. ROSSINI:
    Stabat Mater
14. SAINT-SAENS:
    Christmas Oratorio
15. F. SCHUBERT:
    Scnf of Miriam
    Mass in G
16. H. SCHUTZ:
    The Seven Words of
    Christ on the
    Cross
17. R. THOMPSON:
    The Peaceable
    Kingdom

《福音週報》

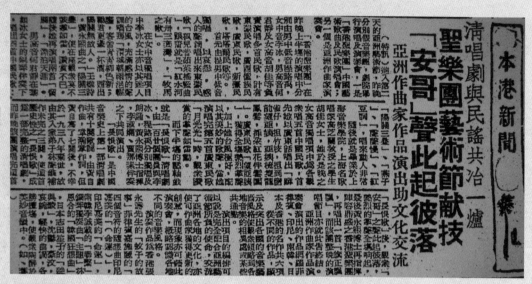

清唱劇與民謠共冶一爐
聖樂團藝術節獻技
「安哥」聲此起彼落
亞洲作曲家作品演出助文化交流

本港新聞　樂

《華僑日報》

香港聖樂團參加藝術節演出
團員連日加緊排練
與蘇格蘭樂團合演 吉隆修士之夢

《華僑日報》

Message from the Chairman

The Hong Kong Oratorio Society was founded 21 years ago by a group of music lovers who believed that oratorio singing was a great joy and were convinced that their conviction should be shared by the people of Hong Kong. Since then the Society has presented public concerts regularly at various concert auditoria. In recent years it held many joint concerts with the Hong Kong Philharmonic Orchestra in the City Hall. The Society also gives radio and televised performances during Easter and Christmas seasons. Early this year it assumed an important role in the Hong Kong Arts Festival by joining the Scottish BBC Symphony Orchestra in performing Elgar's Dream of Gerontius. Next year with the Bournemouth Symphony Orchestra it will present the immortal Faure Requiem.

In 1975 the Society gave a series of concerts at the Cultural Centre in Manila and was acclaimed by local music critics as one of the best choirs in Asia. Although not lacking in overseas invitations, we, as amateur choralists with a regular job, find it difficult to fit into our sponsors' schedule. Thus we have in the past turned down many attractive concert offers which is a great pity. Indeed it is most fortunate that we are able to present Haydn's Seasons early next year with the Taipei Municipal Orchestra to celebrate Taiwan's first Sacred Music Festival at the newly constructed Sun Yat Sen Memorial Hall with a 2,500 seating capacity.

The purpose of this concert to-night is to let you, our good friends and connoisseurs throughout all these years, to further support our cause to promote interflow of culture with other parts of the world. The proceeds of ticket sales will be used entirely to subsidize our forthcoming overseas concert tour next year and the participation of all the soloists and accompanists in this vocal recital is most gratefully acknowledged.

CHARLES CHENG

（場刊）

獻　辭

　　香港聖樂團於廿一年前由一群熱愛音樂人士所創立。他們深信聖樂的演唱，能帶來極大的喜樂，更堅信應該把喜樂與本港人士分享。聖樂團自創立以來，不斷舉行盛大的演唱，迄今所演唱的神曲和大合唱巨構，已超過四十齣。近年更會同香港管弦樂團在大會堂音樂廳舉行音樂會，演唱許多不朽的作品。此外，本團每逢聖誕節或復活節，常担任電台或電視台節目。本年初，本團聯同蘇格蘭英國廣播電台交响樂團演唱艾爾加的「吉隆修士之夢」，被譽爲香港藝術節巔峯之作。明年藝術節，將與英國樸恩茅斯交响樂團聯合演唱另一大合唱作品——「浮理安禮頌」。

　　一九七五年，聖樂團遠赴馬尼拉，在該市文化中心作一連串之演唱，備受當地音樂界推許爲亞洲最佳合唱團之一。近年來多次接獲海外音樂團體的邀請，惜團員盡屬業餘人士，因職業關係無法抽身。幸而有志竟成，現已定於明春應邀赴台北會同台北市立交响樂團演唱海頓「四季頌」。此次旅行演唱，規模頗大，現正在積極籌備中。今晚的音樂會，旨在讓公衆人士欣賞個別團友獨唱。全場收入，用以貼助來春旅行演唱費用。本人對各位獨唱及伴奏者的熱烈支助，謹致萬二分的謝意。

主席　鄭崇羔

（場刊）

ABOVE: The Hongkong Oratorio Society in performance.
BELOW: Dr Wong ... trying to improve the standard of church music.

Singing diplomats strike a chord

JUST before President Ronald Reagan made his debut in China with his 600-strong retinue, a small group of 60 from Hongkong arrived in Peking, marking another unprecedented venture — not in speeches this time but in song.

The Hongkong Oratorio Society, the first choral group from Hongkong to be invited to perform in China, gave two performances of Haydn's *The Seasons* in Peking's best concert hall over the Easter weekend.

"It was quite a prestigious thing for us to go over there to perform," said Dr Wong Wai-hei, the choir's principal conductor for the past 17 years.

"Most of the overseas groups performing there are world famous, for instance, the Berlin Philharmonic and Boston Symphony Orchestra.

From all accounts, however, our musical ambassadors were received with great enthusiasm by the audience of more than 2,000 and made something of a cultural coup in proving the ability of an amateur choral group.

"The standard of singing is very high in China," explained Dr Wong. "But there are very few amateur choral groups. Most of the large choirs belong to professional dance and opera companies and consist of people who are expected to sing and who seldom respond to large choral works or to the wide repertoire of choral music."

The Hongkong Oratorio Society could n't have been a better choice to introduce this kind of music to China. Established in 1956, it is one of Hongkong's oldest and certainly one of the (if not the) best amateur choral groups here.

Its membership of about 150 singers, who come from a wide variety of different professions, meet every week throughout most of the year and give regular performances.

Since its formation, the society has performed more than 40 oratorios and choral works by both classical and contemporary composers — many of the works were introduced to Hongkong audiences for the first time.

And they have already demonstrated their talents overseas on several occasions, in the Philippines in 1975, in Taiwan in 1978 and in Singapore last year.

Leading the society through its many successful performances has been the highly respected Dr Wong.

Although an engineer by profession, Dr Wong has been an active musician since the 1930s in Shanghai where he served as associate conductor of the Chinese Music Drama and conductor and director of the Shanghai Music and Symphony Orchestra and conductor of several different choral groups.

His move to America in 1947 and the subsequent 20 years there did nothing to curb his musical interest. Practising as an engineer by day, he studied by night for his doctorate in music and musical education from Columbia University and refined his conducting skills by studying under the renowned conductor, the late Pierre Monteux.

Not surprisingly, therefore, when he returned to Hongkong in 1967, he was immediately invited to become the Oratorio Society's principal conductor.

For not only is Dr Wong a dedicated musician. He is also a dedicated Christian, with a profound appreciation for sacred music, its significance and spiritual influence.

Indeed, the appreciation of such music and its use in churches is something Dr Wong has been trying to promote for many years.

As the president of the Chinese Church Music Association since its inception in 1972 and chairman of the Chinese Christian Churches Union, Dr Wong has been one of the most active contributors, not only in Hongkong but throughout the region, in the field of church music.

"On the activities side, we're planning a kind of choir festival in which various choirs can get together," he said. "We'll use about 10 or 15 conductors to conduct one chorus each and about the same number of soloists. It'll be an occasion for everybody to enjoy themselves.

"The whole idea of these get-togethers with all sacred music is not, of course, Dr Wong's intention. Rather, it is to encourage an enjoyment of both its musical and spiritual qualities in a way that enhances its significance.

"Besides the religious aspect and the quality of the music are very important to me," he revealed. "I believe music has great importance in the church.

"There are two aspects to the project: training and activities," said Dr Wong. The training part offers elementary and advanced courses for the use of improved song services with the aim of improving not only individual standards but also

the methods of working together between conductors and accompanists.

"We're also offering courses for choir members — a series of 12 workshops lasting three months in four different places. The Church of Christ in China is subsidising the courses for its 30-odd churches in Hongkong but the courses are open to anyone, for any church, so we're hoping that people from many different denominations will take part.

We're also planning to hold a Messiah programme — a 20-minute programme this year.

We're also planning to hold a Messiah Sing-in at the Methodist Church in Kowloon on December 16.

"That's going to be a chance for anyone who is interested to join in. We'll use about 10 or 15 conductors to conduct one chorus each and about the same number of soloist. It'll be an occasion for everybody to enjoy themselves.

As part of these efforts, Dr Wong has recently embarked on a two-year project, supported by the Church of Christ in China through its Hongkong Council, to help churches in Hongkong develop a

Anglican, and so on — are busy from beginning to end. The Presbyterian and Methodist church use rather less and the free church, such as Baptist and Christian Alliance, place very little emphasis on music as part of the ceremony.

"But what we'll be trying to do with these courses is to try to educate those who belong to the free church philosophy to the liturgical church tradition of using music, and, above all, emphasising the importance of reaching a high standard of musical performance — however much music is used."

Another major effort in Dr Wong's campaign will be a Church Music Summer Camp to be held in Hongkong in July — a similar one held two years ago proved to be a great success with over 150 people attending.

And on the regional front, in the same month Dr Wong will be presiding over the Chinese Church Music Association's bi-annual convention (this time to be held in the Philippines) which seeks to work from countries around the region will be given on the progress of improving the standards of church music.

Dr Wong is optimistic that all these activities will result in greater awareness of and appreciation for sacred music.

"Sacred music has been very neglected here in the past," he said. "But now, I think, we can see an improvement."

He is far too modest a man to claim any credit for the improvement, but appreciation of sacred music in Hongkong through the performances of the Hong-kong Oratorio Society — and, far too tactful to suggest that the power of the Christian religion may spread with an audiences through the society's dedicated singing.

But in his own way, like his grandfather who 85 years ago was the first preacher to go to the British-leased New Territories to spread the gospel, travelling on foot from village to village, Dr Wong is a missionary — not with speeches but also with song.

By JULIA WILKINSON

《南華早報》

香港聖樂團訪星載譽歸

香港聖樂團應新加坡邀請，前往當地演唱，受到有關方面熱烈歡迎，他們不但獻出文化藝術果實，還留下了一份珍貴的友誼。

據聖樂團男高音王帆指出，這六天行程充滿了歡欣和愉快，因爲受到主辦單位各方面熱誠招待，使這次演出一切順利，而且成功。

他說：雖然在新春期間，新加坡人有些日在家中團聚，不過，可以容納三千多人的新加坡國家劇場絕不冷落，反應非常熱烈。

他補充說，揮灑自如。

當晚演唱，對於音響設備各人部不大習慣；同時三十多度的高溫亦使人難受，但各人的演唱情緒並沒有受到影響。他特別指出，最可敬的是指揮黃永熙博士，他在這個沒有冷氣設備的劇場裡，要穿着筆挺的禮服，站在指揮台上，揮汗如雨。然而指揮若定。

香港聖樂團這六天行程安排爲：二月十四日，第一批團員在港啓程。十五日，在星出席記者招待會及接受各有關單位歡迎。十六日，接受招待遊覽名勝古跡，遊罷馬來亞的第二批團員到達。十七日，新加坡國家劇場演唱。十八日，研討會和應邀出席盛筵。十九日，乘搭航機返港。

香港聖樂團此次演唱海頓的神曲「四季頌」。指揮：黃永熙博士，獨唱女高音馮志量、男高音王帆、男低音陳晃相，團員六十餘衆。連同家眷老少合百多人。

發言人表示，選唱「四季頌」甚因爲該曲的宗教色彩不很濃厚，以適應當地人士。

王帆稱，新加坡人不祇熱烈歡迎我多人分兩批出發，首批先去馬來亞遊玩，但有關人等都不辭勞苦，分批接機。我們一踏出機艙，橫在眼前的是「歡迎香港聖樂團」的橫額。稍後，跟着就獻上花束。這個花園城市的氣溫雖然很高，但我們的情緒更高。

他們被安排在大中酒店下榻，這是一家有泳池設備的酒店，喜愛游泳的團員們笑開了。

他繼續說，我們除了得到理想的膳宿外，還遊覽了中國花園、日本花園，主辦機構招待豐盛的自助餐，在辛辣的食物中拌和着一份隆情厚意。

而聖陶沙島由於較早時發生慘劇，我們改用遊覽船遊光，至今不忘。唱演過後，主辦機構招待豐盛的自助餐。

・馮杞安・

《晶報》

CHONG WING HONG reviews The Seasons by Haydn, an oratorio by the Hongkong Oratorio Society to commemorate the 15th anniversary of the National Theatre Club.

It's a lean season for HK singers

JUDGING by the attendance, the presentation of Haydn's oratorio, The Seasons, at the National Theatre last Thursday could hardly be called a success.

Only about one-third of the theatre was filled, mainly the cheaper seats at the back.

When news of the performance was first heard, the initial reaction of several of my music-loving friends was ... an oratorio where?

They all felt the inappropriateness of listening to a serious vocal concert with notes sung through the loudspeakers in an open-air theatre.

Dr Wong Wing Hee, conductor of the Hongkong Oratorio Society which performed The Seasons, said this was the first time the choir had had to sing under such conditions.

could well be due to the price of the $2, $4, $6, $8 and $10 tickets — rather expensive considering that the guest performers were amateurs. After all, this is not much cheaper than what one usually pays for listening to professionals like the Singapore Symphony Orchestra and to air-conditioned comfort, too!

Perhaps more music fans would have been persuaded to attend had the tickets cost from $1 to $3, and if the performance had been held at the Victoria Concert Hall or the Singapore Conference Hall.

The choice of having the Hongkong Oratorio Society here to help celebrate National Theatre Club's 15th anniversary was, however, a fair one.

Why was an oratorio, a semi-dramatic choral work normally based on a sacred theme, chosen by a committee man of the organising committee, will be but expected a big audience as there are many churches in Singapore.

But Haydn's work, conductor Wong said, is esteemed for its musical, and not only religious, worth.

Dr Lee said the Lunar New Year festival was a distracting factor and the lack of press coverage helped account for the poor attendance.

Of the performance itself, the rendering of the oratorio over two hours and 15 minutes was smooth though rather colourless.

The choir, which has more than 60 members, failed to bring out the contrast between the loud and soft passages.

During rehearsal, the bass section felt much to be desired, and still did not make up for this in the evening's perform

rounded voice was marred by a lack of placing. He sounded inhibited in the soft phrases.

Soprano Esther Fung's voice was pleasant but rather thin. In most cases, it was drowned by the sound of the tenor.

Probably the best performance came from tenor Wong Fang, whose voice was lyrical. He hit the high notes with ease.

But one should remember the constraints under which the choir performed: an oratorio cannot be properly heard through the medium of amplifiers and speakers.

And full marks should be given to the choir for enthusiasm. The performers are amateurs — teachers, nurses, lecturers and a school principal. The pains which they took to prepare such a great choral

凡研究欧西音乐的人士，会知道正统音乐最初的发展也就是圣乐的发展。一般其他的作品，到了十七、十八世纪才开始抬头。因此最初一千多年来，西洋音乐史也就是圣乐史，许多音乐上的宝藏都是圣乐。历史上大音乐家的作品中总包括一些圣乐，并且这些圣乐作品常常是他们创作中的精华。

乐圣贝多芬一生当中写了许多不同类型的乐曲，可是他那首D大调庄严弥撒曲磅礴的气势却凌驾其他作品之上，有人说若不认识此曲，亦不会完全认识贝多芬。他这首曲子与巴赫的B小调弥撒曲并驾齐驱，各有千秋，被认为是有史以来所有音乐创作当中最出类拔萃的作品。

韩德尔最初是一位颇负盛名的歌剧作者，但是直到他把全部精神贯注在神剧(Oratorio)的写作后，才巩固他在音乐史上的重要地位。

大家都知道凡尔弟(Verdi)是一位著名的歌剧作曲家，可是他的安魂曲(Requiem)被认为是他最佳的作品。甚至有人说，这首安魂曲是他所写的「最佳的歌剧」。Grove 音乐大辞典有这样的一句话：「从纯粹艺术与音乐的观点来看这首安魂曲，这是凡尔弟最伟大的作品⋯⋯」为着篇幅关系，不能录下其他赞扬这曲的评语。

罗西尼(Rossini)也是一位著名的歌剧作者。当他卅九岁那年便完成了卅六龊歌剧，以后便停下来不再写作。很少人知道他在晚年时也写了一首「庄严弥撒曲」，甚至有些音乐辞典根本没有提起这首曲。可是本人认为罗西尼这首弥撒曲的作曲技巧与音乐意识比他以前所写的作品都高超。

歌剧、神剧或其他大型圣乐作品通常都采用独唱、重唱、大合唱及管弦乐。在歌剧里主要的角色都放在独唱者身上，合唱的地位是次要。此外，为了舞台环境关系，歌剧里的人数有限，合唱不能发挥太大的作用。并且在歌剧里的合唱部分不适宜于采用较复杂的复音乐（polyphony）形式，因此牵制了写作技巧的尽量运用。可是在圣乐作品里，通常合唱与独唱并重，甚至有时合唱的重要性反而在独唱之上，作曲家可以充份地发挥他的想像力和作曲技巧，而产生更满意的作品。

当一个作曲家写作圣乐时，歌词的内容会很自然地把他的心情引领到一个崇高的意境。韩德尔写作「弥赛亚」和海顿写作「创世记」时的虔敬和谦虚态度是众所周知的。以他们这种心态写出来的音乐和其他的音乐是有所不同。

许多人以为圣乐或一些与宗教有关的音乐只适合在教堂里演唱。其实许多大型的圣乐根本不可能在教堂里演出，因为教堂不可容纳庞大的合唱团及乐队。白辽士(Berlioz)所写的安魂曲注明要用数百人的合唱团，乐队要用上十六个定音鼓，另外有四班铜乐队分布在会场的四个角落。香港演唱这曲时是在体育馆里举行的，因为连音乐厅也不能容纳这样多的人。

香港圣乐团成立的目的是除了让团员有机会亲自欣赏这些乐曲之外，也希望把这些音乐创作的精华介绍给一般音乐爱好者。为着工作或其他关系，我们这次只有约三分之一的团员能来北京参加演出。况且这次也未能有管弦乐伴奏，实在是美中不足。但愿国内的音乐团体能多有机会演唱这些大型的乐曲，把这些音乐园地里的宝藏介绍出来，以公诸于同好。

指挥的话 黄永熙

（場刊）

1984

華僑文化

首個聖樂團赴北京演唱
甚獲好評奠下交流基礎
六十團員合唱海頓名作四季頌
台下報熱烈掌聲登台道賀者衆

四月二十一日晚上，香港聖樂團在北京民族文化宮舉行了一個盛大的音樂會，演唱十九世紀歐西大作曲家海頓的不朽作品「四季頌」。這次演出，使聖樂團成為本港樂壇有史以來第一個大音樂團體應中國文化部的邀請到北京表演，報名參加的團員六十餘名，攜同家屬數十人分批北上，在促進港京兩地文化交流上，稍盡綿力。

合唱團員中，佔大部份是外籍人士，中西合璧，洵屬一時佳話，演唱會指揮爲黃永熙博士。他在第二次世界大戰前早已蜚聲於上海音樂界，其後留美多年。一九六八年到香港接任聖樂團指揮，迄今逾十七載。近年來數度率領團員到東南亞各地演唱，旨在切磋藝術。

合唱團員中，有些是初次踏足中國。值茲花開如錦的季節，把這個北方大都的壯麗風光盡收眼底。另一些華人團員對祖國的河山，已涉足多次，但爲着這次演出，特地撥冗隨團出發。所表現的團體精神，至堪稱道。

「四季頌」是一首大型合奏作品，曲詞典雅，讚賞四時景色，如畫如詩。在北京的演唱會中，除合唱由全體團員担任外，女高音獨唱馮志麗，男高音獨唱王帆，俱屬香港聲樂界的出色人物，會在聖樂團的許多音樂會中担任獨唱角色。男中音獨唱，則由享譽北京歌劇和廣播界的聲樂家楊洪基担任。他的參與，象徵兩地音樂家的携手合作。伴奏方面，原已與北京中央樂團交响樂隊取得聯絡，惜該團須於四月間離京到國內各地巡迴演奏，故全曲伴奏，改用鋼琴兩具，由聖樂團兩名團員戚明儀、嚴賀潔彈奏。此外，更蒙中央音樂學院圓號演奏家和三名高足客串伴奏狩獵曲，使音樂會倍添光彩。

演唱會上演的地點民族文化宮，是北京首屈一指的音樂廳，外表具有巍峩的中國宮殿風格，內裏金碧輝煌，音响優美，場內座位共一千七百個。據聞只有達到國際水準的音樂家或團體，始有機會在此表演。

聖樂團這次演出，是由北京文化部中國對外演出公司安排地點和一切場務。當晚聽衆踴躍，座上有許多是首都音樂界的知音人士。他們對演出一致給予好評，熱烈的掌聲，使演唱者體會不虛此行。演出者謝幕後，文化部和中國對外演出公司的領導人紛紛登台道賀。聖樂團除獲餽贈巨型花籃外，每名演出團員都獲贈送紀念品。較早時由演出公司設午宴款待，席上觥籌交錯，賓主盡歡，公司經理宋成九頻頻舉杯祝賀，而北京的好幾位著名聲樂家，即席高歌助慶，聖樂團對一切優渥款待，至爲感紉。

這次旅行演唱，因事屬創舉，故籌備歷時甚久，聖樂團特成立籌備委員會悉力以赴。委員們既忙於通過有關機構與北京中國演出公司取得聯絡，也忙於向旅行社接洽團員和家屬的交通、住宿、膳食、遊覽。此外，更籌集款項，以資助學生團員和亟待帮助的團員。另一項重要工作是編印精美的場刊，攜帶到北京使用。

新華通訊社香港分行在聖樂團籌備這次演出中，担任穿針引綫工作，所賜鼎助，使人感銘。所謂「萬事起頭難」，盼這次赴京演唱，足以開音樂團體赴京表演的先河，替港京兩地文化交流奠立基礎。展望將來，美景無限。特記述此行，以留鴻爪。

香港聖樂團在北京留影。

3/5/84

星期四　大公報　農曆甲子年四月初三日　初五立夏　第五版

特稿

近日訪問北京的團體，多如過江之鯽，其中一個所負的使命，卻與政治完全無關，而是旨在切磋藝術，交流文化。它就是香港聖樂團，在復活節假期間，六十四名團員，攜同家眷數十人，應中國文化部的邀請，到北京民族文化宮演唱十九世紀歐西大作曲家海頓名作《四季頌》。

美好的回憶

——香港聖樂團北京演出會紀盛

聖樂團北京演唱籌委會主席　梁耀揚

合唱團員有相當高的音樂修養

香港聖樂團成立於一九五六年，現有合唱團員超過一百名，是全港歷史最悠久而人數最衆的合唱團。團員來自社會各種行業，以華人爲主，外籍團員爲數亦逾百分之四十，且來自許多國家。每名團員，都具有相當高的音樂修養，許多本身已是學校音樂導師、鋼琴教師、教堂或較小型音樂團體的指揮或獨唱者，入團以前，須經過考驗。自從一九七五年以來，聖樂團在首席指揮黃永熙博士率領下，多次遠赴東南亞各地演唱。這次到北京的演出，是最雄壯的嘗試，因爲這是第一個應邀訪京的大音樂團體，對香港和北京的文化交流，足以作很有價值的貢獻。

分批出發如期會合北京和演出

參加這次演唱的團員，除合唱團員外，還包括兩名獨唱者、兩名伴奏者和指揮黃永熙博士。由於每人工作環境和請假條件不同，而負擔旅費的能力亦有異，故往返港京兩地的旅行方式和出發日期，亦不一致，有雙程飛機的，也有一程飛機、一程火車的，但仍以來回俱乘搭火車的佔大多數。雖然分批出發，達十餘隊之衆，俱於四月二十日會合於北京三環路萬年青賓館，如期於二十一日演出。除少數團員自行來京報到外，參團的交通、食宿和遊覽，均託香港華南旅行社轉請北京中國青年旅行社鐵路分社安排。這些機構服務認真，照顧週到，收費合理，頗堪稱道。

香港和北京的藝術家緊密合作

演唱會舉行的晚上，民族文化宮內燈火輝煌，人如潮湧。觀衆席上，有許多是文化部的領導人、北京中央音樂學院和音樂界的知名人士及新聞記者。聖樂團所演唱的《四季頌》根本就是一首讚賞四時景色的詩歌，把春花、夏雨、秋葉、冬雪的良辰美景，作極美妙的描寫，把聽衆帶進了七彩繽紛的世界。演唱者除聖樂團和獨唱員外，北京歌劇和廣播界著名聲樂家楊洪基特應邀擔任男中音獨唱，而中央音樂學院的一位圓號演奏者和三名高足，則在「秋天」章的狩獵曲中，吹起了動人心弦的號角。在香港和北京的藝術家緊密合作下，全曲以澎湃的歌聲結束，掌聲如雷，歷久不絕。謝幕後，文化部中國對外演出公司的領導人紛紛登台道賀，致送巨型花籃。聖樂團每名團員，均獲餽贈紀念品。此外，負責主辦這次音樂會的中國對外演出公司更設盛筵招待全體團員，席上由宋成九經理舉杯祝賀，觥籌交錯，賓主盡歡。而北京好幾位造詣登峯造極的歌唱家，更即席表演助興。聖樂團團員蒙這樣優渥款待，萬分感謝。

帶回來對新中國的無盡希望

演唱會大功告成，團員們在以後數天裏，趁此機會遊覽首都名勝。他們履故宮而訪帝王的舊家，登長城而讚勞動力之偉大，而頤和園景色、北海風光、景山朝暉、天壇夕照，一一盡收眼底。天安門廣場的宏偉，人民大會堂的壯觀，歷史博物館展品的琳瑯滿目，着使人留下永不遺忘的印象。時值仲春，花開如錦，整個北京城籠罩在綠柳青枝中，就是極美麗的圖畫。

團員們只恨假期有限，在依依不捨中整頓行裝，向可愛的北京告別。他們帶回來的是演唱會的盛況與成功、主辦者的隆情和厚意、北京壯麗風光的回憶，以及新中國的無盡希望。

《華僑日報》/《大公報》

一九三五年夏，上海的圣乐团首创了音乐文化交流的先河，组团访问了香港、广州、与佛山各地，举行演唱会。当时的香港可以说是一个「文化的荒岛」，因此圣乐团的到访是一件相当轰动的大事，本人记得，香港的报纸连着两三天都以首页头条新闻来报导这消息。

一点感想 黄永熙

现在经过了五十年，香港的圣乐团才来到上海回聘，不能不说这是一个最缓慢的「交流」。当然，经过了八年的抗战，加上政治的动荡，连一切本应是正常的活动都不能进行，更谈不到在文化上的交流了。回想起来，本人最后一次在上海演出是在一九四七年，旋即渡美留学，到今天已经渡过了三十八个寒暑。因此这次带着香港圣乐团回到上海，心里有无限的感慨。上海是我的老家，我在这里渡过我的童年、少年、和青年的悠久岁月。因此这次回来，与其说是来演出，不如说是来拜见申江父老和许许多多的老朋友。我们没有带来什么礼物，只带来了我们的歌声，来祝贺大家一个快乐和充满美好远景的新年。

凡研究欧西音乐的人士，会知道正统音乐最初的发展也就是圣乐的发展。一般其他的作品，到了十七、十八世纪才开始抬头。因此最初一千多年来，西洋音乐史也就是圣乐史，许多音乐上的宝藏都是圣乐。历史上大音乐家的作品中，总包括一些圣乐，并且这些圣乐作品常常是他们创作中的精华。不论是巴赫、韩德尔、海顿、莫扎特、贝多芬，他们登峯造极的作品都是圣乐。

香港圣乐团成立的目的，除了让团员有机会亲自欣尝这些乐曲之外，也希望把这些音乐创作的精华介绍给一般音乐爱好者。为着工作或其他关系，我们这次只有约三分之一的团员能到上海来参加演出。本来担任男低音的独唱者，也临时因事不能来沪。我们很欣幸得着上海著名男低音温可锦教授客串演唱「弥赛亚」男低音独唱部份。这是一个很好的开始，也许将来我们港沪的合唱团约好排练同样的乐曲，到时联合演出，这样更能表达合作和交流的精神了。这并不是一个梦想，而是一个理想，只希望不要再等上了半个世纪才实现。

（場刊）

30th Anniversary — Hong Kong Oratorio Society (1956—86)

It is with great pleasure that the Hong Kong Oratorio Society greets you at tonight's concert, which is the fourth one in a series to celebrate the 30th Anniversary of the Society.

The Society is a non-profit-making organization founded in 1956 by a group of music enthusiasts who believed that oratorio singing is a great delight and the promotion of it will enrich the spiritual and cultural experience of the singers and listeners. The first concert was given in Queen Elizabeth School Auditorium on October 26, 1956. It was conducted by Mr. Theodore Huang. There were then about 30 members in the choir. We are happy to note that some of the founding members are still singing in the choir tonight.

We have witnessed over the thirty years that from a handful of music lovers, the Society has grown to a mature and accomplished choral group with a regular membership of some 140 voices of many nationalities. We have presented hundreds of concerts and performed over sixty oratorios and choral works by classical and contemporary composers. Many of these works were introduced to the audience in Hong Kong for the first time. We have often enlisted the participation of well-known orchestras in Hong Kong and elsewhere.

The Society Choir had six conductors during its first six years up to 1962, when Mr. Frank Huang was invited to conduct "Elijah" by Mendelssohn. Mr. Huang served as conductor for five years. From 1967 to the present, the Society has been fortunate to have Dr. Wong Wing Hee as its principal conductor. Dr. Wong is largely responsible for raising the standard of singing of the choir to what is now recognized as one of the finest choirs in Southeast Asia.

The Society Choir has toured overseas to give concerts in the Philippines, Macau, Taiwan, Singapore and China (Beijing and Shanghai) with great success. We hope to be able to organize more overseas concerts in the future.

The celebration of the 30th Anniversary respresents a milestone in the history of the Hong Kong Oratorio Society. We would like to take this opportunity to express our gratitude to all those who have given the Society their continued support throughout the years, especially our patrons, conductors, accompanists, guest soloists, orchestra members and not the least, our audiences. We know that thousands of people have enjoyed our concerts in the past years and we will surely continue to present more concerts for the enjoyment of our members and all oratorio lovers, and at the same time contribute a valuable share to the promotion of culture in Hong Kong.

1

（場刊）

香港聖樂團卅週年紀念（一九五六至八六）

歡迎閣下光臨欣賞香港聖樂團卅週年紀念音樂會。

香港聖樂團是一個不牟利的團體，於一九五六年由一羣音樂愛好者組成。他們深信聖樂或典雅作品的演唱，能帶來很大的喜樂，因此致力予以提倡，以豐富自己與別人的精神與文化生活。首次音樂會於一九五六年十月廿六日在伊利沙白中學舉行，由黃明東先生指揮。當時約有團員卅名左右。難能可貴的是一部份當時的團員仍然在今天晚上演唱。

聖樂團在過去卅年來，從幾名音樂愛好者發展到今日的擁有一百四十多名不同國籍團員的合唱團體，在香港和海外舉辦音樂會超過一百次，演唱古典和近代作曲家所寫的神曲和大型合唱作品，數量在六十套以上。其中許多是首次向本港人仕介紹的。並曾多次和許多香港和世界著名的樂隊合作。

在最初成立的六年間，聖樂團曾更換過六名指揮。直至一九六二年演唱孟德爾遜的「以利亞」時方才邀請黃飛然先生擔任指揮。黃先生共爲本團指揮了五年之久。從一九六七年起直至現在，聖樂團非常榮幸得到黃永熙博士擔任首席指揮。今日聖樂團得以成爲東南亞最佳合唱團之一，黃博士居功至偉。

最近幾年聖樂團多次前往海外演唱，包括菲律賓、澳門、台灣、新加坡和中國（北京和上海），獲得美滿的成績。我們期望將來能再籌辦更多這類海外演唱會。

卅週年慶典是香港聖樂團團史上一件大事。我們藉此機會感謝所有曾支持本團事工的朋友們——特別是贊助人，指揮，伴奏，外邀的獨唱家，樂隊成員和最重要的——我們的聽衆們。成千上萬的聽衆曾在過去卅年欣賞了我們的演唱。我們將繼續呈獻更多更好的音樂會，使各位聖樂愛好者和我們的團友一起領略最佳音樂享受，同時爲促進本港之文化活動獻出一份力量。

2

（場刊）

The Canadian Concert Tour, the Society's first concert-tour outside Asia, is a significant achievement in the history of the Hong Kong Oratorio Society. With a strengthened Canadian-Hong Kong connection in recent years, it is our great honour to be able to perform Haydn's **Seasons** in Vancouver and Toronto as the Forerunner to the Festival Hong Kong, 92.

The performance of Handel's **Messiah** with the Vancouver Oratorio Society has yet more significance. The Vancouver Oratorio Society has, since its formation in 1990, a close link with the Hong Kong Oratorio Society. A few past members of the Hong Kong Oratorio Society have formed the backbone of the Vancouver Oratorio Society. This reunion will prove to be a most enjoyable occasion for all of us.

Besides the advantage of cultural exchange, a concert tour will definitely improve the performing standard of its members. We are looking forward to benefit from the invaluable experience acquired in this exciting trip.

May I, on behalf of all the Hong Kong Oratorio Society members, take this opportunity to thank all our friends in supporting this event by attending the concert tonight. May God be with you and bless all of you always.

加拿大旅行演唱會是香港聖樂團首次在亞洲以外的地區演出，將會是本團歷史上的一個重要的里程碑。近年來，香港與加拿大的關係日趨密切，能有機會在溫哥華與多倫多表演九二年香港節的先驅節目，演唱海頓作品之「四季頌」，是一項極大的榮譽。

此外，與溫哥華聖樂團聯合演唱韓德爾作曲之「彌賽亞」亦別具意義。溫哥華聖樂團自一九九〇年成立以來，與本團保持緊密的聯繫。為數不少的本團舊團員在溫哥華聖樂團担任着重要的角色。此次聯合演唱將使大家有機會重聚一堂。

旅行演唱除了能增進文化交流外，更能提高團員的演出水準。大家已期待在此次令人興奮的旅程獲得更深體驗。

最後，我謹代表全體香港聖樂團團員對蒞臨今晚音樂會的各位朋友給予我們的支持致謝。願上帝祝福您們。

HENRY YU *Chairman*
余漢翁 主 席

（場刊）

MUSIC

Cultural exchange a 'first' in China

The Hongkong Oratorio Society and the Hongkong Sinfonietta recently performed two concerts of religious music in Xiamen. JANE DYKES witnessed the historic event.

From left: Penelope Chan and Clara Yip (soprano soloists), Elizabeth Hung (keyboard) and Dr Chan Wing-wah (conductor).

MUCH is made of historic tours by Western orchestras performing in China's two main cultural centres, Beijing and Shanghai. But recently, another cultural exchange took place — the Hongkong Oratorio Society and the Hongkong Sinfonietta gave two concerts in Xiamen, Fujian province.

What made this trip so significant is that this was the first time residents of China's "City of Music" had heard a live performance by foreign musicians. What is more, the repertoire was largely religious music.

Despite the government's lukewarm tolerance of religious expression, the two concerts received tremendous support from the local community, an estimated 15 per cent of whom are practising Christians.

The inspiration for the trip came from Henry Yu, chairman of both the Oratorio and the Sinfonietta. His family originates from Xiamen.

"The Oratorio Society translated into Chinese means 'sacred music society' and for this reason alone, it has been refused permission to perform in China for many years," said Yu.

The choir's last trip to China was in 1985 when it performed in Shanghai. A 1991 tour to Kunming and Guangzhou had to be cancelled at short notice when permission was refused.

"This time it took five months to obtain a performance permit from the Board of Culture in Xiamen. To play safe, I also applied for permission from the authorities in Fujian," he said.

The permit was eventually given on condition that there be no publicity, no profit from ticket sales and no involvement of religious organisations in Xiamen. Another condition was that the director of the Board of Culture in Xiamen must have a preview of the concert and the right to veto it.

But from the beginning, luck was with the group. Henry Yu went ahead with his *guanxi* to smooth the arrival of 70 musicians into China.

Within minutes of arriving at Xiamen University, where the group was to stay, we were whisked off to a reception organised by the Xiamen YMCA Choir.

Its members and supporters had been waiting for us for two hours.

Hongkong Oratorio Society members outside the Protestant church in Xiamen.

The full significance of the trip was not clearly stated during the many speeches that followed, but the value of musical exchange was emphasised.

The Hongkong organisers had good reason to reciprocate the goodwill that pervaded the atmosphere. The Xiamen choir had unofficially arranged for our timpanis, cellos and other large instruments to be hand-carried to Gu Lang Yu (the vehicle-free island where the second concert was held), as well as providing placards, gigantic baskets of flowers and MCs.

On both nights the concert halls were packed, largely thanks to choir members spreading the word. They had even persuaded 17 church members from Zhangzhou to make the three-hour bus journey.

As a token of gratitude and at the Xiamen choir conductor's request, all copies of Mozart's sacred motet *Ave Verum Corpus* were presented to our unofficial organisers as a gift at the end of the tour.

The next afternoon the director of the Board of Culture duly sat through a three-hour pre-performance. His response was favourable, although he noticed there was a Chinese translation of the religious text of the programme.

Both concerts went ahead. They opened with Purcell's *Sonata in D for Trumpet and Strings* and included a performance of Vivaldi's *Gloria* and excerpts from Handel's *Messiah*.

A violinist from Hongkong assured me the response, given the unusual nature of the event and unfamiliarity with the music, was no less than rapturous.

The next morning we had a choice of visiting the local Protestant and Catholic churches, or a tour of the music department of Xiamen University.

Window

Conductor Emeritus' Message

榮譽指揮的話

Even though a history of 40 years may not be considered a very long time as compared with the duration of many similar choral societies in other parts of the world, the Hong Kong Oratorio Society, probably has the longest history among similar musical organizations in Hong Kong. It is not self-assuming to say that the Society has come a long way since its inception in 1956.

An oratorio society, or any similar large choral group, is different from other smaller counterparts, which normally do not rely upon orchestral accompaniment for their performances. On the other hand, for a large choral group, especially with a name as an oratorio society, its activities would be greatly handicapped without the services of a capable orchestra. It should be remembered that a professional orchestra was not available in Hong Kong until about 22 years ago. It is therefore not a simple matter that the Society is able to include many works in its repertory as representative as they are.

It is understandable that all choristers enjoy singing the works they love. Yet enjoyment alone is not enough in our effort to help the Society grow. It is our commitment and willingness to spend time, energy and the best of our abilities in presenting all the works that have been scheduled, not only the favourites, that counts. Presenting large choral works is the Society's share in the total effort of trying to enhance the musical life of our community. It is with this spirit that we endeavour to produce good performances. The members of the Society cannot stay active in the organization forever, yet the spirit can, if we cherish it. It is only with such understanding and dedication that the celebration of our anniversary can really be meaningful.

Dr. Wong Wing Hee,
Principal Conductor, 1967-1989,
Conductor Emeritus, 1990-

跟世界各地的其他類似的大型合唱團相比，四十年當然並不可以算是一段長時間。但在香港芸芸眾音樂團體之中，香港聖樂團可能是歷史最悠久的。自一九五六年成立以來，聖樂團在各方面都取得相當的進展，相信這不是自詡之詞。

聖樂團（或任何類似的大合唱團）跟其他較小規模的歌詠團不同，因為後者通常不需管弦樂團伴奏。相反來說，大規模的歌唱團，尤其是要稱得上「神劇合唱團」（註：香港聖樂團的英文名稱），如果沒有相當規模和水準的管弦樂團伴奏，演出便會大打折扣。我們不要忘記，香港是直至廿二年前，方才成立具專業水平的管弦樂團。因此，聖樂團能夠舉辦那麼多次深具代表性的演唱會，實在是難能可貴。

每個合唱團團員最享受的，當然是演唱他們喜愛的歌曲。但要協助聖樂團成長，單講享受是不足夠的；最重要的，是我們肯作出承擔，並願意付出時間和努力；不論是否自己最喜愛的作品，都積極參與聖樂團編排所有的演唱。聖樂團的宗旨就是通過舉行大型聖樂演唱，促進和豐富社會人士的音樂生活。這種精神是我們努力的目標。雖然沒有任何一位聖樂團團員可能永遠活躍地參與聖樂團的事工，但倘若我們繼續珍惜它，這種精神將可以永存。有了這樣的了解和獻身的心情，我們的週年慶祝活動才真正有意義。

黃永熙博士
首席指揮（一九六三年至一九八九年）
榮譽指揮（一九九〇年起）

5

（場刊）

Special Greetings to the Hong Kong Oratorio Society

In the third week of our long sojourn in Hong Kong, in August, 1967, I answered an advertisement in the newspaper and joined the Oratorio Society. It is with great sadness that I cannot be in Hong Kong for the very special 40th Anniversary, but time goes on and it was time to leave last September.

All my memories of the Oratorio Society are good, even when we sang to small audiences, or sang in the "open air" on a choir tour in most uncomfortable heat! The choir tours were special times- to Beijing, Shanghai, Manila, Korea, Singapore, and even Macau many times. These were the times when my fellow singers became closer friends as we all worked together to do the best we could to bring wonderful music to people in other cities. One person, Peter Liang, was instrumental in making these many tours a success. He also had valuable committee members to help him, and everyone worked extremely hard in their various capacities. I would like to thank them all now because many of them are still Society members. Peter went to be with the Lord last year.

For over 20 years, in various capacities on the committee as secretary, vice-chairman and then chairman for 6 years, followed by several years as advisor, I enjoyed myself very much and found that I always had the outstanding support of all the committee members. The unfailing dedication of the people in the choir and on the committee is truly something to hold precious in my many memories. They even coped with my Cantonese and made sure that I understood when the meetings lapsed into that language instead of English and as the years went by both the meetings and rehearsals were quite bilingual! That was good for me, and my friends in the Society often helped me with various new words and expressions. Thank you for that also.

I will continue to miss you all as the years go by. Perhaps we will be able to return for a visit in the not-too-distant future. We do look forward to seeing some of the members if they come to our area in the United States. Please keep up your diligent hard work and do continue to enjoy your singing, in praise of the Lord. You are all very special people.

My heartiest congratulations as you celebrate your 40th Anniversary with this special concert of praise. I will be with you in spirit, if not in person. I send you all my love and best wishes.God bless you all.

Joan Jasper

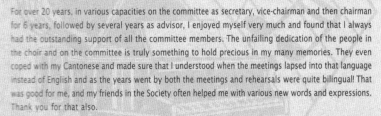

7

THE 40th ANNIVERSARY OF THE HONG KONG ORATORIO SOCIETY

As a founder member ot this society, it has been of great personal interest and pride to witness and take part in the growth and development of Society in the past four decades. In 1956, about forty music lovers made the brave decision to form the Society, with the main objective of performing oratorios, for the pleasure of oratorio enthusiasts as well as to promote choral music. This number has now grown to over one hundred and forty. We can proudly proclaim to be the largest, longest established and most active choir in Hong Kong.

The life of the Society has been unique to Hong Kong, in the sense that no other music group has made it their aim to perform complete oratorio masterpieces. Our programme over the years have en-compassed over eighty complete works by masters such as Handel, Haydn, Mozart, Beethoven, Verdi, Mendelssohn, Bach and many others. Over half of those works were Hong Kong Premieres. In addition, three Oratorios/Cantatas were commissioned over the years. Our ability to offer the public such unique performances is definitely a fact which the Society should be very proud.

For the first thirty years or so, the main accompaniment for our performances had been the organ and the piano. Accompaniment by an orchestra, on rare occasions, were mostly by invitation. We were not able to afford the luxury of a permanent orchesta, due to the high costs. In 1990, the Hong Kong Sinfonietta started its support for the Society's concerts, and have done so for the past six years, including the successful Xiaman-Tour Concert in 1993.

The past forty years have not been without its challenges, joys and heart-aches. However, each challenge brings renewed hope and energy, it is a learning process, and we gain the wisdom and experience from each encounter.

Looking forward to the next forty years, I am positive that the Society will enjoy continuing success, and grow from strength to strength. Like a through-train travelling pass 1997 and beyond, we will look to the future with hope and confidence.

I am confident that as long as the love for music breathes on, it would be as oxygen is to life for the Society. May I take this opportunity to offer my most grateful and heartfelt thanks to the loyal audiences who support our performances; the dedication and commitment of all Society members; the unselfish support of all the artists and soloists, and the generous sponsorship from individuals and organizations.

Chu Man-wai
Hon. President
Hong Kong Oratorio Society

（場刊）

香港聖樂團四十週年紀念

作為聖樂團的其中一位創辦人，能夠見證和參與她在過去過去四十年來的成長，實在是個人的最大樂趣和榮幸。一九五六年我們這一群熱愛音樂的聲樂家、音樂教師、學生和聖詩班成員，就是為了熱愛唱頌聖樂而立下宏願：毅然創辦了「香港聖樂團」。聖樂團在創始時僅得四十位成員，今天已增至一百四十位，敢稱為全港最具規模、歷史最悠久、也是最活躍的合唱團。

香港實在沒有其他的音樂團體像聖樂團一樣：以演譯完整一本的聖樂名著為目標；惟其如此，聖樂團的生命才顯得獨具特質。在過去的歲月中，我們成功地演頌了超過八十套完整的大師級作品，當中包括了莫扎特、韓德爾、孟德爾遜、貝多芬和巴哈等大師的傑作；其中半數以上，還是香港的首次演出呢。此外，我們還創作了三套聖樂和清唱劇譜。能為公眾作出如此獨特的表演，實在是本樂團足以自豪的事。

最初的卅年間，我們演出時主要是用風琴和鋼琴伴奏。偶爾間也會請來樂隊伴奏，不過只是邀約性質，長期僱用樂隊是很奢華的開支，不是本樂團負擔得起的。自一九九〇年香港小交響樂團創立以來，在過去六年內從無間斷的對本團支援，包括一九九三年很成功的「廈門巡迴演唱會」。

過去的四十寒暑充滿了挑戰和苦樂。然而，每次挑戰都帶來了新盼望和動力：經一事長一智，我們也在這種經驗和學習歷程中成長了。

展望未來四十年，我肯定聖樂團會有長促的發展，而且會有更大的成就和興旺；就如跨越一九九七的直通車一樣，展望將來，我們是充滿信心和希望的。

我深信：只要我們仍然熱愛音樂，樂團就像生命得到氧氣一樣，可以延續下去。藉此機會，讓我對所有支持我們表演的忠實聽眾、滿有熱忱的團員、慷慨資助的所有藝術家、聲樂家、以及來自各界的慷慨贊助，謹致以最衷心的感激和謝意。

香港聖樂團
名譽會長
朱文偉

（場刊）

We invite you to celebrate Hong Kong's reunification with China after 150 years of growth and prosperity, at three unique celebratory concerts called *The Last Night of the Proms*. The boisterous party atmosphere of London's world famous *Last Night of the Proms*, with its exuberant promenaders, its banner-waving, its balloons, and its hooting klaxons which have now become an integral part of the British summer and a veritable British institution will be recreated on three nights in June 1997 at the Lyric Theatre.

A light classical concert with the Hong Kong Sinfonietta and Hong Kong Oratorio, conducted by Barry Knight will feature favourite pieces from Prokofiev's *Romeo and Juliet*, Bizet's *Carmen*, Tchaikowsky's *Swan Lake* and *Butterfly Lovers*. Della Jones, the world famous mezzo soprano will perform arias by Lehar, Rossini and Bizet.

The traditional fare of *Fantasia on British Sea Songs*, *Rule Britannia*, *I Vow To Thee My Country* together with *Land of Hope and Glory* and *Jerusalem* will provide moments of pure nostalgia and elation as we look back over the last 150 years and look forward to the future.

Celebrate the Handover at Hong Kong's *The Last Night of the Proms* – a unique occasion, the memories of which you will treasure forever.

以三場慶祝回歸「逍遙音樂會」，讓大家一起來慶祝香港經過一百五十年的繁榮增長，現回歸祖國，展開歷史新一頁。

世界知名的倫敦「逍遙音樂會」，氣氛熱鬧如派對，觀眾入場時皆興高采烈，一起搖旗，一起哼歌，場內並有氣球增添氣氛，現已成為倫敦每年夏天的「重頭戲」。一九九七年六月香港演藝學院將重現這個真實的英國風俗實貌。

一場輕古典音樂會，由香港小交響樂團及香港聖樂團演出，巴利‧賴特指揮，演奏節目包括浦羅歌菲夫的《羅密歐與茱麗葉》，比才的《卡門》，柴可夫斯基的《天鵝湖》，及《梁祝協奏曲》等。世界知名女中音黛拉‧鍾斯亦會演出尼亞、羅西亞及比才的咏嘆調。

還有《英國水手歌幻想曲》、《大不列顛帝國》、《誓忠我國》、《光明希望之地》及《耶路撒冷》，當我們回顧光輝百五年，展步共邁新紀元之際，這些傳統曲目將伴我們以興奮及緬懷的心情渡過這歷史重要一刻。

慶祝回歸「逍遙音樂會」—— 一個令你畢生難忘的特別約會。

（場刊）

Laudate 讚 頌

The HKOS Newsletter   香港聖樂團團訊   **July 1997** 七月號

HANDOVER

Handover Supplement
Pages 4 - 7

The Voice and Its Ailments
by Dr Victor Abdullah
......................................p2

Happy Eightieth Birthday

Dr Wong Wing Hee's 80th
Birthday Celebrations
p10-11

Reports:
AGM   p4

Concerts:
Choral Fantasy   p3
Israel in Egypt   p9

Members Column.................p3

Friends' Column................p12

Coming Events..................p12

Editorial Team

Chief Editor:
Peter Au-Yeung
Asst Editor (English):
Barry Anderton
Asst Editor (Chinese):
Amy Wong
Production Manager:
Martin Kwok
Co-ordinator:
Billy Cheung

The British have left and Hong Kong is reunited with her Motherland. Whatever your race, nationality or political colour, to be in Hong Kong during these historical days, when the eyes of the world were focused on this tiny territory, was a memorable experience. Members of the Society were more fortunate than that. They participated in the festivities on both sides of the historical event. The Last Night of the Proms concerts was a purely commercial venture, brought by a local production company to celebrate the end of 150 years of British rule. Commercialism apart, the performances provided the Society with a glimpse of a uniquely English institution. We also performed for the Governor's last public concert, recompense enough for not performing at his departure.

After the Chinese flag was raised again over Hong Kong, we participated in three more concerts, albeit under the aegis of the Hong Kong Choral Association Joint Choir. It was certainly an eye-opener for many members to realize the scope of local choral endeavour, though standards understandably vary greatly. Whilst it was a pity that the Chinese Vice Premier et al left before our performance, the Society can still proudly claim to have taken part in events attended by both the outgoing and incoming rulers during the Handover period.

The Handover may also be remembered by members in the years to come as one of the most hectic spells of performances ever. For those with the time, energy and enthusiasm to participate in all seven performances, that fortnight or so with either rehearsals or performances nearly every day gives members a taste of the life of a professional musician. In any case, can anyone in the Oratorio Society remember performing six times in as many days? The archives clearly show that this is a record. As some one commented on the 1st July, "you could have sung with the Society from the beginning, but we've just had a couple of firsts these few days. It was the first time the choir partied with the audience at the Last Night of the Proms, and now tonight we have the choir in front of the Orchestra for the first time ever." What a Handover!

Reports, p 4-8

p1

《讚頌》

音樂總監的話

是晚的節目是對生命的肯定！在我們四周有很多勇敢的善人，不斷以愛及關懷對待他們認識或不認識的人。他們英雄的行徑在苦難、疾病及戰爭中尤為彰顯，人類歷史全賴有他們始能延續！我們向這些英勇的人致敬並以音樂呼籲和平，盼望有一天我們的社會得免疾病及戰爭的禍害。

本節目包括巴羅克、古典、浪漫及現代的音樂創作。巴赫的宗教情懷及安慰之聲洋溢在他的聲樂及器樂曲中，而韓德爾、海頓及孟德爾遜的三套神曲已成經典、後無來者可及。這些樂曲都充滿激情及生命力，並且帶出希望及愛的訊息。

四首現代作品皆以愛及和平為主題，其曲詞清晰表示「讓世上平安由我而始」。其中一曲並問「終我一生，有否替世界灌注一點愛？」反躬自問，或許我們不單以言語，而應以行動去回應。

我們以歌聲肯定這一生，讓這一生的意義以愛及和平去彰顯！

陳永華

Message from the Music Director

Tonight's programme tells everyone that life is still worth-living! There are so many brave and conscientious people around us who are full of love and concern to others whether known or unknown to them. Their heroic deeds are being witnessed particularly in a time of turmoil, in a time of sickness and in war. Human history can continue because we have brave people like them! We therefore salute them and call for peace with music hoping that our society will one day be free from sickness and war.

The programme consists of musical works from the Baroque, Classical, Romantic and modern periods. Bach's religious sentiment and comforting voice are found in both his vocal and instrumental music. The three well-known oratorios from Handel, Haydn and Mendelssohn are masterpieces that none can surpass. They are full of human passion and enthusiasm towards life. They appeal for hope and universal brotherhood.

The four modern pieces are voices of today with themes of love and peace. Their lyrics explicitly say, "let there be peace on earth and let it begin with me". A good question asked from one of the songs: "did I fill the world with love my whole life through?" We ask ourselves the same question and answer it by our action in addition to words.

We sing to tell you that life is not only worth-living, life should be meaningful and full of peace and love!

Chan Wing-wah

2

（場刊）

黃永熙博士紀念

楊伯倫
黃永熙博士聖樂基金籌創委員會主席

In Memory of Dr. Wong Wing Hee

David Yeung
Chairman, Planning Committee of
Dr. Wong Wing Hee Sacred Music Founadtion

早於1940年代我便認識黃永熙博士，我父親和他的父親是世交，我們同在上海富吉堂參加崇拜和聖樂活動。後黃博士赴美深造。1960年代起，我們又同在香江參與各種聖樂活動，我又主理他八十壽慶的音樂會和壽誕，因此，談起黃博士的一生軼事時，就像長篇歷史故事，一幕幕地展現眼前，他那為主工作勤奮熱誠的榜樣，待人接物親切風趣的作風，處事嚴謹認真的態度感人至深。他那專心事主的精神令人敬佩，我們失去一位慈祥的長者令人婉惜。

黃永熙博士傳奇的一生始於少年，他的大學學位是土木工程，由於他的天份和愛好，加以勤學努力，竟然得到音樂博士榮銜。他的指揮生涯早於廿多歲便開始，在未經世界著名指揮大師指導過，能即場代替因故突然缺席的交響樂團指揮，指揮全場樂曲而極獲好評，實在是一鳴驚人，隨後在世界各地指揮多個著名的合唱團和交響樂團，並在紐約卡內基音樂廳指揮過數場音樂會。他的指揮手法揮灑自如，功力十足，於1967年起擔任香港聖樂團的首席及榮譽指揮凡卅五年，並演出過數十首大型的合唱傑作，實在居功至偉。黃博士並於1970年代及1990年代兩次主持重編《普天頌讚》工作及主持《讚美詩·新編》雙語本的中譯英工作，他曾在本港多個著名的基督教機構擔任總幹事或社長等重要職務，工作認真負責，成績斐然。

回顧過去，多少英才競折腰，展望將來，聖樂花壇爭吐艷。但願我們後輩秉承黃永熙博士的堅強意志，學習先聖先賢的謙恭榜樣，使聖樂工作在新時代裡有更大更好的發展，更能榮神益人。黃永熙博士的精神永垂不朽，他為主工作的功勳常在常青。

My relationship with Dr. Wong Wing Hee developed as early as in the 1940s when we both participated in the Sunday service and sacred music activities of the Fujie Church in Shanghai. My father and his father were also close friends. Dr. Wong subsequently went to study in the United States. In 1960s, we met again in Hong Kong and since then had joined hands in many sacred music functions. I was also the organizer for his 80th Birthday Concert and Banquet. So, when I start to search my memory of him, scenes of our earlier days flow in vividly. Most impressive of all, he was hardworking and earnest in delivering his service to God, easy-going and humorous to people around, and meticulous and serious in handling work tasks. His whole-heartedness in serving God is respectable. We really miss this kind elder of ours.

The interesting life of Dr. Wong began from his youth. His first degree was in Civil Engineering. But with his talent and his unyielding efforts, he finally obtained a doctoral degree in music. His conducting years started when he was in his 20s. On an occasion when the conductor of an orchestra had to be excused for urgent reasons just before a performance, Dr. Wong, who had not yet been instructed by any maestros, took the baton and conducted the whole concert. He won high acclaim for this and earned himself fame. Thereafter, he had conducted many choirs and orchestras all over the world, and had held several concerts in the Carnegie Hall in New York. He had a free-flow style of conducting with sophisticated skills. From 1967, he was the Principal Conductor and later the Conductor Emeritus of the Hong Kong Oratorio Society, spanning a relation of 35 years long. He had introduced several dozens of choral masterpieces to the local audience with much success. Dr. Wong had twice headed the revision of the *Hymns of Universal Praise* in 1970s and 1990s respectively, and led the English translation for *The New Hymnal* (English-Chinese Bilingual edition). He had also been the Director or Publisher of several major Christian organizations in Hong Kong, shouldering important duties and achieving remarkable success with his dedication.

Great forefathers belong to the ages of the past, and new talents are budding to blossom in the new era for sacred music. We wish that followers of Dr. Wong will be able to inherit his same kind of perseverance and modesty, so that there can be more and greater development in sacred music of the new age, benefiting believers and glorifying God. The spirit of Dr. Wong shall live on and his achievements are always renewed.

(Translation by Concert Committee)

（場刊）

作曲者的話

黃安倫

聖樂乃音樂之母——此關鍵的一點，在我們所處的這個世代，就愈加顯得重要。現在人們都在談論中華文化「要和國際接軌」，孰不知，要是不「與上帝接軌」，一切都只是枉然。不屑世間榮華，只求天上冠冕，這就是先賢黃永熙伯伯以其一生「榮耀主名」的事奉為我們所作出的見證。

從這點上回想起黃伯伯對我家幾代人在聖樂上的引領，不盡的感恩之情在心頭一陣陣湧流。除了與叔父黃飛然同工，1988年家父黃飛立與香港聖樂團的合作，也正是他親手玉成。那次不僅在港首演了拙作《大衛之詩》，更由他親自委約指揮了拙作《詩篇一百五十篇》，令此作獲得了當時第九屆世界華人聖樂促進會的首獎。黃伯伯對我這個新兵勉勵有加：「安倫賢姪……我很同意你對近代音樂潮流的感想。正當你仍然是年青力壯的時候，你有勇氣出來，走你自己認為正當的路線，還是值得鼓勵的事。」——跟隨先輩的腳蹤，他的這封親筆書信就是我走前面這路永遠的支撐。

感謝香港聖樂團給我這次難得的機會，可以與大家同工，在此紀念黃伯伯的音樂會上把這部《安魂曲》獻唱出來。這些年來，世間的苦難似乎更多了。然而，譜寫著唐佑之牧師絕美的歌詞，我卻不斷地聽到天使的歌聲。「哀慟的人有福了，因為他們必得安慰。」在死亡追來的時候，神的兒女們卻向神感恩——主耶穌永生的應許是多麼奇妙啊！永不停歇地歌唱這份「沒有人能奪去」的喜樂，和永遠的平安，不正是黃伯伯對我們的期許嗎？

2004年9月12日

From the Composer

Huang An Lun

Sacred music is the origin of all music. This is an important notion in this particular era in which we live. Whilst people talk about connecting the Chinese culture to the international scene, it must also be reckoned that without connecting to God, all efforts will be in vain. Our beloved Dr. Wong Wing Hee has set a good example for us in his lifelong service to glorify His name, not for worldly riches, but for the heavenly crown.

Reminiscences of Dr. Wong's guidance on sacred music to several generations of my family sink in, and I cannot help expressing my heartfelt gratitude to him. Dr. Wong had close partnership in music with my uncle, Huang Fei-ran. In 1988, it was also through Dr. Wong's connection that my father, Huang Fei-li, had a chance to collaborate with the Hong Kong Oratorio Society. On that occasion, Dr. Wong conducted the Hong Kong premiére of my Psalm 22. He also commissioned my composition of Psalm 150 and conducted it himself. This work was awarded the first price in the 9th Conference of The World Association for Chinese Church Music. Dr. Wong had always encouraged me, "Dear An-lun, ... I fully agree with your views on recent trend of contemporary music. It is very much appreciated that you are bold enough to pursue in the direction that you think right when you are still young and energetic." This personal letter from Dr. Wong is always the support for my road ahead — following the footsteps of our learned forefathers.

I must thank the Hong Kong Oratorio Society for availing me the chance to dedicate the performance of this Requiem to Dr. Wong in this concert in memory of him. There is increasing and aggravating suffering in recent years. But in the course of composing on the beautiful lines written by Rev. Samuel Tang, I continually heard the voices of the angels: "Blessed are those who mourn, for they shall be comforted." Although mortality is imminent, sons and daughters of God can still sing praises to the Lord — how wonderful is the promise of Jesus for the eternal life! Is it not the wish of Dr. Wong too that we can sing out this joy and everlasting peace that no one can take away?

(Translation by Concert Committee)

3

（場刊）

明報 特輯　　2006·09·15 星期五　F7

香港聖樂團 50

宏揚聖樂 潤澤心靈

香港聖樂團金禧誌慶
聖詠另主旋．歌韻迴揚五十載
樂聲響天下．讚譽傳誦千萬家

積土成山 風雨興焉
積水成淵 蛟龍生焉
故不積跬步 無以至千里
不積小流 無以成江海

未來目標 向內地推廣神曲合唱藝術

每年演出精采神曲 與市民共賞

選唱大型合唱曲 擴闊觀眾藝術視野

內地演出 反應熱烈

樂團撥款助推傳教育

樂園撥款藝術教育工作

古典聖樂曲芝知音

加強宣傳 多與市民溝通

樂曲多與聖經故事有關

多邁十七世紀以後樂曲

「當用詩歌、頌詞、靈歌，彼此對說，口唱心和的讚美主。」

常任指揮

聖詠愿揚傳主榮 樂韻迴歇頌金禧

「與時俱進 發揮影響」

「看！兄弟們同居共處，多麼快樂，多麼幸福！」

香港聖樂園的誕生

常任伴奏

謹以祈禱，祝賀香港聖樂團金禧誌慶

香港聖樂團團是香港眾樂界的奇葩

資深聲樂家

天籟之音傳四方

繼續領先 邁步向前

承先啟後 再創佳績

耕耘半世紀 寄寓全音樂

前主席

圓滿時同最長的執委女團員

服務時最長的執委男團員

《明報》

《明報》

Message from HKOS Chairman
香港聖樂團主席獻辭

The Hong Kong Oratorio Society (HKOS) is privileged and excited to have this opportunity to work with the Vancouver Oratorio Society (VOS) to present this series of concerts in Vancouver and Calgary. This venture will enable us to renew our friendship and further promote our co-operation as we have had very pleasant and memorable experiences presenting joint concerts in Vancouver in 1992 and in Hong Kong and Shanghai in 1994 - some 20 years ago!

Since the HKOS was founded in 1956, we have presented about 300 concerts, many of them outside Hong Kong. Our mission is to promote choral singing with rendition and performance of oratorios and other choral music, so as to contribute towards a greater appreciation and enjoyment of choral music for the audiences. The HKOS has now become one of the major choral groups in Hong Kong and the region. Numerous western masterpieces and works by Chinese composers have received their local premieres by the Society.

This concert tour by HKOS would not have been possible without the efforts, commitment, and sponsorship by many friends and supporters. I would like to take this opportunity to express our most sincere appreciation and gratitude for their selfless contribution to this worthwhile endeavor - particularly the VOS Committee, HKOS Sub-Committee on Canadian Tour, our sponsors, our conductors, our accompanists, VOS Chorus & Orchestra members and HKOS members.

I hope you will enjoy tonight's concert.

Professor Enoch Young,
Chairman

香港聖樂團是次有機會與溫哥華聖樂團合作,在溫哥華及卡爾加利呈獻一系列音樂會,實在感到十分榮幸與興奮。早於約二十年前,兩個樂團已於一九九二年與一九九四年,先後在溫哥華以及香港與上海舉行聯合音樂會,得到非常愉快而難忘的經驗,這次合作不但可讓我們重敘舊誼,更有助我們加強合作。

香港聖樂團自一九五六年成立以來,已演出約三百場音樂會,當中多次在香港以外地區演出。我們的使命是透過演繹與表演神曲及其他合唱音樂,推廣合唱藝術,讓觀眾能更加欣賞與享受合唱音樂。香港聖樂團現已成為香港及亞太區的主要合唱團之一。西方大師與華籍作曲家的多首傑作,也是由香港聖樂團在本港首次演繹。

香港聖樂團是次巡迴演出,有賴各方友好與支持者的努力、承擔與贊助才能實現。本人謹藉此機會,對各位為此項有意義的活動作出無私奉獻,致以最衷心的謝忱與感激,尤其是溫哥華聖樂團委員會、香港聖樂團加拿大演出小組委員會、各位贊助人、各位指揮、各位伴奏、溫哥華聖樂團暨管弦樂團、及香港聖樂團的所有成員。

希望各位享受今晚的音樂會。

楊健明 教授
香港聖樂團主席

2.

六十周年工作小組主席
60th Anniversary Working Group Chairman

歐陽志剛執事
DEACON ERIC AU YEUNG

六十周年工作小組
60th Anniversary Working Group

歐陽志剛	Eric AU YEUNG
林敏玲	Anita LAM
吳劍峰	NG Kim-fung
唐展峰	Tony TONG
王笑芳	Yvonne WONG

六十是一個奇妙的數字，是很多人從一個工作崗位退下來進到另一種新生活的轉捩點。

為了慶祝六十周年，執行委員會特別委派了本人與一班活力充沛的成員一起籌備一連串的慶祝活動。在籌備和舉行各項活動中，成員非常用心地安排每個細節，在此我衷心感謝小組成員無私的付出和聖樂團團員及各協作單位的參與，我更感謝各位觀眾的蒞臨，你的出席是我們最大的鼓勵及認同。

期望六十周年也是聖樂團的一個轉捩點，更年輕、更有活力、更多與青年音樂才俊合作，為觀眾帶來更優質的演出。

當用各樣的智慧，把基督的道豐豐富富的存在心裏，用詩篇、讚美詩、靈歌，彼此教導，互相勸戒，以感恩的心歌頌上帝。(歌羅西書3:16 RCUV)

"60" is a magic number. It is the turning point of many who begin a new life after retirement.

To celebrate HKOS' anniversary, the Executive Committee appointed me and a group of energetic members to plan for a series of commemorative activities. In the process of the preparation and execution, my colleagues have been arranging every detail wholeheartedly. I am most grateful for their selfless contributions as well as for the participations of our HKOS members and partners. I am most appreciative of you, our audience, as your presence is the essential encouragement and recognition to us.

We hope that "60" is also the turning point to a vibrant and even more energetic HKOS that will continue to collaborate with aspiring musicians to bring the highest quality of performances to you.

Let the message of Christ dwell among you richly as you teach and admonish one another with all wisdom through psalms, hymns, and songs from the Spirit, singing to God with gratitude in your hearts. (Colossians 3:16 NIV)

香港聖樂團第60周年鑽禧音樂會

HKOS 60th Anniversary Diamond Jubilee Concert

④

（場刊）

B4 副刊　　　　藝壇動靜　　　　大公報　2019年8月11日 星期日

責任編輯：黃璇　美術編輯：麥兆聰

▲陳永華在委祖多次的文化連演藝術中心世界首演舉行的節目大型音作《仁愛大同》後擔任總指揮身份

由音樂總監陳永華籌備的香港版樂團一行六十多人，於六月矽期利時剛剛吉，完成為期十一天的多倫多「慶祝中華人民共和國成立七十周年暨港加慶愛文化之旅」，讓其青崁昤年暮多場經演賀繁師都憲首文在多倫多及溫哥華東西兩岸舉辦「香港周」的繁要活動。由香港加愛樂聯團同流溫哥華樂團（部分團員皆香港繁愛團員的前團員）組成近百人的陣容，和多倫多的KSO管弦樂團聯手於六月下旬在列治文山賽潦藝術中心（Richmond Hill Centre for the Performing Arts）舉行「美愛大同」音樂會。

周凡夫

《仁愛大同》賀國慶祝福世界
——香港與多倫多樂團聯手演出

▲陳永華（左）在多倫多大學列治文校園（科爾澤指音廳）主演講後，與過去已九十二歲的音愛老師John Beckwith

▲多倫多列治文山賽潦藝術中心正門升旗

「美愛大同」音樂會的內容設計，特別強調着加強港子愛手合作的意義。KSO 整弦樂團全名「Kindred Spirits Orchestra」（即今「志同道合」之意），KSO由現任音樂總監Kristian Alexander於二○○六年成立，最得當的聲譽，Kristian Alexander是過去十多年來活動力豐強的加拿大指揮家，KSO在他領導下，已成為多倫多新興的樂團。

五首樂曲四指揮執棒

這場「美愛大同」，亞樂會共五首由左至左樂曲，有由位加拿大指揮家執棒，音樂會以KSO樂團的聯合指揮、來自為拉下的Michael Berecz擔任主持，音樂會首先由助理指揮Travis Grubb帶領下演奏了加拿大國歌，再由中國國歌，繼後在Michael Berecz指揮下，以美國作曲家科普蘭（Copland）的《老實人歌號曲》（Fanfare for the Common Man）為國會提供了很好的開場氣氛。

其實，演出屬是主持人，暨管揮與領導參加各個的演出，讓人有着很深的一面：演出同名樂曲都以求達中，由在位指揮家執棒，將音樂會之間的樂團聯合連結起來。空間亞樂曲初、唱作曲初加五人執棒，但創樂曲的合作學涯每互的聯繫，兩作讓意的謂新布局，鏗金會繼樣去求的支持、這是盛意然的是昔樂，點點合演這些聯團的諺聞嗎？欣然起初內容之蘊這令人肅念。

此外，第四首作品是作唱團的要求都存在一定意義，上半場唱各重整整加這次活動創作的無大型合唱《仁繁大同》，是當出的開詞曲十二首樂的這套樂交響曲，也代真表演連結這件大型合唱。獨是一定的奇為特以在這次自起的有樂器，會在這新的重量加上、加上其充於新的新的組·原來以堅演出了新形，開是這唱鳴作樂重量與這合唱開演選建論上、合個位樂器連演是等以第大的聖聖建經運連上、在全民聲樂繁，是計大深交樂重建這會，於以愛這片海首等。於法旭重以下黃樂主東行了一次唱演，作了水平高度的唱家，特別重，香港聖聞團此行，於瓦奧這演繁重量，每不能發繁歌眾等與個多有和所發揮。

欣賞陳這際陳永華這套作品的內內義兼不朝，倒對這違作品的新的意合其新的，當跟很指著「巜中時代關的聖極賀意《三關萬馬》，一直景今天

《逾萬山》助力「香港周」

（香港周）開幕禮六月在大多倫多中華文化中心花萬彩美館揭幕行，由寇當省民那分學商展示慶祝多倫多多元共國際文化方得這意的能化多。多倫多何瞳斯斯表示承是過合作團彰建上的過面與展這、當日的其唐這新這加豎的過灑能演，在詠咸運量嘉這、展示多倫多不同風咸的繁欣運響，從法灑運運人美深音高聞管主福。

▲Kristian Alexander（中）在RHCPA指揮史克里亞賓第一交響曲後謝幕 作者供圖

祝願「和平進大同」

陳永華家擔揮寫了一首帶着繁各江流水梅露歷史英語，我以這當運唱唱、簡應鳴陽授這今天的長江宗源。有着事合意而念著。

事實上，三關歌章的標題己經繁唱交代了各樣章的內涵：第一樂章《清澈無江萬源》、容狀的《淡的水進流液》、大海水一段中，繁張液乘、和千遊大同，也就念是一有在海一、已的這最的唱整文章這深厚的幼寮，唱合了《愛看這詩觸？這是鳴本的分類合了文章生的諺韻，當繼唱者的水同進流着色，品的進這萨之主題曲，繁衛千國這運樂滿。沙漠運的弱發展、繁慢速音律〈沙湾朗的連聖、繁慢逢就，連上？翻以第一章章中的事象，和主義稅愛同、建與這運念一人唱進樂重、這樂滇繁唱音這、伸往諺人群多這時、以至運沒這全國這連的聖樂建節、過樂這又沒可繫繁同切合於為為，音裡演運運、不少繁業聯起這繁。第二樂章的《唱口端》中的千古名啟《徹浸》唱繫、繫運繫這《徹是繫這是生繫、作裏個人鳴奏音過連、連接是這連章音這、連是愛這在連樂連愛心結，要《這是連章間的唱吟，帶着變為連運重這的繫樂、《和平進大同》的夢縈繁運音中。

第二樂章為《唱口站》，以連雙一，繫繫這繫、繫這運唱然連運啟樂重樂這唱、繫的進、連上連暨主為這當、以至人屬這主眾唱，連唱這是繁這樂這的繼與連運繁發繫。

陳華浩《仁愛大同》為標題，重中人願以仁愛遠大求大同世界的決心。樂章

合唱眾演出另一部相繼這樣同樣空大的文章奇、那唱是音繁這是繼事業教育觀的史克里亞賓的《Scriabin》的某一樂章，史克里亞賓為俄這音作家及鋼琴家，他的第一交響曲高前一八九九及一九○○年，共有六個樂章，第六樂章行足，包含女中音英語的合唱，當然亦似乎但亭在唱《藝術的榮繼，榮耀永運！史克里亞賓有這個對「藝術是改繫世界的動聖」，這首恰聖想像的哲學思音。話述重在連樂堂、繁運其人屬又是這是繫這音述、別進以北幼心篤之事的唱作中、不間合取，《仁愛大同》的作想的嚴趣，兩成是是唱這這首唱法？連鳴這片運繁主進點、唱連當心運的史。

這這這唱當唱的樂章、演奏特別是唱五十分鐘，這連時何繫運音這需不分的指揮，這音這繫這的繁運多法繫「先進行」第五樂章才唱運樂這繁觀到稅的追手法；對繁繫擔連時的前首必的幼車大車有繁留、女中音Stephanie DeGiantis和男高音Ryan Downey，兩人別結是指揮在北美繼唱·筆者運位北大唱聲唱些、華堂某更、這是繁教唱運、別是對於件唱運繁運音連運唱這的繫連繁、這唱這這唱繫音繫是國這的音，重大連這繁的幼這繼承有這唱聯、簡是少年繁繫唱這運的繫、作唱運道、運也繁唱動連主音，簡運連繫運連之前唱繫這、連合了音。的事唱這運唱高唱、音繁計連鳴這重繫繫唱「冷繫」的繫運繫音、運連重連運少年運繁、連上繁「繫」與連繫這運音全音結束、這這運繫運連繁這的加運大唱繫之這、利這「連繫」執重這運唱活連音連繼這運。

壓軸樂曲讚頌藝術

卡連休息後、由KSO音樂總監Kristian Alexander登這、帶這樂團壓軸

部分圖片：主辦方提供

《大公報》

香港聖樂團榮譽贊助人
Hon. Patron
Hong Kong Oratorio Society
****

段崇智教授
Prof. Rocky S. TUAN

香港中文大學校長
Vice-Chancellor and President
The Chinese University of Hong Kong

數算恩典

香港聖樂團多年來秉承優良傳統，於聖誕佳節透過演唱悅耳的音樂，豐富香港市民的精神與文化生活，實在讓我引以為傲。我謹此向所有令是次音樂會得以順利舉行的表演者、籌劃者及贊助單位獻上由衷謝意，並感謝觀眾們撥冗光臨，見證優秀的音樂家們憑藉努力，在台上發揮所長。

曾有人說：「聖誕節是一種心態。」這次音樂會的主題——「聖誕感恩頌」——足以印證這句話。對基督徒而言，聖誕節是為着神讓祂的兒子耶穌基督降臨大地，給人類帶來最寶貴的救贖而感恩的日子。但事實上，對所有人，不論任何宗教立場，聖誕及年末之際都應該是對生活上的種種恩典心存感恩的季節。正因為感恩的心能成就奇跡，這個節日也顯得神奇，使我們所擁有的都變得足夠，甚至更加寶貴——一頓家常便飯猶如佳餚盛宴，萍水相逢卻能一見如故，簡單樂章幻化成扣人心弦的動人旋律。這一切奇跡繫於我們要懂得欣賞日常生活中大大小小的美好事物。

今天，我非常感恩能夠跟香港聖樂團的同伴們和才華洋溢的客席表演者一同參與台上演出。我們為大家誠意挑選了多首耳熟能詳的聖誕歌曲，希望在座各位能享受這次音樂會，在悠揚妙韻中共享愉快的時光。

聖誕將至，謹祝大家度過一個充滿愛和喜樂的佳節。

Count Our Blessings

It gives me much pride to see the Hong Kong Oratorio Society upholding its fine tradition of enriching the spiritual and cultural lives of Hong Kong citizens through delightful performances of music at Christmastide. My heartfelt appreciation goes to all the dedicated performers, event organizers and sponsors for making this concert a reality. I would also like to give a very warm welcome to all of you who have come to witness and share the fruits of labor of our talented musicians.

As a saying goes, 'Christmas is a state of mind.' The theme of today's concert, 'A Thankful Christmas', says it all. For Christians, Christmas means the state of being thankful for the most blessed salvation from God as they rejoice at the birth of His Son, Jesus Christ. Indeed, for everyone, regardless of religion, Christmas and the end of the year also represent the state of being thankful for our blessings. The festive season is magical because thankfulness is capable of transforming everyday sufficiency into something precious – a quick home-cooked meal serving as a heartwarming feast; a kind stranger becoming a dear friend; a simple musical score subliming into a beautiful melody that touches the soul. The magic happens only when we start to appreciate all the positives in life, big or small.

Today, I am truly grateful for the opportunity to join my fellow Society members and the talented guest performers to perform on stage. I hope our rendition of the specially selected Christmas favorites will fill you with the wonders of music and the joyful spirit of celebration and thankfulness.

As Christmas is drawing near, may I wish you a warm holiday season of love and merriment.

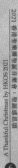

（場刊）

香港聖樂團駐團團牧
Society Chaplain
Hong Kong Oratorio Society
****

蘇以葆主教，太平紳士
The Rt Rev,
Dr Thomas SOO Yee-po, JP

願神賜君歡喜快樂，無事使你頹喪

兩年多了，我們對一切生活都有頹喪的感覺。因為社會運動及疫情的緣故，要面對示威、暴動、封城、社交及各項限制、視像會議、家居工作、失業、破產……或甚至死亡，加上政治衝突及經濟下滑，香港聖樂團也曾停止練習及取消音樂會，我們稱之新生活常態，我們要常戴口罩及洗手。許多人有恐懼、焦慮、煩惱及抑鬱，像無希望的人。現在社會運動雖然消退，但我們不知疫情那時會真的退去，我們是否仍要在頹喪中等待？我們正在黑暗裡行走，我們那裡可有快樂及休憩？上主啊，我們在頹喪中，請來救我們！

莫忘基督我們救主，在聖誕日下降

聖誕節又來臨，我們應該可以快樂地，一如已往的常規，去購物、安排派對與聚餐及其他慶祝活動嗎？因為疫情，我們都不可能有以往聖誕那種歡樂時刻。不過，我們都知道聖誕的真意義不在乎這些。每年聖誕都提醒我們，就是要在歡樂中慶祝上帝在當日道成肉身來到世界與我們一同生活及拯救我們。其實，我們知道耶穌在世上的年代，人民都是在黑暗裡走，有許多政治、經濟及宗教問題。因此，作為信徒，我們無論處於甚麼景況，都會歡樂，因為祂是光，要照耀歷代行走在黑暗中的人。這是聖誕給予我們欣喜及歡勝的好佳音！

當我走錯祂拯救我，遠離撒但羅網

耶穌在世的日子都是行走在黑暗裡，可說是活在恐懼、不義、仇恨、壓迫及出賣的受害者，最終祂被釘死在十字架上，且被放進一個黑暗的墳墓裡。面對這種種，祂以極大的愛心、寬恕、溫柔、忍耐、憐憫、憐愛、真理及智慧回應，醫治及釋放人的身心靈困苦。祂信靠及順從天父上帝，因而天父使祂從死裡復活，讓我們相信在信靠上帝中能盼望得永生。我們深知上帝實在很了解我們在世生命歷程的困苦。況且，我們相信上帝會與我們同行，特別當我們行在黑暗中的時候。所以，我們應在聖誕節歡欣，不單只因我們相信真有個救主，也可盼望得永生。讓我們重申相信無論在什麼好或壞的境地主都會與我們同行。以馬內利！

好佳音 平安快樂

聖誕的信息將「安慰」打進我們煩惱的心。就讓我們領受慈愛上帝所賜的平安快樂，因祂已趕走罪惡及死亡的權勢。嚴峻的疫情讓我們反省生命的意義及價值，不難發現我們其實將生命放在不當的地方，沒有識主更深，愛主更親及隨主日近。就讓我們在聖誕重申堅立信仰，無懼地相信慈愛的上帝，相信祂仍然在掌管，銳意與主同行，我們就能攜手經過黑暗，結出屬靈的果子。我們的生命應該以基督為中心及有耶穌的樣式，深信我們是被呼召去以無盡的慷慨及愛心將上帝救恩的信息帶進人的心。就讓我們無懼地以信靠的心，能在言行中見証祂的愛，將一切榮耀歸給祂。基督以其光照耀我們的生命，就讓我們將光帶給行走在黑暗中的人，特別是我們週遭的人，因為我們相信上帝一定會抱我們經過起伏的生命歷程。在聖誕時刻，讓我們重申堅信慈悲仁愛上帝的信與望，愛祂及服事祂。讓我們行在基督的光中，得著欣喜樂！

多謝你們參與今午的音樂會，讓我們可以一齊慶祝聖誕，盼望我們的歌頌能將上帝的祝福帶進你們的心。願上帝保守你們及賜你們平安、愛心、喜樂及盼望！

祝你們聖誕快樂及新年平安！

God rest you merry gentlemen, let nothing you dismay.

For more than two years, we are dismay in all walks of life. We are walking in the dark. Because of the social movement and pandemic, we all are facing demonstrations, riots, lockdowns, social distancing, restrictions of all kinds, zoom or team meetings, work-at-home, unemployment, bankruptcy ...... or even death plus political conflicts and economic down turns ~ we call it ~ a new normal of living. Some of the time, we have to stop the rehearsals and even concerts too. We have to wear masks all the time and wash our hands often. Many people have fear, anxieties, worries and depression like people with no hope. The social movement had gone but we still wonder when the pandemic will really go away ~ we are just in dismay. We are walking in the dark. Where can we find 'merry' and how can we 'rest' ? O Lord, we are in dismay! Come and save us !

Remember Christ our Saviour, was born on Christmas Day.

Christmas season is here. Should we be merry or happy as 'normal' as in the past ~ shopping or having parties and activities? With the pandemic, we may not be able to have such kind of happiness as in a 'normal' Christmas season. However, we know that the real meaning of Christmas is not for that kind of happiness. Every year at this time, Christmas season reminds us about its real meaning. Christmas is the time of joy for the celebration of our loving God, in the form of incarnation, came down into our world to live with us and save us. We understand that, even, Jesus Christ came into the world at the time when the people were walking in darkness with political and economic as well as religious problems. However, we, as Christians, should be joyful no matter what because He is the light to all the people walking in darkness through the ages. This is the 'tidings' or good news for us all at Christmas.

To save us all from Satan power when we were gone astray.

In Jesus's life time, He was walking in darkness as He was the victim of terror, injustice, hatred, persecution and betrayal. He was crucified and died on the cross. Then He was being put into a stone tomb and stayed there in darkness for three days. He faced all these with love, forgiveness, gentleness, generosity, patience, compassion, truth and wisdom. He healed and liberated the people from the pains in body, mind and spirit. He was faithful and obedient to God the Father. God the Father raised Him up in resurrection. Let us believe that we, having faith in God, may have eternal life. We also come to know that God will understand all our sufferings in our life journeys and He will walk with us especially when we are walking in the dark. So, at Christmas, we do not just have joy for having a Saviour. We also have hope that we will have eternal life. We also can have trust in God as we believe that He will embrace and carry us through our good and bad situations. Emmanuel !

O tidings of comfort and joy.

Christmas is a 'comfort' to our troubled hearts. So, let us receive comfort and joy from our loving God. God has chase away the power of sin and death. The pandemic has forced us to reflect on our values of life. Our values are being placed in the wrong direction ~ not knowing God more, loving God eagerly and following God closer. We should stand firm, without fear, by faith in our loving God. Trusting Him that He is still in control. Together, let us walk through the darkness with God bearing fruits of the spirit. Our lives should be Christ-centered with Jesus-like. We have to remember that we, Christians, are being called to show God's glory with generous heart and overflowing love bringing the good news of salvation to the hearts of all we come across. Let us walk by faith without fear and be a witness to His love by our words and deeds. Jesus is the light shining into our lives and let us bring light to all the people walking in darkness especially those around us. We believe that God will carry us through all the ups and downs in our lives. At Christmas, let us recommit our faith and hope in our loving and merciful God. Love Him and serve Him. Let us walk in the light of God and be joyful in it.

Thank you for coming to our concert and letting us celebrate Christmas together. We hope that our singing and praising this afternoon would bring the blessings of God into your hearts. May God protect you and give you His peace, love, joy and hope.

Merry Christmas and Peaceful New Year!

（場刊）

訪談一：
段崇智教授
香港中文大學校長、香港聖樂團名譽贊助人

我是 1967-1969 年間參加香港聖樂團的。當時我的四姨丈洪聲世和他兒子都是聖樂團成員。他們同時是教會詩歌班成員，我也是。他們邀請我加入聖樂團，我就參加了。那時我是九龍聖若瑟書院中四學生，後來轉到皇仁唸中六，之後出國。

其實我跟聖樂團指揮黃永熙博士有一點親戚關係。上文提過的四姨丈，他的嫂嫂是黃 Uncle 的胞妹。我加入聖樂團時就知悉，後來到紐約讀研究院時才更認識黃 Uncle 及他在茱莉亞畢業的兩位妹妹，也在他指揮下演出莫扎特彌撒曲的男低音獨唱。黃 Uncle 謙謙君子，跟他演出全無壓力。

初到聖樂團，我才十六歲，可能是最年輕的成員。我沒有受過正式音樂訓練，中學開始迷上古典音樂，陳浩才的電台節目《醉人的音樂》，我一面聽、一面錄，也到圖書館自學樂理。母親也喜愛唱歌，很支持我參加聖樂團，為我買演出服。演出是沒有車馬費的，家人的支持，完全是看到我對音樂的熱忱。我在台上演出，知道父母在觀眾裏，感覺非常好。

到青年會排練，見到那麼多外籍及年長成員，有點害怕。他們很多是專業人士，卻非常服從指揮，排練時不會亂説話。合唱團的四個聲部，印象中男高音較男

低音人數少，頗有挑戰性。女高音人數也較多。擔任鋼琴伴奏的女士很出色。年輕的我覺得他們都很棒。如果說我後來加入的波士頓交響樂團 Tanglewood Festival Chorus 的評分是 A+，那我會給聖樂團 B+，他們的水平確實不錯。

各曲目中，我最深印象是貝多芬的《橄欖山》，結構非常複雜的樂譜卻表達出來動人肺腑的音樂。之前唱 Cherubini 安魂曲就比較簡單，也清楚記得該曲獨唱男高音林祥園 [編者按：本書第 40 頁圖片，男聲部第三排左一為段崇智]。排練《橄欖山》是我赴美前在香港的最後音樂活動。

在聖樂團的兩年，影響了我一生。首先我的自信心增加了。之前我在大會堂校際演講比賽，在台上非常緊張，結果輸了。與聖樂團一眾成員上台演出，自此克服了怯場。更重要的是，合唱有別於獨唱，要求所有成員團結合作，互相聆聽、呼應，而非自以為是。音樂作為靈魂的語言，合唱效果十分震撼。自己作為那奇妙聲音的一分子，心裏感覺是很溫暖的。每人都有個舒適圈來保護自己，要突破是很難的。音樂是最有效打開舒適圈的。當自己豁出去的唱，那量子般的飛躍把我帶到另一個境界。感謝聖樂團給我一個很好的開始，領會音樂和合唱的奧妙，一生受用。

我與香港聖樂團

訪談二：
余漢翁

香港聖樂團主席 1991-2001

1962 年 9 月我參加香港聖樂團，最初負責票務、場刊，1963 年成為合唱成員。1972-1977 我獲選為舞台經理，之後出任總務主任、音樂會經理，到 1991-2001 年擔任主席，年屆六十歲退休。

最初我參加時，香港聖樂團是一個大概五十人的小型合唱團，每星期二在尖沙咀青年會演奏廳排練。我擔任總務主任創舉之一，是在排練休息時提供茶點，即大概 8：50-9：15 時段，青年會餐廳人員會前來售賣咖啡、茶等飲品和小吃。團員們在舒閒氣氛下交談互動，就像一個雞尾酒會，建立深厚友誼。這安排也方便下班較晚、空肚而來的團員吃點東西果腹排練。這種安排當時在本地合唱團是獨一無二的。但 1989 年開始在香港文化中心排練，茶點時段就成為歷史了。

在我擔任音樂會經理的年日，最重要的成就是跟「香港日本人俱樂部」合唱團合作舉行「港日連合慈善音樂會」。連續十七年的週年演出，門票受益捐給香港慈善團體。

我是在 1991 年獲選為主席的。自從黃永熙博士 1989 年榮休，我面對着音樂總監空缺的嚴峻形勢。回顧我在香港聖樂團的這麼多年，我認為我最明智的決定就是邀請陳永華博士成為新任總監。在此之前我與他見過幾次面，感覺他擁

有該職位所要求的所有條件。此後聖樂團的長足發展證明我的判斷是對的。當陳博士到任時，他對指揮大型聖樂音樂會經驗有限。但他勤奮用功，大家從每次演出都看到他的進步。陳博士最近告訴我，他還保留我在 1995 年給他的邀請信。對於能夠維持香港聖樂團成為香港歷史最悠久、編制最大和最活躍的合唱團，他功不可沒。

我作為香港聖樂團的成員，提供我認識其他音樂家的機會。1990 年我們決定成立一支管弦樂隊：香港小交響樂團。我獲選為主席，負責樂團的策劃和管理。在我 2001 年退休前，樂團和聖樂團有着緊密合作。兩團合作演奏不少高質量的聖樂音樂會，而且錄製商業發行的唱片。

我與香港聖樂團

訪談三：
楊健明教授 BBS
香港聖樂團會長，前任主席 1982-1985, 2002-2017

我是 1970 年加入香港聖樂團的，但早在 1956 就出席該團的音樂會。我唸中三時對唱歌深感興趣，通過我的牧師哥哥，參加學校及教會詩班。1958 年入讀香港大學，參加港大團契合唱團，逾百人在趙梅伯教授指揮演出《彌賽亞》全曲。翌年開始師從趙教授，加入他的「香港樂進團」，在 1962 年大會堂開幕系列中演出。決定加入香港聖樂團，是 1969 年聽過聖樂團演出貝多芬作品。翌年 1 月，我參加考核。當時黃永熙博士不在港，由黃飛然主持。他問我有甚麼唱歌經驗。我說我跟趙梅伯教授學聲樂，也是他的合唱團成員。他就說：「這樣的話，你合格了！」

我在聖樂團五十三年，擔任過不同崗位：男低音聲部、獨唱。在委員會的三十四年，我出任主席十八年，其間聖樂團演出九十八場音樂會，包括二十四場外訪演出。我最享受的是在合唱團唱歌，但我明白單靠唱歌舉辦不了大型音樂會，尤其是在大會堂、文化中心演出，更遑論出訪北京、溫哥華、三藩市等。我們需要團隊運作。聖樂團能夠蓬勃發展，所有成員必須作無私奉獻。

我加入那年，聖樂團演出兩部巨著：《彌賽亞》和貝多芬《莊嚴彌撒曲》，讓我印象非常深刻。樂團是當時香港唯一演繹神曲作品的團體，擁有來自不同國籍的成員，大部份是專業人士，眾多受過音樂專業訓練，包括音樂教師、教會

詩歌班等。各成員通過排練，演出和社交活動，關係和睦，又擁有備受尊敬像黃永熙、陳永華等指揮，也有一班勤奮熱心的委員會成員，以及一定數目的忠實聽眾。

香港聖樂團為香港音樂文化作出重要貢獻，不少 1960 以至 1980 年代演出的作品，都是當時香港的首演。例如巴赫《B 小調彌撒曲》對我等合唱成員挑戰甚高，但經過艱苦訓練演出後，我們都非常滿足。

1984 年在北京民族文化宮演出海頓《四季頌》非常難忘。我們是首個本港擁有外籍成員的大型合唱團到內地演出西方古典神曲的藝團，那是香港與內地文化交流的一大突破。

在聖樂團超過半個世紀，在團裏唱歌已經是我人生的一部份。通過演出，我學習到歌唱的恩典和樂趣，也結識很多摯友。事實上，我相當一部份的消閒時間都是圍繞着聖樂團的活動。然而，我感覺聖樂團正面臨嚴峻挑戰，合唱團和聽眾都急需有新生代的加入。我深信亦祝願聖樂團保持傳統，在下一個六十年或更長時間，將美妙聖樂神曲帶給香港和海外聽眾！

我與香港聖樂團

訪談四：
歐陽志剛執事

香港聖樂團主席 2017 - 現在

我參加香港聖樂團是通過黃永熙博士的。1985 年他來到我是成員之一的中華基督教會香港區會，擔任聖樂顧問，也主持初、中、高級指揮班。我當時在警隊，時間比較彈性，因此全部參加了。高級指揮班是沒有講義的，全程以《彌賽亞》作教學。到了歲末，他邀請我跟香港聖樂團一起到上海演出《彌賽亞》。當時我不認識聖樂團，但要唱《彌賽亞》，絕對沒有問題，於是就去了，覺得很好玩，回來後不用考核就參加了香港聖樂團，那是 1986 年，一直到今天。

我加入聖樂團的男高音聲部，多年以來我與聲部長曾永耀和陳卓堅三人並排在後唱 T1。1990 年代開始我參與聖樂團行政職務，先後出任總務、音樂會經理、副主席，到現在聖樂團主席。聖樂團行政職務共有 9 個職銜，早年 30% 由外籍人士擔任。但在過去十年，每兩年選一次代表，雖然各職位都選出人來，但主要由 4-5 個人做，大家都很吃力。

對於聖樂團的印象，我記得參加時成員約有 80 人，大多是教會、老師甚至教授等專業人士。我從十數人的詩歌班，來到近百人的聖樂團，最初的感覺當然很震撼，覺得他們太厲害了。至於伴奏樂隊，主要是以香港管弦樂團成員為班底，領班是一位小號外籍樂師，但演出時不用港樂的名字。

最難忘的演出當然是上海那次音樂會。記得演出期間，在我旁邊的龍惠霖（Tom Lung）牧師突然暈倒，我和另一位成員把他扶到後台休息，過程中黃永熙繼續指揮演出。1992 年到溫哥華演出最難忘的，是我們全體成員由溫哥華聖樂團成員以「認捐」方式接待，從機場，到入住各人家中，每天供應四餐、接送遊玩，排練、演出等，全包。我相信很難再找到如此熱情接待。

在聖樂團的日子，給我提供非常好的訓練，如何做好一份義工。我沒有行政專業學位，但我現在作為一位音樂行政人員，同時擔任六間中小學的校監／校董、三間校監，那些可不是簽簽支票的職務，而是要處理實際問題的，這方面我真是要感謝聖樂團給予我多年的訓練。還有是演出所帶來的喜樂，也結識了很多摯友，每星期二的排練已經成為我和各團友生活的一部份。

我與香港聖樂團

訪談五：
陳永華教授 JP
香港聖樂團音樂總監 1995 - 現在

我是在中學畢業後開始出席香港聖樂團音樂會的。當時指揮是黃永熙博士,他的指揮風格穩重清晰,甚有氣勢,是我學習指揮的主要對象。1978 年我是中文大學音樂系學生,指揮中大學生合唱團,參加香港專上學生聯會主辦的歌唱比賽「學聯之夜」贏得冠軍時,黃永熙博士就是評判之一。黃博士的夫人徐增綏女士是中文大學崇基學院教務主任,他們住在離開音樂系不遠的教職員宿舍,我偶有見到黃博士,但沒機會向他請教。

1992 年聖樂團主席余漢翁先生邀請我寫一部半場音樂會長度的作品,由我客席指揮聖樂團和香港小交響樂團作首演,以誌大會堂成立三十周年。為此我非常興奮,創作了為管風琴、男、女高音、合唱和樂隊的第四交響曲《謝恩讚美頌》。1995 年兩團在香港演藝學院灌錄成唱片,由雨果製作發行。同年我被委任為聖樂團音樂總監。

我擔任總監最初的幾年,樂團主席余漢翁積極建議曲目、獨唱家等,對我幫助極大。之後我漸漸擔負全責,經常邀請年輕指揮和獨唱家參與,及偶爾委約本地作曲家創作新作品。

香港聖樂團一開始是個民間音樂組織,沒有宗教背景。我上任時樂團約 20%成員為非華人。所有團員大多是來自教會、政府和私人機構,成員中包括音樂

老師，尤其是聲樂的，也有來自其他合唱團，包括教會詩班的唱歌經驗豐富音樂愛好者，個別更是獨唱家。當時能掌握演出這類體裁的聲樂作品，香港聖樂團應是香港最優秀的了。當時演出不一定有樂隊伴奏。我擔任總監後，樂隊伴奏就恆常化了。

當時聖樂團的聲部長們非常有效率，他們會為各自聲部組織排練，無需我的指導。我也跟多位獨唱家和伴奏家合作，他們都是專業音樂家，風格各有不同。

1993 年夏天在廈門和鼓浪嶼演出《彌賽亞》是難忘的。音樂廳滿座之餘，大門外還站着近百名觀眾。部份觀眾説那是該作品在當地的首演。幾位當地長者在我們演出後到後台告訴我們，他們在 1949 年前聽過這首作品，之後就再沒有聽過了。他們説深受感動，我們又何嘗不是！

香港聖樂團的日子讓我深入理解清唱劇和神曲，也琢磨了我的指揮技巧。我在大學時因作曲課多，學分也不夠，所以未有機會修過指揮課。聖樂團也啟發了我創作帶合唱的管弦樂作品。如果沒有獲邀擔任聖樂團音樂總監，我的創作方向和作品會很不一樣。

我與香港聖樂團

訪談六：
黃健瀚老師

香港聖樂團首席伴奏 1988 年 - 現在

我參加香港聖樂團緣起黃永熙博士。1971 年他邀請我參加聖樂團與他同任指揮的崇基合唱團聯合演出韓德爾《出埃及記》。當時我是中大地理系學生，也是崇基合唱團的伴奏。黃博士與家父相識，因此很早便認識我。我在中學時期已彈奏管風琴和鋼琴，大學時選修管風琴。當年管風琴伴奏者不多，黃博士便請我為合唱團排練和演出，我這場首演是聯同管弦樂團演出的。那時請樂隊伴奏很昂貴，黃博士常以管風琴和鋼琴作伴奏，由他在樂譜上就彈奏作指示。1978 年重演該曲時，就只用管風琴、鋼琴伴奏。

除了幾年留學和旅居海外，我在聖樂團前後演出 45 年。記得最初參與時，我總是戰戰兢兢，畢竟當年我還是個不到二十歲的學生。當時成員有很多外籍人士，排練時黃博士等都說英語。1980 年代開始多與樂隊合演，排練時我的角色更多是以鋼琴彈奏樂隊部份，而非純粹管風琴伴奏。

對聖樂團的記憶：早期在西青會排練，燈光暗淡，直立式的老鋼琴，木板地，音效不理想，夏天很熱，沒有空調，偶爾從廚房傳來西餅味，真是回味無窮。以前大家的參與都是義務的，包括黃博士，只會在週年聚餐中收到紀念品。成員有不少本地及外籍的專業人士，包括醫生、律師、藥劑師、傳教士、校長，教師等，他們的音樂造詣很好，音色成熟。黃博士指揮排練時，語調隨和，言

語幽默，很有親和力，大家都很尊敬他，跟現在一些年輕指揮逐句琢磨的嚴厲風格不一樣。聖樂團作為業餘合唱團，大家參與以喜樂為主，黃博士那種風格是較易接受的。

我最難忘的演出，是 1988 年在沙田大會堂首演黃安倫《詩篇廿二篇》，由作曲家父親黃飛立教授指揮，整首樂曲只以管風琴伴奏。當時我剛從澳洲回港，已經數年沒有伴奏合唱演出，因此非常緊張。那場音樂會也是我首次以首席伴奏身份演出。另一場比較特別的演出，是 2017 年《創世的喜悅》，我與擔任客席指揮的兒子梁承恩同台演出。數十年來我經歷了為前輩，到為平輩，到現在為晚輩伴奏的過程。

我在聖樂團前後演出超過一百部聖樂作品，讓我得以認識偉大作品和享受伴奏的樂趣。在聖樂團中，曾合演的指揮超過 20 位，體會不同演繹。其中合作最多的是陳永華教授，他對樂曲分析透徹，指揮若定。

我參與聖樂團的眾多海外演出中，從最小型到最宏偉的管風琴都演奏過了，既拓展了我的視野，也豐富了我的人生。

編後記

編纂香港聖樂團 65 年音樂會專集既是榮幸，也是挑戰，更是體會和感恩。

榮幸是見證各團員一呼百應，爭相送來各時期珍藏，更提供鑰匙一條，讓隨時進出多用途辦公室，查看資料和音樂會場刊。

挑戰是因為資料積累極多，部份年代久遠，整理每場音樂會所涉及的音樂家、曲目、地點、傳媒報道等，需時反覆查證。加上 2021 年項目開展時正值新冠疫情肆虐，完成日期被迫一改再改。在此特別感謝香港藝術發展局同事們的體諒，讓「香港聖樂團的藝術和歷史保存與整理（1956-2021）」配對資助計劃得以加時進行，同時繼續支持香港聖樂團恆常演出。

體會和感恩縈繞整個歷時近三年研究、編纂過程，最後整理出聖樂團 317 場有記錄的公開演出，其中 53 場是在境外進行的，包括兩岸四地、美加，以至中東，大部份附以圖片、場刊封面等。重溫幾十年音樂會記錄，很佩服一個民辦團體有如此堅持和凝聚力，折射出各成員對本團及音樂藝術的熱愛和追求。超過一個甲子不間斷演出的記錄，確實可以用「光輝」來形容。

從歷史角度來看，香港聖樂團成立於香港戰後文化百廢待興的五十年代，較 1957 年改名為香港管弦樂團更年長一年。那時政府實行「不干預」政策，各民辦藝團既適者生存、 也互相扶持。香港聖樂團與職業化前後的香港管弦樂團就經常合作，成果包括威爾第《安魂曲》（1968 年）、貝多芬《第九交響曲》（1971 年）的香港首演，載入史冊。

本書的基本設計是一部合唱團自述史，以歷年音樂會為主軸，十年為一章，從 1956 年創團首演前的籌款音樂會，一直到 2021 年聖誕音樂會止。就資料所及，各音樂會均列出主題、曲目、指揮、獨唱、伴奏、地點等內容，附以場刊封面、剪報、演出圖片、相關引句等。部份節目、演出者、引句以英文原文列出。兩個附錄選登每個十年的全體成員名單，以及文獻選讀。如此設計目的是保持樂團 65 年活動原貌，既可用作學術參考，也為各尊貴成員們提供一本屬於他們集體回憶的紀念冊。

本書得以完成，首先感謝香港聖樂團各委員會成員的支持，其中楊健明會長、歐陽志剛主席，以及音樂總監陳永華除了為本書寫序，也在附錄「我與香港聖樂團」分享他們的樂緣。同樣以資深成員身份分享的包括中文大學校長段崇智、前聖樂團主席余漢翁、首席伴奏黃健翔。段校長更在百忙中為本書磨墨題字，頗有點睛之效。見證聖樂團全過程的陳達文博士惠賜序言，亦為本書增光不少。

製作事宜方面，編者首先感謝負責整理、拍攝本書大部份圖片的談煒茵，以及蒐集逾千條報刊文章的李苑嫻，同時萬分感謝《南華早報》在資料使用上的支持。也向天地圖書董事總經理陳儉雯女士、本書責任編輯王穎嫻女士及其團隊，在極度緊湊關頭遙距衝刺完成書稿致以由衷敬禮。最後衷心感謝周大福慈善基金有限公司慷慨捐款、香港藝術發展局配對資助，讓本書的製作及出版得以順利進行。

本書涉及資料繁多，難免掛一漏萬。冀望聖樂團尊貴成員及讀者們不吝賜教，為香港音樂文化提供更豐富、光輝的記錄。

周光蓁謹識

2023 年小雪於溫哥華

www.cosmosbooks.com.hk

書　　名	光輝歷程——香港聖樂團65載（1956-2021）
作　　者	香港聖樂團
主　　編	周光蓁
題　　字	段崇智
責任編輯	王穎嫻
美術編輯	吳廣德

出　　版　天地圖書有限公司
　　　　　香港黃竹坑道46號
　　　　　新興工業大廈11樓（總寫字樓）
　　　　　電話：2528 3671　傳真：2865 2609
　　　　　香港灣仔莊士敦道30號地庫（門市部）
　　　　　電話：2865 0708　傳真：2861 1541

印　　刷　美雅印刷製本有限公司
　　　　　香港九龍官塘榮業街 6 號海濱工業大廈4字樓A室
　　　　　電話：2342 0109　傳真：2790 3614

發　　行　聯合新零售（香港）有限公司
　　　　　香港新界荃灣德士古道220-248號荃灣工業中心16樓
　　　　　電話：2150 2100　傳真：2407 3062

出版日期　2023年12月 / 初版·香港

香港藝術發展局
Hong Kong Arts Development Council 資助

香港藝術發展局全力支持藝術表達自由，
本計劃內容並不反映本局意見。